Europe and the Recognition of New States in Yugoslavia

Europe's recognition of new states in Yugoslavia remains one of the most controversial episodes of the collapse of Yugoslavia. Richard Caplan offers a detailed narrative of events, exploring the highly assertive role that Germany played in the episode, the reputedly catastrophic consequences of recognition (for Bosnia and Herzegovina in particular) and the radical departure from customary state practice represented by EC's use of political criteria as the basis of recognition. The book examines the strategic logic and consequences of the EC's actions but also explores the wider implications, offering insights into European security policy at the end of the Cold War, the relationship of international law to international relations and the management of ethnic conflict. The significance of this book extends well beyond Yugoslavia as policymakers continue to wrestle with the challenges posed by violent conflict associated with state fragmentation.

RICHARD CAPLAN is University Lecturer in International Relations and Fellow of Linacre College, University of Oxford. He is the author of *International Governance of War-Torn Territories: Rule and Reconstruction* (2005) and co-editor of *Europe's New Nationalism: States and Minorities in Conflict* (1996) and *State of the Union: The Clinton Administration and the Nation in Profile* (1994).

Europe and the Recognition of
New States in Yugoslavia

Richard Caplan

UNIVERSITY PRESS

CAMBRIDGE UNIVERSITY PRESS
Cambridge, New York, Melbourne, Madrid, Cape Town, Singapore, São Paulo

Cambridge University Press
The Edinburgh Building, Cambridge CB2 2RU, UK

Published in the United States of America by Cambridge University Press,
New York

www.cambridge.org
Information on this title: www.cambridge.org 9780521821766

First published 2005

Printed in the United Kingdom at the University Press, Cambridge

A catalogue record for this book is available from the British Library

ISBN -13 9780521821766 hardback
ISBN -10 0521 82176 2 hardback

For Luisa

Contents

Acknowledgements

In the course of researching and writing this book, I benefited from the assistance and encouragement of a great many individuals and institutions without whose support this undertaking would have been a far more arduous one.

I owe a debt of gratitude to the many libraries and documentation centres whose staff responded patiently to my requests for official publications and archival materials. These include the Bodleian Library, the British Library, Cambridge University Library, the European Commission, the Institute of Advanced Legal Studies, the Liddell Hart Centre for Military Archives, the Royal Institute of International Affairs (Chatham House), University of London Library, the Organisation for Co-operation and Security in Europe, the Western European Union, and the Widener and Pusey Libraries at Harvard University.

For their generous financial support, I am grateful to the MacArthur Foundation and the Department of War Studies, King's College London. I am also grateful to the British Association for Slavonic and East European Studies (BASEES) for helping to defray the costs of my field research. The Department of Politics and International Relations at the University of Oxford was generous in granting me leave to complete this book.

For their critical reaction and/or practical assistance, I am grateful to Anthony Borden, Norman Cigar, Zlatko Dizdarević, Geoffrey Edwards, John Feffer, Gorana Flaker, Lawrence Freedman, Samantha Gibson, James Gow, Peter Gray, Mirza Hajrić, Martin Kruger, Eli Lauterpacht, Diana Lewis, Jenny Little, Tihomir Loza, Paul Mitchell, Zoran Pajić, Mario Petrović, Oliver Ramsbotham, Adam Roberts, John Roper, George Schöpflin, Jane M. O. Sharp, Brendan Simms, Cornelia Sorabji, Alenka Suhadolnik, Cedric Thornberry, Karin von Hippel, Marc Weller, Jim Whitman, Paul Williams, Stefan Wolff, Davorka Zmiarević and the three anonymous reviewers of this manuscript. I owe a particular debt to Lawrence Freedman for his patience and guidance in supervising this research in its earlier guise as a doctoral thesis. I would also like to thank the many government officials, former and current, who gave so generously of their time in interviews with me.

I am grateful to Neven Andjelić, Branko Manojlović, Lisa Petrović, and Uliva Tanović for their assistance with the translation of Serbo-Croatian texts, and, finally, to John Haslam at Cambridge University Press for his unstinting patience and encouragement.

Portions of this manuscript have appeared previously in revised form. A version of Chapter 1 appeared as 'Conditional Recognition as an Instrument of Ethnic Conflict Regulation: The European Community and Yugoslavia' in *Nations and Nationalism*, vol. 8, no. 2 (April 2002). Part of Chapter 4 appeared as 'The European Community's Recognition of New States in Former Yugoslavia: The Strategic Implications' in *The Journal of Strategic Studies*, vol. 21, no. 3 (September 1998) and as 'International Diplomacy and the Crisis in Kosovo' in *International Affairs*, vol. 74, no. 4 (October 1998). I am grateful to the publishers for their permission to reproduce selections of this material.

Introduction

Since the end of the Cold War, more than a dozen new or nascent states have emerged in Europe as a consequence of the break-up of three multinational federations: the Soviet Union, Czechoslovakia and Yugoslavia.[1] This second 'springtime of nations' has proved to be more sanguinary than the first a century and a half earlier. While in most cases the establishment of new states has proceeded in a peaceful manner, in other instances it has been accompanied by violent conflict, either because the federal authorities have not acquiesced in the assertions of statehood on the part of rebel entities or because population groups within the emergent states have contested the independence claims. The wars of Yugoslav dissolution, triggered by Slovenia's and Croatia's declarations of independence on 25 June 1991, have been the most prominent example of this violent trend.[2]

The response of the international community to the Yugoslav crisis – still ongoing – has taken many forms. One of the more controversial initiatives has been the European Community's recognition of new states in Yugoslavia beginning in December 1991.[3] To some, EC recognition of the break-away republics was but a matter of bowing to the inevitable; to others, it was an act of reckless diplomacy. To its proponents within the Community, however, recognition was thought to have broad utility

---

[1] The dissolution of these three states led, by January 1994, to the creation of nineteen new or successor states: Armenia, Azerbaijan, Belarus, Bosnia and Herzegovina, Croatia, the Czech Republic, Georgia, Kazakhstan, Kyrgyzstan, Macedonia, Moldova, Russia, Slovakia, Slovenia, Tajikistan, Turkmenistan, Ukraine, Uzbekistan and Yugoslavia (Serbia and Montenegro). In addition, three states – Estonia, Latvia and Lithuania – regained their independence. Several other sub-state entities – among them Chechnya in Russia and Kosovo in Serbia – were engaged in struggles for independence.

[2] For other conflicts associated with the establishment of new states in Europe after the Cold War, see Michael E. Brown (ed.), *The International Dimensions of Internal Conflict* (Cambridge, MA: CSIA/MIT Press, 1996).

[3] The European Community (or 'the Twelve') and the European Union are used interchangeably throughout this study. The EU superseded the EC with the coming into force of the Treaty on European Union on 1 November 1993.

1

for the purpose of conflict regulation. The prospect of recognition, it was argued, might deter the Belgrade authorities from continuing to prosecute the war. Actual recognition would alter the nature of the conflict – that is, transform an internal dispute into an interstate war – and thus endow the protagonists with additional rights and obligations as well as create new opportunities for third-party intervention. Recognition would also confer legitimacy on, and therefore strengthen, one political option – independent statehood – that some thought would provide the basis for a permanent solution to the conflict. Finally, recognition could be granted on conditional terms, allowing the EC a degree of leverage with which to mould the strategic environment in a manner more conducive to peace in the region.

This latter use of recognition – conditional on criteria relevant to regional security – is the central focus of this book. When in December 1991, six months after the outbreak of hostilities, the EC Council of Ministers chose to recognise the Yugoslav (and Soviet) republics seeking independence, it conditioned recognition on the acceptance of various 'Helsinki norms' by the new state authorities. The EC stipulated, *inter alia*, that the new states would have to have constituted themselves on a democratic basis; to have accepted the provisions of the UN Charter, the Helsinki Final Act, and the CSCE Charter of Paris, especially with regard to the rule of law, democracy, and human rights; and to have demonstrated a commitment to settle by agreement all differences arising from state succession. The Yugoslav republics were further required to accept extensive provisions for safeguarding the rights of national minorities within the new state borders and to adopt constitutional and political guarantees ensuring that they harboured no territorial claims towards 'a neighbouring Community state'.[4] The prospect of recognition, the EC reasoned, would induce the emerging states to adopt policies that might mitigate and perhaps even eliminate some of the presumed sources of the conflict.

The EC's initiative, although not unprecedented, represented an innovation in EC security policymaking.[5] It also represented a significant departure from recent state practice, where the tendency had been to recognise states on the basis primarily of non-political criteria. Despite

[4] 'Declaration on the "Guidelines on the Recognition of New States in Eastern Europe and in the Soviet Union"' and 'Declaration on Yugoslavia', Extraordinary EPC Ministerial Meeting (Brussels), EPC Press Releases P. 128/91 and P. 129/91, 16 December 1991.
[5] New states established by the Congress of Berlin (1878) and the post-First World War settlements were also bound by national minority provisions, as discussed in ch. 1.

these novelties, scholars have given scant attention to the strategic logic governing the EC's use of recognition.[6] There are two reasons that explain this lacuna. First, the controversy surrounding the initiative has tended to overshadow many other considerations – controversy arising in part from Germany's precipitate moves towards recognition (of Croatia especially) but also from the reputedly baleful consequences of recognition itself. Second, the EC's weak implementation of its policy, notably its tolerance for derogation from its own requirements for recognition, has led many analysts to treat the initiative as a mere face-saving gesture, the real purpose of which was to mask a fundamental policy reversal so as to forestall a heightening of divisions among the Twelve.[7] But while 'extra-strategic' factors clearly had important bearing on the EC's decision to extend recognition, they alone do not explain the specific design of the recognition policy, the provisions of which reflected several months of thinking about the requirements for peace in the region. It is apparent from EC official documents, political memoirs, and other evidence examined in this study that the architects of the EC's policy were motivated to a large degree by the security dividends that they expected conditional recognition to yield, however modest those dividends might be.

One aim of this study, then, is to recover the strategic thinking behind the EC's recognition policy. What were the sources of the policy? How was it expected to contribute to peace and stability in the region? What led to its adoption in the face of strong objections or warnings from leading EC member states, the UN secretary-general and diplomats in the field? Another aim is to explore the strategic consequences of the policy. While recognition was intended ostensibly to help dampen the hostilities, critics maintain that it did more to aggravate and extend the Yugoslav wars than perhaps any other single factor – by encouraging the republics (and the Kosovo Albanians) in their drives

---

[6] Partial exceptions include Robert Cooper and Mats Berdal, 'Outside Intervention in Ethnic Conflicts', 35(1) *Survival* (1993), 133–4; Jennifer Jackson Preece, *National Minorities and the European Nation-States System* (Oxford: Clarendon Press, 1998), pp. 44–8; and Karen E. Smith, 'The Use of Political Conditionality in the EU's Relations with Third Countries: How Effective?' 3 *European Foreign Affairs Review* (1998), 268.

[7] See, for instance, Johan Galtung, 'The Problems of Recognition', *YugoFax* No. 9 (1991), 1; Simon Nuttall, 'The EC and Yugoslavia – *Deus ex Machina* or *Machina sine Deo?*' 32 *Journal of Common Market Studies*, Annual Review (1994), 17–19; Susan L. Woodward, *Balkan Tragedy: Chaos and Dissolution After the Cold War* (Washington, DC: The Brookings Institution, 1995), pp. 183–9; and Mario Zucconi, 'The European Union in the Former Yugoslavia', in Abram Chayes and Antonia Handler Chayes (eds.), *Preventing Conflict in the Post-Communist World* (Washington, DC: The Brookings Institution, 1996), pp. 263–70.

for independence; by undermining the EC peace talks under the direction of Lord Peter Carrington; by intensifying the fighting in Croatia; and by triggering the bloodiest phase of the conflict, the Bosnian war. Are these valid criticisms? Did the EC's policy help in any way to mitigate or prevent violent conflict in the region? Did it create opportunities for more effective international action, whether or not those opportunities were exploited? Or would the interests of peace have perhaps been better served by a further delay in recognition? These are some of the key questions at the heart of this study.

Recognition and conflict management

Although there has been little scholarly treatment of the EC's use of conditional recognition as an instrument of conflict management, the scholarly literature on conflict management itself provides a useful lens through which to view the EC's initiative in relation to other approaches to the regulation of conflict. Much of this literature is concerned with conflicts between identity groups that occur *within* states, where these groups are often aggrieved national minorities seeking to redress what they perceive to be unjust patterns of state governance by the dominant identity group or groups, including the denial of self-determination in the form of independent statehood.[8] Of course, many internal conflicts have a trans-boundary dimension that involves cross-border identity affinities (e.g., Northern Ireland, Cyprus), while some interstate conflicts also have a basis in communal competition (e.g., India–Pakistan, Rwanda–Burundi). The Yugoslav wars have had elements of all of these different categories: internal conflict, interstate war, communal strife and intragroup competition.

Scholars typically distinguish conflict management from two other modes of third-party diplomatic and/or military engagement in a crisis (other than war-fighting itself): conflict prevention and conflict resolution. Conflict prevention refers to measures that aim to impede the escalation of a non-violent dispute into an armed confrontation. Conflict resolution occurs during or, more likely, after the cessation of hostilities and refers to efforts to eliminate the sources of violent disagreement or to impose a partial settlement. Conflict management or regulation (the

---

[8] Representative works of contemporary scholarship in this field include Milton J. Esman, *Ethnic Politics* (Ithaca, NY: Cornell University Press, 1994); Ted Robert Gurr and Barbara Harff, *Ethnic Conflict in World Politics* (Boulder, CO: Westview Press, 1994); and Donald L. Horowitz, *Ethnic Groups in Conflict* (Berkeley: University of California Press, 1985).

terms are frequently used interchangeably) occupies the broad middle ground between the two and refers to attempts to contain, suspend, mitigate or channel conflict after the eruption of violence and while resolution is being sought.[9] These are by no means hard and fast distinctions; the lines between the different categories are often blurred. For instance, the mitigation of conflict may be so thorough as to constitute effective elimination. Some scholars, for that matter, treat conflict resolution as an aspect of conflict management.

In their study of the macro-political regulation of ethnic conflict, John McGarry and Brendan O'Leary provide a taxonomy of the methods of ethnic conflict regulation that is a useful scheme for classifying conditional recognition as conceived of by the European Community.[10] McGarry and O'Leary identify eight methods of ethnic conflict regulation, four of which aim at the elimination of group differences (genocide, forced mass-population transfers, partition and/or secession, integration and/or assimilation) and four of which seek to manage group differences (hegemonic control, arbitration, cantonisation and/or federalisation, consociationalism or power-sharing). States may employ different methods at the same time, choosing even to combine aims. Thus, for instance, South Africa under white minority rule pursued both a strategy of partition and one of hegemonic control through its homelands and apartheid policies respectively.

To the extent that the EC's recognition policy can be characterised by its efforts to ensure a large measure of autonomy for national minorities adversely affected by the break-up of Yugoslavia, this approach clearly belongs to the class of methods seeking to manage rather than to eliminate group differences. The form of autonomy that the EC envisioned for its target minorities in Yugoslavia had a cultural, political and, in some cases, territorial component to it. None of the four methods within McGarry and O'Leary's family of management techniques corresponds precisely to this full range of entitlements but cantonisation comes very close. Under cantonisation political power is devolved to a delimited

---

[9] Luc Reychler, 'The Art of Conflict Prevention: Theory and Practice', in Werner Bauwens and Luc Reychler (eds.), *The Art of Conflict Prevention* (London: Brassey's, 1994), pp. 1–21; Sophia Clément, *Conflict Prevention in the Balkans: Case Studies of Kosovo and the FYR of Macedonia*, Chaillot Paper No. 30 (Paris: Institute for Security Studies of the Western European Union, 1997), pp. 7–9; and Raimo Väyrynen (ed.), *New Directions in Conflict Theory: Conflict Resolution and Conflict Transformation* (London: ISSC/SAGE Publications, 1991).

[10] John McGarry and Brendan O'Leary, 'Introduction', in John McGarry and Brendan O'Leary (eds.), *The Politics of Ethnic Conflict Regulation: Case Studies of Protracted Ethnic Conflicts* (London: Routledge, 1993), pp. 1–40.

area of the state where a national minority, numerically superior in that area, is permitted to enjoy 'mini-sovereignty'.[11] (National minorities outside the region may also possess certain entitlements – as they did under the EC's plan – but these will necessarily fall short of territorial autonomy.) Examples of cantonisation would include the Basque region of Spain, the German-speaking region of Italy (Alto Adige/South Tyrol) and the transfer of authority from Westminster to Scotland and Wales within the United Kingdom (the latter more accurately, perhaps, a form of 'semi-federalisation').

By allowing minorities to be masters of their own house, at a local level at least, autonomy arrangements are meant to mitigate the effects of majority rule in an ethnically divided society. And where ethnic divisions have already led to violence, these arrangements may enhance the security of the affected population. Because cantonisation enshrines rather than eliminates ethnic differences, it can be attractive to identity groups who wish to preserve their distinctiveness within a society rather than to transcend their differences through integration and assimilation. Since it requires less cooperation among competing ethnic groups than power-sharing arrangements, it is also thought to be especially well suited to deeply divided societies. Where the divisions are so profound as to give rise to secessionist demands, the expectation is that the devolution of power will defuse these pressures. Central authorities, however, are often concerned that cantonisation may in fact have the effect of encouraging state fragmentation.[12]

In many cases in recent history, autonomy agreements have proved to be an effective means of managing internal conflicts. In his study of communal conflicts between 1945 and 1990, Ted Robert Gurr found that autonomy agreements resulted in a de-escalation of violence in seven out of eleven instances in which they were adopted.[13] (Of the four failures – marked by the commencement or resumption of civil war – two were attributable to central government defections from their agreements.) While a communal group may choose to reject autonomy arrangements because they fall short of the group's ultimate aspiration (i.e., independent statehood), it may also be discouraged from accepting

---

[11] *Ibid.*, p. 31.

[12] Donald L. Horowitz, 'The Cracked Foundations of the Right to Secede', 14(2) *Journal of Democracy* (2003), 10.

[13] Ted Robert Gurr, *Minorities at Risk: A Global View of Ethnopolitical Conflicts* (Washington, DC: United States Institute of Peace Press, 1993), pp. 300–5. Hurst Hannum, *Autonomy, Sovereignty, and Self-Determination: The Accommodation of Conflicting Rights* (Philadelphia: University of Pennsylvania Press, 1990), pp. 123–327, provides details of nine regional autonomy arrangements.

such arrangements under pressure from outside parties – an observation, it will be seen, that has particular relevance to the Yugoslav case.

While this book is concerned with the EC's use of conditional recognition as an instrument of conflict management, it draws to a limited extent from the field of development studies for insights into the utility of this approach generally. For more than two decades states and multilateral organisations have been employing political conditionality in their relations with developing countries, tying aid, trade and other concessions to prescribed changes in a recipient state's political behaviour.[14] Often conditional development assistance has been in pursuit of objectives akin to those of the EC in Yugoslavia, including the promotion of human rights, democratisation and 'good governance'. The EC/EU itself has used political conditionality extensively as part of its trade and development assistance programmes, sometimes imposing on recipient states requirements relating to their domestic political structures in many ways not unlike the requirements it stipulated for the new state authorities in Yugoslavia. Another aim of this study, therefore, is to examine these early and parallel uses of political conditionality for what they suggest about the potential for and limitations of conditional recognition as an instrument of conflict management. How effective has aid and trade conditionality been and what accounts for its successes and shortcomings? Bearing in mind the relevant differences, can the lessons drawn from these experiences inform the use of conditional recognition in support of conflict mitigation and prevention?

Recognition and norms

The question of norms is central to this study and provides the overarching framework for a discussion that spans a broad range of topics. Norms are shared understandings of standards for behaviour; they inform beliefs and expectations about how an actor with a given identity will or ought to behave.[15] In the case of the EC and Yugoslavia, norms were the very basis of the Community's criteria for the recognition of new states.

Norms may find expression in ethically or prudentially prescriptive terms, as in the assertion: 'It is immoral (or unwise) to sell arms to states that may use them to suppress internal dissent.' In this sense of the term,

---

[14] For an overview of these practices, see Olav Stokke, 'Introduction', in Olav Stokke (ed.), *Aid and Political Conditionality* (London: Frank Cass, 1995).

[15] Audie Klotz, *Norms in International Relations: The Struggle Against Apartheid* (Ithaca, NY: Cornell University Press, 1995), p. 14.

the EC's use of political conditionality can be said to raise important normative issues concerning equitable relations between states. Is it fair to expect new states – and select new states at that – to satisfy requirements for recognition that established states have not had to meet and in many cases could not meet? Is it legitimate for some states to insist on the adoption of standards that do not have universal currency as well as on the mode of their implementation? The difficulty is compounded by the fact that conditionality, whatever form it takes, is predicated on fundamental asymmetries in the global order that the major powers have exploited historically for purposes evidently more self-serving, yet no less nobly proclaimed, than those that would appear to have guided the EC in this particular instance.[16]

The normative dimension of this study, however, does not extend principally to questions of international morality, although these are given some consideration. There is another, more fundamental sense in which norms are central to this study, and that is in the constitutive and regulatory functions they perform in the international system. As Peter Katzenstein explains the distinction:

In some situations norms operate like rules that define the identity of an actor, thus having 'constitutive' effects that specify what actions will cause relevant others to recognize a particular identity. In other situations norms operate as standards that specify the proper enactment of an already defined identity. In such instances norms have 'regulative' effects that specify standards of proper behavior.[17]

These two functions are inter-related: norms help to define the distinguishing characteristics of an actor, and the actor's identity in turn shapes expectations about its behaviour. Consider the principal actor in the international system: the state. The state's identity is in part constituted by shared beliefs, which are embedded in international conventions and customary law about what a state is: notably, an inhabited territory with a government capable of exercising effective control over that territory and of entering freely into relations with (other) states. A trust territory is not a state because it lacks the attributes of internal and external sovereignty. If such a territory were to become a state, our expectations about its formal capabilities would change

---

[16] For a representative statement of this view, see Samir Amin, 'The Issue of Democracy in the Contemporary Third World', in Barry Gills, Joel Rocamora and Richard Wilson (eds.), *Low Intensity Democracy* (London: Pluto Press, 1993), pp. 59–79.

[17] Peter J. Katzenstein, 'Introduction: Alternative Perspectives on National Security', in Peter J. Katzenstein (ed.), *The Culture of National Security: Norms and Identity in World Politics* (New York: Columbia University Press, 1996), p. 5.

accordingly – as would its behaviour.[18] For instance, only states sit on the United Nations Security Council, only states petition the International Court of Justice and only states participate in the Nuclear Non-Proliferation Treaty regime. Contrary, then, to the claims of neo-Realists and other materialists who maintain that one can explain the behaviour of states principally with respect to the balance of their relative capabilities, norms are not mere epiphenomena. Rather, they are of fundamental importance in part because they help to shape the modal character of statehood itself.[19]

Norms are also important because they reduce the complexity of choice-situations with which states are confronted and in so doing bring a measure of order and stability to an otherwise anarchic world.[20] By making it possible to establish what a state is, norms provide a means by which a unique set of rights and obligations are conferred on some entities and not on others – even entities whose power, in the case of major multinational corporations, may in important respects exceed that of certain states. Thus do states avoid the chaos that would no doubt arise were myriad entities around the globe to lay claim to such entitlements as the right of self-defence and freedom from intervention.

The conferment of rights and obligations is, of course, achieved through the recognition of states, which itself is a norm-governed process. The relevant norms have their basis in both treaty and customary law, although recognition has also always been something of a discretionary political act. A broad degree of uniformity in the application of these and any norms would seem necessary, however, if they are to perform any meaningful role, and such uniformity does indeed exist. Yet, as we noted earlier, the EC's adoption of security-relevant criteria for the recognition of new states in Yugoslavia represented a significant departure from the prevailing norm tending towards recognition on the basis primarily of non-political criteria. The question arises, then, how pertinent was the normative legal tradition to the EC's actions? And

[18] The degree of actual sovereignty may differ from the formal sovereignty required for statehood, as evidenced by the international community's tolerance of a large measure of control by Moscow over the foreign and domestic policies of the Soviet vassal states during the Cold War.

[19] Ronald L. Jepperson, Alexander Wendt and Peter J. Katzenstein, 'Norms, Identity, and Culture in National Security', in Katzenstein, *The Culture of National Security*, pp. 35–6.

[20] Friedrich V. Kratochwil discusses the simplification of choices that norms help to achieve. See his *Rules, Norms, and Decisions: On the Conditions of Practical and Legal Reasoning in International Relations and Domestic Affairs* (Cambridge: Cambridge University Press, 1989), p. 10.

what are the implications for international order of the EC's use of unorthodox criteria?

Answers to these questions depend, in part, on how one understands international law to function. If international law is understood as the mere application of neutral rules in a disinterested fashion, then its relevance to the case at hand would seem slight. If instead international law is understood as a dynamic process of which policy considerations are an integral part, then there may be scope for 'deviations' of the kind the EC practised.[21] But surely there are limits to innovation within any normative order, beyond which certain actions would be considered to be an unacceptable violation. How are these limits determined? In exploring these questions, this study draws on the interdisciplinary dialogue that has been taking place in recent years between scholars of international law and scholars of international relations.[22] One result is to suggest a different way of thinking about recognition: not as a set of rules but as an informal regime governed by a set of norms (political as well as legal) whose 'compliance pull' derives largely from the contribution that recognition is perceived to make to the maintenance of a stable international order. While the EC may have departed from customary practice by conditioning its recognition of new states in Yugoslavia on unorthodox criteria, it can be said to have done so in a manner consistent with trends in international law – in particular, what some scholars view as an emerging right to democratic governance.[23] The general explanations of state behaviour advanced in this book thus seek to accommodate the EC's actions while at the same time retaining the notion of meaningful normative constraints.

The structure of the book

The EC's use of recognition as an instrument of conflict management can best be appreciated within several different contexts, notably European strategic considerations at the end of the Cold War; the relevant international law and legal norms; and the intended and actual policy outcomes of EC actions. Accordingly, this book is organised

---

[21] Rosalyn Higgins explores these two views of international law in her *Problems & Process: International Law and How We Use It* (Oxford: Clarendon Press, 1994), ch. 1.

[22] For a useful overview of this dialogue, see Anne-Marie Slaughter, Andrew S. Tulumello and Stepan Wood, 'International Law and International Relations Theory: A New Generation of Interdisciplinary Scholarship', 92 *American Journal of International Law* (1998), 367–97.

[23] Thomas M. Franck, 'The Emerging Right to Democratic Governance', 86 *American Journal of International Law* (1992), 46–91.

around a number of broad thematic areas. The result is not a linear recounting of events but an analytic exploration that moves backwards and forwards and pauses periodically to examine associated questions. Readers interested in the short, 'straight' narrative can read just Chapters 1 and 4.

Chapter 1 focuses on the development, terms of reference and implementation of the EC's recognition policy. Particular attention is given to the strategic logic behind the initiative and what it reveals about thinking within the Community regarding strategies for achieving a peaceful settlement of the Yugoslav conflict. It argues that however much extrastrategic considerations may have informed EC policy and however imperfectly that policy may have been implemented, conditional recognition represented a genuine attempt to address some of the presumed sources of violent conflict in the region.

The recognition of states occupies an important place in international legal doctrine and historic state practice, and this tradition is examined in relation to the EC's recognition policy in Chapter 2. Although recognition has always been something of a discretionary political act, by the end of the Cold War it would seem to have become codified around general requirements for statehood that enjoyed broad support internationally. The EC's use of conditional recognition, it is shown, exhibited continuity with tradition but also departed from the prevailing norms in significant ways.

Given that there exists a large body of legal theory and practice relating to the creation of new states, the EC's unorthodox use of recognition raises important questions about the relevance of international legal norms to the Community's actions and to international politics generally. Are the critics right to suggest that international law had little bearing on the EC's actions? Is any invocation of the law but a conceit, masking what were fundamentally political choices? These questions are explored in Chapter 3.

Chapter 4 examines the impact of EC recognition on the strategic environment in the former Yugoslavia. Although its proponents defended recognition on the grounds that it would ameliorate the crisis, conventional wisdom holds that EC recognition contributed to the intensification of hostilities in the region. It is argued in this chapter that the responsibility that recognition is thought to bear for the violent conflict in the former Yugoslavia is overstated – that the forces of violence in the region were to a large degree operating independently of the factor of recognition. Recognition, in fact, created opportunities for more effective international action but these opportunities were not exploited.

Finally, Chapter 5 returns to the question of the strategic logic behind the EC's use of conditional recognition but this time in an attempt to reach some tentative conclusions about its possible utility. This chapter looks at prior uses of political conditionality, especially politically conditioned aid, for what these experiences suggest about the possibilities for and limitations of the use of conditional recognition as an instrument of conflict management. Conditional recognition, it is argued, can play a limited role in support of conflict mitigation, especially if reinforced by complementary measures such as conditional membership in regional organisations. The allure that the European Union and its affiliated bodies hold for the rest of Europe means that the EU enjoys particular influence in this regard – a form of 'soft power', to use Joseph Nye's term – although not as much influence, perhaps, as its more optimistic leaders imagined on the eve of the post-Cold War era.[24]

This is an interdisciplinary study that draws principally on empirical and theoretical investigations in four fields of social scientific research: strategic studies (for the nature and regulation of communal conflict); development studies (for prior and potential uses of political conditionality); international law (for general legal theory and the theory and practice of state recognition); and international relations (for evidence and explanations of cooperation in world politics). The book derives its core findings from comparative case study, analysis of official documents and interviews. Yugoslavia is treated here as both a single and multiple case study because the differentiated response of the EC to the crisis allows for consideration of three distinct aspects of the policy – recognition (Slovenia, Croatia, and Bosnia and Herzegovina), delayed recognition (Macedonia) and non-recognition (Kosovo) – although developments in each of these regions were, of course, interconnected. Cases concerned with the use of aid conditionality are drawn entirely from the secondary literature.

The documents used for the purposes of this study include international legal materials relevant to the recognition of states in general and to the EC's recognition of states in Yugoslavia in particular; official statements, parliamentary hearings, defence planning and budget documents, and foreign office reports and memoranda of several EC member states relating to security policy and policy towards Yugoslavia; and official documents of the former Yugoslavia relevant to political and strategic developments in that region. Other important sources include

[24] Joseph S. Nye, Jr, *Soft Power: The Means to Success in World Politics* (New York: PublicAffairs, 2004).

interviews with officials of the EC, its member states and the former
republics of Yugoslavia in the period from 1995 to 1999. These have
been supplemented by the research interviews conducted by Brian
Lapping Associates for the 1995 BBC television series, 'The Death of
Yugoslavia', the transcripts of which have been deposited at the Liddell
Hart Centre for Military Archives in London. For developments within
the European Community and the former Yugoslavia in the period
under consideration, this study also makes use of the extensive reportage
and secondary literature on the subject.

There are inherent limitations to any study of events as recent as those
of the wars of Yugoslav dissolution, and these limitations are worth
noting. Chief among them, perhaps, is the paucity of archival materials.
To the extent that official papers can shed light on some of the key
questions explored here, many of these papers may not be available to
the public for several years to come – if at all. Thus, for instance, Bosnian
Serb preparations for war, the details of which might clarify the role that
EC recognition played in the outbreak of hostilities in Bosnia and
Herzegovina, may only become better known as Serb military planning
documents become available. Such documents, however, do not necessarily exist in all cases. As Vojislav Šešelj, a Serbian MP who commanded a paramilitary unit during the war, explained in an interview
in 1992: 'Plans of that type [ethnic consolidation] are not written down
for the general public. He who holds power or who has the capability of
implementing a plan writes it down [only] for the benefit of his own
guidance and that of the necessary circle of people around him who
participate in implementing the national plan.'[25] Furthermore, the prospect of an indictment by the International Criminal Tribunal for the
Former Yugoslavia – the first war crimes tribunal to be operational in the
course of hostilities – has no doubt prompted some parties to destroy key
documents that they may have feared could incriminate them. These
difficulties are compounded by a trend that has seen the replacement of
many traditional forms of communication (e.g., internal memoranda
and telegrams) with paperless forms of communication (telephone calls,
emails) that are likely to be less accessible to posterity.[26]

[25] Šešelj interview with *Srbija* (Belgrade), January 1992, cited in Norman Cigar, *Genocide in Bosnia: The Policy of "Ethnic Cleansing"* (College Station, TX: Texas A & M University Press, 1995), p. 47.
[26] Richard Holbrooke discusses the challenge for historians posed by the obsolescence of these traditional forms of communication in his *To End a War* (New York: Random House, 1998), p. 372. See also 'E-Mail Nightmare' (editorial), *The Washington Post*, 2 December 1998.

The limitations of researching the present, then, may not be entirely overcome with the passage of time. Moreover, these limitations are offset by distinct advantages to present-oriented research – among them, the availability of the principal and supporting actors. These individuals are important not only for their first-hand knowledge of events but also for their private papers, many of which are unlikely ever to find their way into public repositories.[27] Of course the scholar must approach the admissions of any participant with circumspection – but no more so, perhaps, than he or she would the memoirs of a former diplomat, which, while generally acknowledged to be unique and valuable sources of information, may nonetheless be marred by incomplete knowledge, lapses of memory and the tendency of memoirists to present themselves in a positive light.[28]

The recognition of new states in Yugoslavia represents one of the most important episodes in recent European history. Its significance, however, extends well beyond history as we continue to wrestle with the challenges posed by violent conflict associated with state fragmentation – in the Western Balkans and elsewhere. It is hoped that this book can contribute to an understanding of these challenges and thus make it possible for scholars to comprehend better the dynamics of violent self-determination disputes and for policymakers to play a more effective role in the management of them.

---

[27] The testimony and material evidence being gathered in The Hague, however, is already a store of incalculable value.

[28] For an eloquent defence of present-oriented research, see Timothy Garton Ash, *History of the Present* (London: Allen Lane/Penguin Press, 1999), Introduction.

1   The EC's recognition policy: origins and terms of reference

The European Community's decision to recognise the republics of Yugoslavia seeking statehood was taken at a Council of Ministers meeting in Brussels on 16 December 1991, six months after the war began following Slovenia's and Croatia's declarations of independence on 25 June 1991.[1] Initial confidence in the EC's capacity for effective mediation in the crisis had by that time been displaced by a conviction among some member states that more radical measures were urgently needed to stop the fighting. A few governments, notably those of Germany and Denmark, had spoken openly about recognising the break-away republics as a means to achieve that goal soon after the outbreak of hostilities,[2] and as the war progressed Germany especially became more outspoken in support of recognition. But because of the importance attached to maintaining political consensus within the Community,[3] persistent objections from other member states – particularly France, Britain and the Netherlands – meant that EC recognition would not be forthcoming until the opposing states finally yielded at the December foreign ministers' meeting.[4]

Numerous accounts have been written about the events leading up to the EC's fateful decision; these events, therefore, are discussed here

---

[1] The declarations marked the culmination of more than a decade of sharp economic decline and rising inter-republic tensions. For an account of the crisis, see Lenard J. Cohen, *Broken Bonds: Yugoslavia's Disintegration and Balkan Politics in Transition*, 2nd edn (Boulder, CO: Westview Press, 1995).

[2] 'Some Western Nations Split off on Yugoslavia', *New York Times*, 3 July 1991; and 'European Community Freezes Arms Sales and Aid', *New York Times*, 6 July 1991.

[3] For a discussion of the importance and achievement of consensus among the Twelve in the early phase of the Yugoslav crisis, see Reneo Lukic and Allen Lynch, *Europe from the Balkans to the Urals: The Disintegration of Yugoslavia and the Soviet Union* (Oxford: SIPRI/Oxford University Press, 1996), ch. 13.

[4] Several European states were to extend recognition before the EC, notably Estonia, Latvia, Lithuania, the Vatican, Iceland and Ukraine. See 'Recognition of Croatia and Slovenia', *RFE/RL Research Report*, *'Weekly Review'*, 24 January 1992, p. 76.

only briefly.[5] This chapter focuses instead on the content of the EC's recognition policy for what it reveals about thinking within the Community regarding strategies for achieving a peaceful settlement of the Yugoslav conflict. Of course, the more parochial interests of individual member states – Germany's in particular – were not irrelevant to the formation and implementation of the EC's recognition policy, and these are discussed as well. But however much these interests may have guided or even dominated policy considerations, they alone do not explain the specific *design* of the EC's policy. The architects of that policy, it will be seen, gave serious thought to how recognition might be used effectively to mitigate the conflict and to prevent its further expansion. To ignore the EC's use of recognition for this purpose, or to suggest that this was merely a face-saving gesture that cloaked the 'real' interests of certain member states, as many observers maintained at the time, is to overlook an important dimension of the EC's diplomatic intervention in the Yugoslav crisis.

Three sets of documents provide the framework for the EC's recognition policy and they are given particular emphasis here. These documents are: the EC Conference on Yugoslavia's draft Convention of 4 November 1991 (the 'Carrington Plan'), whose minority rights provisions were retained as key conditions for EC recognition; the opinions of the arbitration commission (the 'Badinter Commission') that the EC established in part to advise it on legal questions arising within the context of the EC's peace negotiations; and the actual policy of conditional recognition adopted at the 16 December Council of Ministers meeting and articulated in the EC's twin 'Guidelines on the Recognition of New States in Eastern Europe and the Soviet Union' and the 'Declaration on Yugoslavia'.

The road to recognition

With the declarations of independence by Slovenia and Croatia, the EC was inescapably implicated in the Yugoslav conflict. For whatever choice

---

[5] See, for instance, Cohen, *Broken Bonds*, ch. 8; Mihailo Crnobrnja, *The Yugoslav Drama*, 2nd edn (London: I.B. Tauris, 1996), ch. 13; Misha Glenny, *The Fall of Yugoslavia: The Third Balkan War* (London: Penguin, 1992), chs. 3 & 4; James Gow, *Triumph of the Lack of Will: International Diplomacy and the Yugoslav War* (London: Hurst & Co., 1997), chs. 3 & 4; Laura Silber and Allan Little, *The Death of Yugoslavia* (London: Penguin, 1995), chs. 12–14; Susan L. Woodward, *Balkan Tragedy: Chaos and Dissolution after the Cold War* (Washington, DC: The Brookings Institution, 1995), ch. 6; and Henry Wynaendts, *L'engrenage: Chroniques yougoslaves, juillet 1991–août 1992* (Paris: Denoël, 1993), chs. 6–12.

Map 1. New Balkan states after 1991.

the EC or its individual member states might make – immediate recognition, non-recognition or delayed recognition of the two republics[6] – that choice would almost certainly have a bearing on events in the region. States differed in their assessments of the probable consequences that any particular démarche might have for the course of the war. They were concerned, moreover, about the wider ramifications of the EC's actions at a time when borders were being called into question across the continent. 'Tomorrow what we have done for Yugoslavia would be applied to other cases', Roland Dumas, the French foreign minister, cautioned in early July 1991.[7] West European leaders were especially concerned about the implications that the dissolution of Yugoslavia

---

[6] None of the four other republics sought recognition until later that year.

[7] Cited in 'European Community Freezes Arms Sales and Aid', *New York Times*, 6 July 1991.

might have for the Soviet Union, where nationalist tensions also threatened to disturb the established order.

Germany was the first EC member state to advocate the recognition of Slovenia and Croatia. Until fighting erupted at the end of June, Germany had, along with the rest of the EC, supported the continued unity of Yugoslavia. As late as 19 June 1991, Germany voted in favour of a statement by the Conference on Security and Co-operation in Europe (CSCE) expressing support for the 'unity and territorial integrity of Yugoslavia';[8] in fact, it was Hans-Dietrich Genscher, the German foreign minister, who supplied the text of the statement.[9] Even after Slovenia's and Croatia's declarations of independence, Germany supported the Western European Union (WEU) declaration of 27 June that expressed regret at 'the recent unilateral decisions' of the two republics and urged all political authorities in Yugoslavia to 'resume the dialogue with a view to securing the unity of the state'.[10] With the outbreak of hostilities that same day, however, Germany began to change course. At the summit of the EC heads of state in Luxembourg on 29 June, German Chancellor Helmut Kohl sided tacitly with Slovenia against Belgrade when he declared, 'The unity of Yugoslavia cannot be maintained with the force of arms.'[11] And in a radio interview on 3 July, Genscher expressed the view that Yugoslavia continued to exist on paper only, and blamed the Yugoslav military for reinforcing the republics' drive for independence.[12]

Germany was not alone in tempering its support for a united Yugoslavia. British Foreign Minister Douglas Hurd, too, felt constrained to qualify an earlier statement supporting the 'integrity of Yugoslavia' by adding that this should not be accomplished through the use of force.[13] Indeed, throughout the summer and autumn of 1991, the differences between Germany and its partners on the question of recognition were largely to do with the modalities of recognition – when and how – and not with whether recognition should be granted. 'No one could seriously suggest that we could have gone on pretending that the old Yugoslavia

---

[8] *Agence Europe* (Brussels), No. 5516 (20 June 1991), p. 4.
[9] Gianni De Michelis, 'Così cercammo di impedire la guerra', 1 *Limes* (1994), 232. De Michelis, the Italian foreign minister, participated in the CSCE deliberations.
[10] WEU Ministerial Statement (Document 1280), Vianden, Luxembourg, 27 June 1991.
[11] Cited in Hans-Heinrich Wrede, 'Die deutsche Balkanpolitik im Einklang mit den Partnern', *Das Parlament* Nr. 40 (1 October 1993), p. 14 (my translation).
[12] Michael Libal, *Limits of Persuasion: Germany and the Yugoslav Crisis, 1991–1992* (Westport, CT: Praeger, 1997), p. 17.
[13] Cited in 'First Test for New Europe', *The Independent*, 28 June 1991.

still existed', Hurd would later say.[14] Even France, the most vociferous critic of German actions throughout this period, had concluded by the end of the summer that recognition would have to be extended to the two republics eventually. In late August, as the Yugoslav People's Army (JNA) began its fierce assault against the Croatian town of Vukovar, Hubert Védrine, secretary-general of the Elysée, received Croatian President Franjo Tudjman and offered him assurances that international recognition would be forthcoming, provided that Croatia guaranteed the rights of its Serb minority.[15] The following month, Foreign Minister Dumas, speaking on French TV, asserted that the question was 'no longer to know if these republics were independent but how they will be so'.[16] And, on 9 October, Dumas fell just short of saying that the EC should recognise the independence of Slovenia and Croatia when he told the French National Assembly:

Yugoslavia no longer exists in its original form and we are forced to take note of a *de facto* partition occurring . . . due to the will expressed by the two republics which were part of the union to break away. The European Community should continue to act in complete solidarity and draw the logical consequences under international law from this situation.[17]

By this time the EC itself had adopted the position that it would eventually extend recognition to those republics seeking it. On 4 October, Hans van den Broek, the Dutch foreign minister, acting in his capacity as president of the EC Council of Ministers, announced that an agreement had been reached between the representatives of the then warring parties – Slobodan Milošević, the president of Serbia; Franjo Tudjman, the president of Croatia; and General Veljko Kadijević, the Yugoslav defence minister – in the context of the EC's Conference on Yugoslavia.[18] As Van den Broek summarised the positions: 'It was agreed that the involvement of all parties concerned would be necessary to formulate a political solution *on the basis of the perspective of recognition of the independence of those republics wishing*

---

[14] Hurd continues: 'We must deal with realities, and the reality was that Croatia existed. Whether it should have been recognised in the autumn, which is what the Germans wanted, or at the end of the year, which is what happened, or a little later, is a matter of dispute. . .' *Parliamentary Debates* (Hansard), House of Commons, vol. 259, col. 334, 3 May 1995.

[15] Hubert Védrine, *Les mondes de François Mitterrand* (Paris: Fayard, 1996), p. 610.

[16] *Agence Europe* No. 5568 (16–17 September 1991), p. 3.

[17] Cited in 'Yugoslavia no Longer Exists, Says France', *The Times*, 10 October 1991.

[18] The EC announced the establishment of the peace conference on 27 August 1991. See Joint Statement, 28 August 1991, 24(7/8) *Bulletin of the European Communities* (1991), 115–16.

it. . .'[19] For the first time, then, the EC was formally proposing recognition as the basis of a political solution to the Yugoslav conflict. However, the agreement also contained an important qualification: recognition was to be granted 'at the end of the negotiating process conducted in good faith [and] in the framework of a general agreement'.[20] In other words, recognition would be granted only after a consensual constitutional settlement acceptable to all six republics had been forged. This fundamental principle, which would be reiterated in the Conference's proposed outline of a general settlement and in both drafts of the Convention,[21] was endorsed by all EC member states, first in a European Political Cooperation (EPC) declaration of 6 October 1991 following an informal meeting of EC foreign ministers at Haarzuilens, and then in a 10 October declaration of the CSCE's Committee of Senior Officials.[22]

Leading German policymakers would later invoke the decisions taken at this time in support of Germany's unilateral recognition of Slovenia and Croatia on 23 December 1991. According to Genscher, the Haarzuilens meeting was a turning point: 'Hereby the EC affirmed the rights of the republics to independence if they wished it.'[23] But it was Van den Broek's subsequent 'translating [of] the results of Haarzuilens into reality', as Genscher puts it,[24] that for the German foreign minister was of crucial significance. Genscher refers to both a press statement that Van den Broek issued on 10 October and an interview that appeared in the Austrian newspaper *Die Presse* on 18 October. In the latter instance Van den Broek set a deadline of a maximum of two months for the negotiating process and indicated that the Twelve would be prepared to extend recognition after that period:

---

[19] Reproduced in Report of the Secretary-General Pursuant to Paragraph 3 of Security Council Resolution 713 (1991), UN Doc. S/23169, 25 October 1991, Annex II, p. 20 (emphasis added).

[20] *Ibid.*

[21] See Arrangements for a General Settlement [18 October 1991], 1.1(e) and Treaty Provisions for the Convention [23 October 1991], Article 1.1(e) in UN Doc. S/23169, Annex VI and Annex VII; and Treaty Provisions for the Convention [4 November 1991], Article 1.1(f) in David Owen, *Balkan Odyssey*, CD-ROM, Academic edition, version 1.1 (London: Apple/Electric Company, 1995).

[22] 'Declaration on Yugoslavia', Informal Meeting of Ministers of Foreign Affairs (Haarzuilens), EPC Press Release P. 98/91, 16 October 1991; 'The Situation in Yugoslavia', Third Additional Meeting of the Committee of Senior Officials (Prague), *Journal* (10 October 1991), Annex.

[23] Hans-Dietrich Genscher, *Erinnerungen* (Berlin: Siedler, 1995), p. 953 (my translation).

[24] *Ibid.*, p. 954.

VAN DEN BROEK: The solution has to be found within a month. The negotiations can be extended for a maximum of another month. By that time there must be a political solution, and the Yugoslav army must have retreated from Croatia completely.

DIE PRESSE: And if it [the JNA] does not do this?

VAN DEN BROEK: If this is not the case, the time will have come for the Community to decide on the recognition of Slovenia and Croatia. At that point we can no longer deny the right to independence if individual republics have expressed it in a democratic way.[25]

Van den Broek was optimistic about securing the peace – he had expected that a general settlement could be achieved within the Dutch six-month presidency – and his resoluteness at this particular moment may have reflected growing impatience with the lack of progress in negotiations, for which he held Belgrade largely responsible since Serbia was the only republic to reject the EC's Arrangements for a General Settlement presented to the parties on 18 October.[26] (The Arrangements were drawn up on the basis of the 4 October agreement between Milošević, Tudjman and Kadijević mentioned above.) But Van den Broek's statements were not supported by subsequent declarations of the Community or other member states. Just a few weeks after the *Die Presse* interview, the EC Council of Ministers, meeting in the margins of the Rome NATO summit on 8 November, reaffirmed the position that 'the prospect of recognition of the independence of those Republics wishing it, can only be envisaged in the framework of an overall settlement. . .'[27] There was no mention of a 10 December deadline; on the contrary, the majority of ministers cautioned against the 'premature recognition' of Slovenia and Croatia, which, in their

---

[25] VAN DEN BROEK: Diese Lösung muß innerhalb eines Monats gefunden werden. Die Verhandlungen können maximal um einen weiteren Monat verlängert werden. Bis zu diesem Zeitpunkt muß eine politische Lösung da sein und muß sich die Jugoslawische Armee aus Kroatien völlig zurückgezogen haben.
DIE PRESSE: Und wenn sie dies nicht tut?
VAN DEN BROEK: Sollte dies nicht der Fall sein, ist für die Gemeinschaft der Zeitpunkt gekommen, über die Anerkennung Sloweniens und Kroatiens zu entscheiden. Dann können wir das Recht auf Unabhängigkeit, wenn es von einzelnen Republiken auf demokratische Weise zum Ausdruck gebracht wird, nicht länger negieren. Helmut Hetzel, 'In zwei Monaten entscheiden wir über die Anerkennung', *Die Presse*, 18 October 1991.
[26] UN Doc. S/23169, pp. 9–10. Norbert Both, *From Indifference to Entrapment: The Netherlands and the Yugoslav Crisis 1990–1995* (Amsterdam: Amsterdam University Press, 2000), pp. 126–7.
[27] 'Declaration on Yugoslavia', Extraordinary EPC Ministerial Meeting (Rome), EPC Press Release P. 109/91, 8 November 1991.

view, would create more problems than it would resolve.[28] Van den Broek seemed even to contradict himself when, just two weeks before the presumed deadline, he was quoted as saying that now was not the time to ask at what point the EC will eventually recognise Slovenia.[29]

Yet there can be no doubt that the trend towards recognition was gathering momentum within the EC as Belgrade was perceived increasingly to be using excessive force in its war against Croatia, to be acting on behalf of Serbian interests alone and to be impeding progress towards a negotiated settlement. A British Foreign and Commonwealth Office memorandum, for instance, faulted the Yugoslav federal army's 'cynical aggression against Dubrovnik in October and the obstructive tactics employed by Serbia at the October discussions' for the suspension of the Conference on Yugoslavia's plenary meetings in early November, after Milošević had rejected the draft Convention that Lord Peter Carrington, chairman of the conference, drew up subsequent to the October 18th Arrangements for a General Settlement.[30] As a consequence of this shift in thinking, other states joined with Germany, which on 13 November had stated its intention to recognise Slovenia and Croatia by Christmas. Italy announced on 28 November that it would extend recognition to the two republics before the end of the year,[31] and on 3 December, Belgium and Denmark announced that they, too, would recognise the two republics by that time.[32] These latter decisions were facilitated by the first of several opinions delivered by the Badinter Commission, the arbitration commission established by the EC at the same time as the Conference, which on 29 November observed that 'the Socialist Federal Republic of Yugoslavia is in the process of dissolution'.[33] By then, moreover, the Soviet Union appeared to be headed inexorably towards disintegration and there was less concern,

---

[28] Wynaendts, *L'engrenage*, pp. 132–3. Wynaendts, Carrington's deputy, was present at the EC's Rome meeting.

[29] 'Reaktion Van den Broeks auf Kohl', *Frankfurter Allgemeine Zeitung*, 29 November 1991.

[30] Foreign and Commonwealth Office, 'Developments in Central Europe: Mechanics of Security and Co-operation (CE 129)', memorandum dated December 1991, in House of Commons, Foreign Affairs Committee, First Report, *Central and Eastern Europe: Problems of the Post-Communist Era* (HC 21–II), vol. II, Minutes of Evidence, HC Session 1991–2, p. 194.

[31] 'Bonn Urges Recognition of Breakaway Republics', *The Guardian*, 14 November 1991; 'UK Ready to Recognise Croatia and Slovenia', *The Independent*, 29 November 1991.

[32] 'Croatia and Slovenia Put Case to Bonn', *The Guardian*, 4 December 1991. See also Both, *From Indifference to Entrapment*, p. 135.

[33] Opinion No. 1, 29 November 1991 (published on 7 December 1991), 31 *International Legal Materials* (1992), 1497.

consequently, about the broader demonstration effect that the break-up of Yugoslavia might have.

Worried that the EC was losing its cohesion just when the Community was engaged in efforts to strengthen its common foreign and security policymaking capacity, Dumas suggested to Genscher at the Maastricht summit of 9–10 December that France and Germany propose to the rest of the Community a set of conditions whose fulfilment would entitle candidate republics to EC recognition.[34] It was a mutually satisfactory compromise. France, although it would still have preferred to extend recognition in the context of a general settlement, would at least be satisfied that the policy was a common EC policy, and one, moreover, that obliged the aspiring republics to agree to conditions that arguably would enhance the prospects for peace. Germany, although it would have preferred immediate recognition, would be satisfied that recognition would soon be forthcoming and that it would not be a German initiative alone.[35]

A few days later, Alain Dejammet, the French political director, and Jacques Blot, director for Europe at the Quai d'Orsay, travelled to Bonn to meet with Jürgen Chrobog, the German political director, to draft a proposal for a policy of conditional recognition that could be presented at the Council of Ministers meeting in Brussels on 16 December.[36] Van den Broek, in turn, wrote to the EC foreign ministers proposing that they agree to the policy at the meeting: '[T]he Twelve should consider to proceed with a policy of conditional recognition. This would imply granting recognition only to republics that have accepted EC proposals.'[37] These preparations belie the impression some analysts convey that German demands for recognition on 16 December were hasty and unanticipated,[38] or that the Brussels principles were designed merely to

---

[34] At an earlier meeting between Kohl and Mitterrand on 15 November, Mitterrand had also stressed the importance of EC cohesion and suggested in more general terms the need to secure guarantees for the respect of minority rights in the event of recognition. See Libal, *Limits of Persuasion*, p. 76; and Védrine, *Les mondes de François Mitterrand*, p. 615.

[35] Genscher would announce one week later, 'Es wird keinen Alleingang der Bundesregierung geben' ['There will be no German going alone']. Cited in 'Die EG berät über Anerkennung Sloweniens und Kroatiens', *Frankfurter Allgemeine Zeitung*, 17 December 1991.

[36] Author interview with Dejammet, New York, 21 November 1996; telephone interview with Chrobog, 3 June 1999. Genscher confirms this account and claims to have checked the draft criteria with Chrobog 'word for word over the telephone'. Genscher, *Erinnerungen*, p. 959.

[37] Cited in Both, *From Indifference to Entrapment*, p. 133.

[38] See, for instance, Richard Holbrooke, *To End a War* (New York: Random House, 1998), p. 31.

cloak French embarrassment at a display of 'German *diktat*'.[39] Two texts
were tabled at the 16 December meeting: a set of general guidelines on
the recognition of new states in Eastern Europe and the Soviet Union
and a set of guidelines specific to the recognition of new states in
Yugoslavia (see Appendices 1 and 2).[40] After considerable debate –
many states still opposed recognition – and with some modification,
the two texts were adopted by the foreign ministers.

The two texts represent a striking departure from historic convention
insofar as they predicate diplomatic recognition on the fulfilment of a
series of novel political conditions by the aspiring state entities. (Legal
thinking and historic state practice with respect to recognition are discussed in greater detail in Chapter 2.) Among the EC's general requirements was acceptance of the foundational documents of the post-Cold
War European order – the Charter of the United Nations, the Helsinki
Final Act and the Charter of Paris – as well as acceptance of certain basic
norms of international society: respect for the inviolability of borders,
acceptance of disarmament and nuclear non-proliferation obligations,
and a commitment to settle any disputes arising from state succession
peacefully.

The guidelines specific to Yugoslavia required, additionally, acceptance of the provisions of the Conference on Yugoslavia's draft Convention and, in particular, those contained in Chapter II on human rights
and the rights of national or ethnic groups (see Appendix 3). In deference to Greek concerns about alleged Macedonian irredentism, a further
condition was that the republics commit themselves to adopt constitutional and political guarantees to ensure that they harbour no territorial claims towards 'a neighbouring Community state', and that they
also refrain from hostile propaganda activities towards such states, including the use of a name that might imply territorial claims.[41] In both

[39] Peter Jenkins, 'Dangerous Consequences of a Bad Night's Work', *The Independent*,
18 December 1991.
[40] 'Declaration on the "Guidelines on the Recognition of New States in Eastern Europe
and in the Soviet Union"' and 'Declaration on Yugoslavia', Extraordinary EPC Ministerial Meeting (Brussels), EPC Press Releases P. 128/91 and P. 129/91, 16 December
1991.
[41] EC governments were generally unfamiliar with the issues surrounding Macedonian
independence and feared that their non-acquiescence in Greece's concerns might
jeopardise Greek ratification of the Maastricht agreement. Moreover, Greece waited
until very late in the meeting to table its proposal (the meeting ended in the early hours
of 17 December) when the ministers were very tired. Author interview with Dejammet;
and Kevin Robert Warnes, 'West European Foreign and Security Policy-Making:
National Interests and Regional Cooperation (1990–1994)', Ph.D. dissertation,
University of Bradford, Department of Peace Studies, 1995, p. 251.

the general guidelines and those specific to Yugoslavia, it was not clear precisely what would constitute 'acceptance', 'respect', 'commitment', 'guarantees' or 'fulfilment' on the part of the aspiring state entities. A role was envisioned for the Badinter Commission to advise the Community in this regard, which was to assess the republics' applications and report its findings prior to 15 January, when, it was agreed, the EC would implement its policy.[42] But the question of evaluation and timing, as we will see below, would bedevil the Community in the critical one-month interval.

Because of the centrality of the EC's recognition criteria to this study, a closer examination of these conditions is warranted. It is particularly useful to view these conditions in light of the various claims that were being advanced at the time for the strategic value of recognition – that is, how recognition might help to prevent, mitigate or even resolve conflict in the Yugoslav region.

The strategic logic of recognition

To the proponents of recognition, its utility as an instrument of conflict management was three-fold. First, recognition was seen as a punitive measure, the prospect of which might deter the Belgrade leadership from pursuing a campaign of violence against the break-away republics. Second, actual recognition would alter the fundamental nature of the conflict: it would transform an internal dispute into an interstate war and endow the antagonists with new legal rights and obligations as well as create new opportunities for intervention by third-party states. A related function of recognition was that it could confer legitimacy on, and therefore strengthen, one political option – statehood for all the Yugoslav republics – that some saw as the basis for a lasting resolution of the conflict.[43] Finally, and most relevant for our purposes, the offer of recognition would induce the aspiring state entities to adopt policies, especially regarding the status of minorities within their territories, that might eliminate or at least mitigate one of the presumed causes of the conflict. Although recognition, strictly speaking, could be used only

---

[42] The Declaration reads: 'The applications of those Republics which reply positively will be submitted through the Chair of the Conference to the Arbitration Commission for advice before the implementation date.'

[43] For a view of the new states in Yugoslavia as 'a peace-enforcing and peace-keeping institution', see Tomaž Mastnak, 'Fascists, Liberals, and Anti-Nationalism', in Richard Caplan and John Feffer (eds.), *Europe's New Nationalism: States and Minorities in Conflict* (New York: Oxford University Press, 1996), pp. 59–74.

once, the EC could and did employ it repeatedly as either a threatened or a promised course of action.

In the early phases of the conflict, recognition was viewed by its advocates largely as a tactical measure to pressure and deter the Serbian and Yugoslav federal authorities from the further use of force. Thus at an EC Council of Ministers meeting in The Hague on 5 July, Genscher argued (unsuccessfully) for inclusion in the common declaration of an explicit warning to the Yugoslav army that any further military actions on their part would raise the possibility of EC recognition.[44] The Yugoslav army should know, Genscher announced shortly after, that the Community 'will seriously consider and also implement recognition' if it interferes in Yugoslav politics again.[45] At this stage of the crisis, Genscher appears to have believed that the Slovene and Croatian decisions were not irreversible – that they left room for negotiation and that democratic reform on the federal level might still accommodate their aspirations.[46] When on 6 August Genscher reintroduced the question of recognition into the debate at an EC foreign ministers' meeting, his interest again was to threaten a course of action that might induce the Serbian authorities to comply with the EC's further demand for a cessation of hostilities.[47] Genscher communicated this threat directly to Belgrade. On 24 August he told the Yugoslav ambassador to Bonn:

If the bloodshed continues and the policy of *faits accomplis* by force supported by the Yugoslav army is not halted immediately, the Federal Government [of Germany] must seriously examine the recognition of Croatia and Slovenia in their given frontiers. It will also commit itself to a corresponding examination within the European Community.[48]

As the fighting in Croatia intensified in the autumn of 1991 and it became apparent that, contrary to Belgrade's claims, the JNA's use of force bore little relation to Croatian cease-fire violations and, moreover, the JNA's intervention was not limited to the liberation of besieged garrisons or the protection of Serb communities, Germany and other member states began to argue in support of recognition as a means of internationalising the conflict – the second use of recognition. Genscher

---

[44] 'If it had been up to me alone, specific mention would have been made of the need to recognise the independence of Slovenia and Croatia in the event of future military action', Genscher said at the time. Cited in 'EC Backs Away from Recognition', *The Independent*, 6 July 1991. See also Both, *From Indifference to Entrapment*, p. 104.

[45] Cited in 'European Community Freezes Arms Sales and Aid', *New York Times*, 6 July 1991.

[46] Libal, *Limits of Persuasion*, pp. 12–13.

[47] *Ibid.*, p. 36.

[48] *Ibid.*, p. 39.

says that he first proposed this option at the 25 July meeting of EC foreign ministers. 'Were the negotiations to be blocked and the war were to continue', [I made clear,] 'then the option would have to be considered of whether we should not seek, as a last resort, an internationalisation of the conflict by recognising both republics in order to end the bloodshed and expulsions.'[49]

Internationalisation of the conflict could have many meanings and implications. In principle, recognition would confer international personality on Slovenia and Croatia and therefore entitle the two entities to a greater degree of protection than they would otherwise enjoy, although even as constituent republics of Yugoslavia they already enjoyed certain rights and freedoms as codified in international humanitarian law, such as the 1949 Geneva Conventions and the Additional Protocol II of 1977, to which Yugoslavia was a signatory.[50] (These protections may have been what the EC had in mind when in late August 1991 it called upon the Federal Presidency 'to put an immediate end to [the] *illegal use of the forces* under its command' – an exhortation that would have made little sense unless Croatia were already a subject of law.)[51] Of course, however clear a legal entitlement may be – extending to the right to self-defence, including collective military actions on the behalf of a state – there can be no assurance that the rights of any state will actually be protected. And while there was talk as early as July 1991 of deploying an armed interposition force to the region, there was insufficient support within the Community for such an option.[52]

Even though Germany, too, at various times advocated the deployment of some kind of intervention force to dampen the fighting,[53] Bonn seems to have imagined that 'internationalisation' of the conflict by itself

---

[49] Genscher, *Erinnerungen*, p. 945.
[50] Milan Šahović, 'International Humanitarian Law in the "Yugoslav War"', in Sonja Biserko (ed.), *Yugoslavia: Collapse, War, Crimes* (Belgrade: Centre for Anti-War Action, 1993), p. 146.
[51] EPC 'Declaration on Yugoslavia', 27 August 1991, EPC Press Release P. 82/91 (emphasis added).
[52] For a discussion of early EC considerations about armed intervention, see Geoffrey Edwards, 'European Responses to the Yugoslav Crisis: An Interim Assessment', in Reinhardt Rummel (ed.), *Toward Political Union: Planning a Common Foreign and Security Policy in the European Community* (Boulder, CO: Westview Press, 1992), pp. 174–7.
[53] On 2 August, Genscher expressed his support for a CSCE or WEU peacekeeping operation and in September, at the CSCE human rights conference in Moscow, proposed the establishment of a CSCE interventionary force. See Sonia Lucarelli, *Europe and the Breakup of Yugoslavia: A Political Failure in Search of a Scholarly Explanation* (The Hague: Kluwer Law International, 2000), p. 203; and *Keesing's Record of World Events* (September 1991), p. 38458.

might achieve the desired result. In a position paper that the Federal Foreign Office produced in March 1993 to explain its earlier actions, Germany argued that because the Yugoslav conflict was not a civil war but a war of conquest by Serbia, the international community had only two choices: it could either respond with a military containment of Serbia or it could pursue 'internationalization of the conflict by political means through formal recognition of the threatened republics in order to thwart any hopes Belgrade might have of *faits accomplis* achieved through the use of force being tolerated'.[54] Recognition, by this reasoning, would deter Belgrade from the further prosecution of its military campaign and even effect a withdrawal of its forces because the Yugoslav army's control of Croatian territory would then be in violation of Croatia's sovereign rights. The Serb authorities, it was assumed, would know that a prolonged occupation of Croatia might invite punitive measures from the international community. Germany applied the same logic to Bosnia and Herzegovina, albeit somewhat less confidently: it was the 'cherished hope', the position paper reads, 'that the internationalization of the Bosnian issue ensuing from recognition would, as in the case of Croatia, have a dampening effect on Serbia's aggression'.[55]

The third use of recognition was as an incentive to induce the would-be states to make changes in their policies, especially towards local national minorities, that the EC believed necessary to ensure peace in the region. The argument, put simply, was that the assertions of state-hood by the Yugoslav republics had threatened the national minorities within those territories – the Serbian communities in Croatia and Bosnia and Herzegovina in particular – and that adequate guarantees for the rights of these minorities on the part of the new state authorities would undercut one of the motive causes of the violent conflict.[56]

---

[54] German Foreign Office, Bonn, 'Recognition of the Yugoslav Successor States', mimeo, 10 March 1993, p. 3 (copy on file with author).

[55] *Ibid.*, p. 7.

[56] The argument that was *not* made, it is interesting to note, was that the EC had any special obligation towards the minority populations made vulnerable as a consequence of the state-creation process that the EC was abetting. Compare with Georges Clemenceau, the French prime minister, in his defence of the minority rights provisions of the treaty that reestablished the Polish state after the First World War : 'It is by their [the Entente Powers'] decision that Polish sovereignty is being re-established over the territories in question, and that the inhabitants of these territories are being incorporated in the Polish nation . . . There rests, therefore, upon these Powers an obligation, which they cannot evade, to secure in the most permanent and solemn form guarantees for certain essential rights which will afford to the inhabitants the necessary protection, whatever changes may take place in the internal constitution of the Polish State. . .' Cited in C. A. Macartney, *National States and National Minorities* (London: Oxford University Press, 1934), p. 238.

The EC's conditions for recognition reflect this logic. As Douglas Hogg, the British minister of state for foreign affairs, put it on 6 November 1991: 'The essential question . . . to be addressed is the question of minority rights [and] one of the major levers that we have in order to get people to address fully and properly the question of minority rights is recognition.'[57] But the link between security and minority rights – a hallmark feature of the Helsinki approach to security[58] – was already evident in the agreement that Van den Broek had negotiated between the presidents of Croatia and Serbia and the Yugoslav defence minister on 4 October. That agreement not only provided for recognition in the context of a general settlement but it also specified that any settlement must contain, *inter alia*, 'adequate arrangements . . . for the protection of minorities, including human rights guarantees and possibly special status for certain areas'.[59] The 4 October agreement, in turn, was the basis for Chapter II of the Carrington draft Convention whose acceptance by the republics, we have seen, was a requirement for EC recognition. As Paul Sizeland, Carrington's principal assistant, would later recall: 'In working on the draft convention it was clear to all those in Lord Carrington's team that the provisions for safeguarding minority rights would need to be very tightly drawn to provide the groups concerned with the necessary confidence.'[60]

As an element of a draft convention, Chapter II was still incomplete at the time of its adoption as a condition for recognition. The Council of Ministers' decision had the effect, therefore, of freezing a work in progress. As a consequence, there are some notable lacunae and inconsistencies, which are discussed below.[61] The main features of the chapter, however – a mixture of general and specific requirements – were by that point fairly well elaborated.[62]

Like the recognition guidelines of which they are a part, Chapter II requires the commitment of the parties to the principal international and regional human rights instruments, including the International

---

[57] Foreign Affairs Committee, *Central and Eastern Europe*, p. 59.

[58] Richard Dalton, 'The Role of the CSCE', in Hugh Miall (ed.), *Minority Rights in Europe* (London: Pinter/Royal Institute of International Affairs, 1994), pp. 99–111.

[59] UN Doc. S/23169, Annex II, p. 20. The EPC Declaration of 6 October 1991 added, similarly, 'The right to self-determination of all the peoples of Yugoslavia cannot be exercised in isolation from the interests and rights of ethnic minorities within the individual republics.'

[60] Letter from Paul Sizeland to the author, 3 November 1997.

[61] I owe this observation to Dr Geert-Hinrich Ahrens, chairman of the Conference's working group on human rights and minorities and the principal author of Chapter II. Letter from Ahrens to the author, 27 November 1997.

[62] See Treaty Provisions for the Convention [4 November 1991], Chapter II.

Covenant on Civil and Political Rights and the International Covenant on Economic, Social and Cultural Rights, as well as to specific human rights guarantees: the right to life, freedom of expression, the right to a fair hearing, freedom from torture and slavery, etc. – all of which have been fairly widely accepted around the globe even if they are often observed in the breach. Many of the national and minority rights are also widely accepted, within Western Europe at least; for instance, the right to identity, culture, religion and the use of one's own language both in public and private, and protection of equal participation in public affairs.

It is those rights that were to be available to members of national or ethnic minorities forming a majority in the area where they live that represented the boldest and most controversial attempt to accommodate the self-determination demands of minority groups in the former Yugoslavia. Chapter II required the establishment of a 'special status' for national minorities, which would provide for the right to have and display national emblems of the group; the right to a second nationality alongside the nationality of the republic; an educational system that 'respects the values and needs' of the group; and, most important, a legislative body, an administrative structure (including a regional police force) and a judiciary responsible for 'matters concerning the area'. There were to be provisions, moreover, for international monitoring of these arrangements.[63] The affected areas were to be listed in an annex to the treaty but since the treaty was not completed, the areas were never specified. (By contrast, the earlier outline of a settlement stipulated that '[t]he [special] status set out above will apply, in particular, to the Serbs living in areas in Croatia where they form a majority'.)[64] There were, however, several candidate regions. According to Sizeland, the Chapter II provisions 'were designed to apply as much to Serbs living in Krajina, as [to] Croats living in Serbia. . .' And 'the intention was that all Albanian communities in Kosovo should [also] benefit'.[65] Henry Wynaendts, Carrington's deputy, indicates that Vojvodina and Sandžak – the Hungarian- and Muslim-majority regions of Serbia respectively – were also considered candidates.[66]

The EC had a model in mind for the 'special status': the autonomy arrangements that had been negotiated for the Alto Adige/South Tyrol

---

[63] *Ibid.*, Art. 2(5B).

[64] Arrangements for a General Settlement (2.5), UN Doc. S/23169.

[65] Letter from Sizeland.

[66] Telephone interview with Wynaendts, 5 December 1997. See also 'Background Briefing on 6 October by Ambassador Geert Ahrens', in B. G. Ramcharan (ed.), *The International Conference on the Former Yugoslavia: Official Papers* (The Hague: Kluwer Law International, 1997), vol. II, p. 1604.

area of northern Italy in the aftermath of the Second World War.[67] The
territory had been ceded by Austria to Italy after the First World War but
because of the large German-speaking population there it was to be a
seat of unrest and a source of tension between the two countries for years
to come.[68] As early as 1946 Italy had pledged to grant autonomy to
the area but Austria objected that Italy was attempting instead to dilute
the majority German presence, first by amalgamating the largely Italian
province of Trentino and the predominantly German province of Bolzano to create a single region (Trentino–Alto Adige) and later by promoting the influx of Italian speakers from other parts of the country.[69]
Frustrated by what it viewed as obstructionism on Italy's part, the
Austrian government took its case to the UN General Assembly, which
on 31 October 1960 unanimously adopted a resolution calling on Italy
and Austria to seek a bilateral solution or, failing that, to seek recourse to
other peaceful dispute-resolution mechanisms such as arbitration.[70]

In response to dissatisfaction among the German-speaking South
Tyrolese that erupted in a brief campaign of violence in 1961, Italy
established a commission to re-examine the problem and resumed bilateral talks in 1963 after the commission presented its findings. These
negotiations led to a series of reforms in 1969 whose implementation,
however, Italy only completed to Austria's satisfaction in 1992.[71] Under
these arrangements (and further constitutional reforms adopted in
2001), Bolzano enjoys a large measure of control over its own fiscal,
economic, social, cultural and educational affairs.[72] Significantly, the

---

[67] Both Wynaendts (*L'engrenage*, p. 124) and Libal (*Limits of Persuasion*, p. 166) indicate
that Alto Adige/South Tyrol was a model for the 'special status' arrangements.

[68] Some 66 per cent of the population of Bolzano, the province in Italy that corresponds
roughly to South Tyrol, identified German as their native language in 1981. See
'Austria–Italy (South Tyrol)', in John B. Allcock *et al.* (eds.), *Border and Territorial
Disputes*, 3rd edn (Harlow: Longman, 1992), p. 21. The 2001 census essentially
confirmed these data.

[69] For accounts of the conflict and peacemaking efforts through the 1960s, see Mario
Toscano, *Alto Adige – South Tyrol* (Baltimore: The Johns Hopkins University Press,
1975) and Antony E. Alcock, *The History of the South Tyrol Question* (London: Michael
Joseph, 1970).

[70] UN General Assembly Res. 1497 (XV).

[71] On 19 June 1992 the Italian and Austrian representatives to the United Nations jointly
informed the secretary-general that bilateral differences over administration of the
region had been resolved. 'South Tyrol', draft memorandum provided to the author
by the Austrian Embassy (London), September 1997.

[72] The 'Autonomy Statute' of 1972 and associated legislation are contained in *Il nuovo
Statuto di Autonomia* (Bolzano: Giunta provinciale di Bolzano, 2003). See also, Stefan
Wolff, 'Settling an Ethnic Conflict through Power-sharing: South Tyrol', in Ulrich
Schneckener and Stefan Wolff (eds.), *Managing and Settling Ethnic Conflicts* (London:
Hurst & Co., 2004), pp. 64–72.

province retains a high proportion of the income tax generated within it, which, because of its prosperity, is quite considerable. The German language enjoys equal status with Italian within the province (there are special provisions for the Ladin-speaking population as well), allowing individuals to request that all court and local administrative proceedings be carried out in their native tongue. Indeed, anyone taking a job in the public sector has to demonstrate linguistic competence in both German and Italian. (Instruction in one's native language is guaranteed to a university entrance standard.) Bolzano also has the right to contest national laws before the Italian Constitutional Court that are thought to encroach on the province's autonomy.

Although the EC's 'special status' arrangements exceeded the package of special rights that the Italian authorities granted the German-speaking community in South Tyrol (as the territory is now known officially), there is a strong correspondence between the two. Both are predicated on the notion that a minority may require special protections that general principles of human rights may not be sufficient to ensure.[73] And both reflect a conception of autonomy that contains political and territorial elements in addition to provisions for cultural self-determination. South Tyrol has continued to be a source of inspiration for the international community's mediation efforts in the region: in 1997, two years before the NATO military campaign against Serbia/Yugoslavia, the Bertelsmann Foundation and the Centre for Applied Policy Research in Munich proposed similar autonomy arrangements as the basis for a solution to the conflict in Kosovo.[74]

For many political leaders throughout the former Yugoslavia, South Tyrol is also a model, but one from which a very different lesson can be drawn. They invoke South Tyrol as evidence of the long and laborious negotiations that may be necessary to achieve a *modus vivendi* with local minority populations, and, for that reason, they caution the international community against undue pressure on them to make immediate and sweeping concessions to these population groups.[75] As for South Tyrol itself, ironically, the ascendancy of self-determination demands in

[73] For a discussion of the weakness of the liberal conception of human rights for the purpose of collective 'cultural survival', see Charles Taylor, *Multiculturalism and "The Politics of Recognition"* (Princeton: Princeton University Press, 1992).
[74] 'How to Settle the Kosovo Conflict', policy recommendations by the Bertelsmann Foundation and the Centre for Applied Policy Research (1997), cited in International Crisis Group, 'Kosovo Spring', *ICG Balkans Report*, 20 March 1998, pp. 48–9, available at http://www.crisisweb.org.
[75] This observation is based on interviews that the author conducted with officials throughout the region.

post-communist Europe in the early 1990s prompted a reconsideration on the part of some among the German-speaking community about the adequacy of existing arrangements. Whereas in 1969 the package of reforms won the approval of the South Tyrolese People's Party (SVP), in November 1991 – just one month before the EC's adoption of its recognition policy – the SVP affirmed its commitment to self-determination for South Tyrol, extending even to the right to seek changes in its international boundaries.[76] (The SVP would later renounce these claims in reaction to the violent conflict in Yugoslavia.) A majority among both the German and Italian communities, however, appear to be satisfied with the autonomy arrangements.[77]

If the specifications of the EC's 'special status' were derived in part from the Alto Adige/South Tyrol experience, the idea of a 'special status' for minorities in general originated from a very unexpected quarter: Slobodan Milošević. When, on 29 September 1991, Wynaendts met with Milošević in Belgrade, the Serbian leader proposed negotiating a 'special status' for the Croatian Serbs within the framework of the Conference on Yugoslavia, suggesting, however, that the concerned parties should be consulted about the details. 'His ideas were not without interest', Wynaendts recalls.[78] The attraction of the proposal for Wynaendts was two-fold: first, it did not require a modification of existing boundaries to regulate the problem of the majority Serb regions in Croatia and, second, the proposal enjoyed the backing of a key regional figure (or so it seemed), whose support was thought to be critical to the success of any plan. Carrington immediately took up Milošević's idea and on 4 October instructed Wynaendts to meet with Croatian Serb representatives, which he did in Paris on 12 and 30 October. Yet as Wynaendts was to discover, and Milošević would already have known, the demands of the Croatian Serb leadership now exceeded the catalogue of rights that the EC was prepared to recommend.

Wynaendts met with both Milan Babić and Goran Hadžić, the 'presidents' of the Serbian Autonomous Regions (SAOs) of Krajina and Slavonia, Baranja and western Srem respectively. (The SAOs were areas of Croatia where, since August 1990, the Serbs had been exercising effective control.) Only Hadžić was interested in the 'special status', for the simple reason that in his region Serbs had not constituted a majority

---

[76] 'Austria–Italy (South Tyrol)', p. 27. At the same time, the SVP acknowledged that such a policy could not, realistically, be pursued in present circumstances and resolved instead to step up pressure for full observance of South Tyrol autonomy.

[77] Wolff, 'Settling an Ethnic Conflict through Power-sharing', p. 73.

[78] Wynaendts, L'engrenage, pp. 113–14 (my translation).

before the war and the 'special status' would thus legitimate Serb control there. For this same reason Wynaendts replied that such a proposition was unthinkable. Babić, on the other hand, wanted to take the notion of a special status further. He demanded that his region have the status of a 'free territory' – in effect, a state within a state. (Six months later the Bosnian Serbs would adopt a similar position.)[79] Milošević supported the Croatian Serbs in their demands. Moreover, when Carrington presented the Yugoslav republic presidents with the first outline of the Convention on 18 October, Milošević indicated that he wanted the Serb areas of Croatia to enjoy a relationship with Serbia identical to any relationship they might have with Croatia.[80] Milošević also insisted that the 'special status' arrangements must not apply to areas outside Croatia – to Serbia, that is.[81] Milošević's main objection to the draft Convention, however, was not the 'special status' provisions as such, but the recognition of the republics' unilateral declarations of independence that acceptance of the treaty would entail, even though Milošević had already endorsed such an outcome in principle when he signed the October 4th agreement. As Carrington would later recall:

After the first plenary, the plenary on October the 4th, we formulated the whole plan, and sent it out to the presidents, and they all came to The Hague, and it then started to unravel, because President Milosevic decided that what he'd agreed to on October the 4th was not satisfactory and he raised all sorts of problems and difficulties about it all. He raised all problems about legality, and whether you could just dismember Yugoslavia or whether that bit . . . I mean everything that you could think of, and it was quite clear that he was back pedalling on what he'd agreed on October the 4th. And indeed I said to him, 'Are you still agreed on what happened on October 4th?' and he said no, he wasn't.[82]

Milošević's reservations meant that the Carrington plan was effectively dead, although this was not immediately apparent as negotiators laboured in vain over the next several weeks to bring Milošević on board.

---

[79] *Ibid.*, p. 127.

[80] UN Doc. S/23169, p. 11.

[81] Although the EC did not yield to Milošević on this point, an important provision of the 23 October version of the draft Convention was eliminated from the 4 November version in an apparent effort to gain the Serbian leader's cooperation. The earlier version stated that 'the republics shall apply fully and in good faith the provisions existing prior to 1990 for autonomous provinces' (Art. 2.C.6) – an obvious reference to Kosovo and Vojvodina, the two provinces of Serbia whose autonomy Milošević had revoked in 1989.

[82] Carrington interview for 'The Death of Yugoslavia' television series, Liddell Hart Centre for Military Archives, King's College London (hereafter LHCMA), 4 April 1995, Box 18, File 1, pp. 7–8.

Despite the objections of Milošević and the protestations of Hadžić and Babić, the EC negotiators and senior statesmen of the member states were still persuaded of the merits of seeking minority rights guarantees. Sizeland points out that there were other minority representatives who were 'quite satisfied' with the Chapter II provisions.[83] Also, both Dejammet and Chrobog, the French and German political directors respectively, saw the guarantees as necessary groundwork for future stability in the region – 'one small part of a longer process', Chrobog would later say.[84] Moreover, once accepted by the new state authorities, it was thought that the guarantees would provide an explicit, agreed-upon standard to evaluate these states' treatment of their minority populations and to demand improvements, if necessary, in states' behaviour.[85] Yet how meaningful the guarantees would be in the end would depend, in part, on the seriousness of the EC in seeking adherence to them.

Implementing recognition

Having opted on 16 December to extend recognition to those Yugoslav republics seeking it, it remained for the EC member states to determine which republics now merited recognition and how the Community would proceed to grant it. Here it seems more evident that principle yielded to political expedience and whatever attempt had been made originally to harness the power of recognition in the interest of conflict mitigation was abandoned for reasons of parochial concern.

The EC's 'Declaration on Yugoslavia' invited all Yugoslav republics to indicate by 23 December whether they wished to be recognised as independent states and whether they were willing to accept the EC's conditions for recognition. Croatia and Slovenia requested recognition on 19 December, and Bosnia and Herzegovina and Macedonia on 20 December. (Serbia and Montenegro, still challenging the legality of the other republics' unilateral declarations of independence and contending that the EC's policy represented unlawful 'interference in the internal affairs of a sovereign state', did not seek recognition and would later declare themselves to be the successor state to Yugoslavia.)[86] As

---

[83] Letter to the author.
[84] Interviews with the author.
[85] De Michelis claims, in this respect, to have sought to disabuse Tudjman of any 'illusions' he might have about 'unilateral support outside of the 16 December criteria' when the two met at Davos in February 1992. De Michelis, 'Cosi cercammo di impedire la guerra', 235.
[86] 'The Position of the SFRY Presidency on the Legal Aspect of the Yugoslav Crisis', statement of the Embassy of the Socialist Federal Republic of Yugoslavia (London),

indicated earlier, there was, and remains, some debate as to who was to determine whether the republics had satisfied the criteria for recognition. At the Council of Ministers meeting on 16 December, a role was envisioned for the EC's arbitration commission in this regard, and on 11 January the commission delivered four opinions in response to each of the applications for recognition.

It might seem unusual for an arbitration commission, ostensibly concerned with settling disputes between parties, to play the role of fact-finder and assessor for the EC in its recognition of states, but the commission served a curious function from its inception. Established by the Community on 27 August 1991 in the framework of the Conference on Yugoslavia, the commission was expected to help resolve legal differences that might arise in the context of negotiations among the Yugoslav republics over a political settlement.[87] Yet unlike other arbitral processes, where the procedures to be followed and the rules of law to serve as the basis of judgements have typically been made explicit, the commission was established on the basis of very general terms of reference.[88] The 27 August declaration only stated that 'the relevant authorities will submit their differences' to an arbitration commission,[89] and left it to the commission to adopt its own rules of procedure, which, moreover, were never made public.[90] Usually arbitration also requires the consent of the parties to all aspects of the process – what is known as an implementing *compromis*. But while the Yugoslav republics can be said to have approved the establishment of the commission through their endorsement of the 27 August declaration, their assent cannot be interpreted as a formal obligation to accept the outcome of an

---

11 December 1991; and letter of the SFRY Presidency to the president of the UN Security Council of 19 December 1991, Embassy of the Socialist Federal Republic of Yugoslavia (London), 23 December 1991.

[87] Libal, *Limits of Persuasion*, p. 40. Pierre Hassner has suggested that the arbitration commission, a French initiative, was also seen as a way to slow the German march towards recognition. Hassner, 'The European Union and the Balkans', unpublished background paper submitted to the International Commission on the Balkans, 1996, p. 14.

[88] These observations on arbitral procedures are drawn from Matthew C. R. Craven, 'The European Community Arbitration Commission on Yugoslavia', 66 *British Year Book of International Law* (1995), 333–413.

[89] Joint Statement, 28 August 1991.

[90] Steve Terrett, *The Dissolution of Yugoslavia and the Badinter Arbitration Commission* (Aldershot: Ashgate, 2000), p. 137. See also Alain Pellet, 'Note sur la Commission d'arbitrage de la Conférence européenne pour la paix en Yougoslavie', 37 *Annuaire français de droit international* (1991), 332. With respect to the rules of procedure governing its evaluation of applications for recognition, see Opinions No. 4–7, where in each case the Commission refers to, but does not specify, 'the rules of procedure adopted by the Arbitration Commission on 22 December'. Opinions No. 4–7, 31 *International Legal Materials* (1992), 1501–12.

unspecified dispute-resolution process. Instead, as Matthew Craven has observed, their support 'appears to [have been] in the form of a "gentleman's agreement" incorporating a declaration of intention or preliminary agreement to submit disputes to arbitration'.[91] Indeed, when in April 1993 the Federal Republic of Yugoslavia (FRY) – the self-proclaimed successor state to the Socialist Federal Republic of Yugoslavia (SFRY) – challenged the commission's competence, it maintained that it 'shall consider null and void and non-binding any opinion of the Commission adopted in the procedure to which it has not agreed'.[92]

The questions arising over the commission's competence, however, have had largely to do with matters of international law bearing on statehood and succession,[93] whereas the commission's 'opinions' with respect to recognition, we have noted, dealt with how well the candidate republics satisfied the EC's criteria. These opinions, too, were contentious, but for very different reasons. Greece rejected the commission's finding that Macedonia met all of the EC's requirements, maintaining that the Yugoslav republic harboured territorial claims against it – notwithstanding the commission's view that 'the Republic of Macedonia has . . . renounced all territorial claims of any kind in unambiguous statements', including in amendments to its constitution that the Macedonian legislature adopted expressly to assuage Greek concerns.[94] (Greece's real fear may have been that the existence of a Macedonian state would encourage the Greek Slavophone community to seek greater national rights.)[95] As a consequence of Greece's persistent objections, EC member states were constrained to withhold their recognition of Macedonia until December 1993.[96] Germany, on the other hand,

---

[91] Craven, 'The European Community Arbitration Commission', p. 341.

[92] Statement of 30 April 1993 by the Government of the Federal Republic of Yugoslavia, 32 *International Legal Materials* (1993), 1581. The FRY was challenging the competence of the commission to deliver opinions on the division of assets and liabilities of the SFRY.

[93] These judgements are examined in Chapter 2.

[94] Opinion No. 6 (11 January 1992). On 6 January 1992, the Macedonian legislature adopted two amendments to the constitution. Amendment I states that Macedonia 'has no territorial pretensions towards any neighbouring state' and that its borders 'can only be changed in accordance with . . . generally accepted international norms'. Amendment II states that Macedonia 'will not interfere in the sovereign rights of other states or in their internal affairs'. *Constitution of the Republic of Macedonia* (Skopje: NIP Magazin 21, 1991 [amendments inserted]).

[95] Gow, *Triumph of the Lack of Will*, p. 82. For a discussion of Greek government efforts to restrict the rights of its minority populations, see Adamantia Pollis, 'Strangers in a Strange Land', *War Report* No. 25 (March/April 1994), p. 12.

[96] On 16 December 1993, six member states of the European Union recognised Macedonia under the name 'Former Yugoslav Republic of Macedonia' (FYROM). See *Keesing's Record of World Events* (December 1993), p. 39785. However, Harris

fearful of the commission's probable reservations with respect to Croatia's application, chose to extend recognition to that republic on 23 December – some three weeks before the commission would report its findings. And, indeed, the commission concluded that Croatia did not meet the necessary conditions for its recognition because Croatian law did not fully reflect all the provisions of the draft Convention of 4 November 1991, 'notably those contained in Chapter II, Article 2(c) under the heading of "special status"'.[97] Bosnia and Herzegovina, meanwhile, was subject to an additional requirement beyond any that the EC had specified: the provision of evidence, 'possibly by means of a referendum', of the will of the people to constitute their republic as a sovereign and independent state.[98] The additional requirement would prove to be an incendiary measure that would further alienate the Bosnian Serb community, but the commission apparently entertained hopes that in the two or three months necessary to organise the referendum, diplomacy could be made to work.[99] The only opinion relative to recognition that was not contentious was the commission's judgement that Slovenia had satisfied the EC's requirements.[100]

The case of Croatia deserves closer attention because the controversy surrounding its recognition raises important questions about the strategic premises of the EC's policy, the role of the arbitration commission and, ultimately, the relationship between international law and international politics. At the 16 December Council of Ministers meeting, Genscher declared that Germany would accept the conditions for recognition but made it clear that it would not feel bound by the findings of the commission. Three days later the German federal government formally announced its intention to recognise Slovenia and Croatia on 23 December.[101] (In an attempt to square the circle, Germany added that it would not implement its decision until 15 January – the date set by the EC in its Declaration on Yugoslavia.) Genscher claims that '[t]he resolution of the federal government took into full account the criteria laid down by EC', and that Germany had already satisfied itself that Croatia met the most critical requirement: minority rights guarantees.[102] At the end of November, the German Foreign Ministry

suggests that EU recognition was implied by member state support for Macedonia's admission to the UN General Assembly on 8 April 1993. See D. J. Harris, *Cases and Materials on International Law*, 5th edn (London: Sweet & Maxwell, 1998), p. 151.
[97] Opinion No. 5 (11 January 1992).
[98] Opinion No. 4 (11 January 1992).
[99] Védrine, *Les mondes de François Mitterrand*, pp. 619–20.
[100] Opinion No. 7 (11 January 1992).
[101] Libal, *Limits of Persuasion*, p. 86.
[102] Genscher, *Erinnerungen*, p. 962.

had dispatched the legal scholar Christian Tomuschat to Zagreb to advise the Croatian government on the drafting of minority rights legislation – what was to become the Constitutional Act on Human Rights and Freedoms and the Rights of Ethnic and National Communities and Minorities of 4 December 1991. Tomuschat, particularly satisfied with the results of his efforts, declared that the legally anchored protection of minorities in Croatia 'should serve as a role model for the further development of minority rights in Europe'[103] – a remarkable claim in light of the Croatian government's disregard for Serb rights in the years to follow.

It is true that the commission's findings, strictly speaking, were meant only to be 'an element of appreciation [and] not of decision', as Genscher would say in his defence in January.[104] Indeed, if the findings were expected to have been determinative of EC member states' actions, then the commission's favourable evaluation of Macedonia's application ought to have led the Twelve to recognise that republic. But it is also true that Germany did not pause long enough in its march towards recognition even to consider the commission's findings, and therefore, can hardly be said to have acted in the spirit of the EC's 16 December decision. (The ministers of foreign affairs had decided on 16 December that their political directors would meet on 15 January to examine the findings of the commission.)[105] With Germany breaking ranks, Italy followed suit, announcing on 20 December that it would recognise the independence of candidate republics that satisfied the 'criteria of democracy' established by the EC – notably, it specified in the same communiqué, Slovenia and Croatia.[106] A charitable reading of events would have it that Germany was sincere in its appreciation of EC policy but that the policy was too ambiguous, predicated as it was on a compromise formula that masked rather than resolved the differences among the Twelve. At the very least it seems fair to say that all the member states – in the case of both Croatia and Macedonia – chose to take liberties with the very conditions they had established for recognition.

The commission itself would later offer a judgement of Croatia slightly at variance with its original opinion. When on 4 July 1992 it re-evaluated Croatia's Constitutional Act in light of amendments to the legislation, it offered this restatement of its original opinion: 'In Opinion 5 of 11 January, the Arbitration Commission took the view that the Republic

---

[103] Cited in *ibid.*, p. 961.
[104] Cited in *Agence Europe* No. 5644 (11 January 1992), p. 3.
[105] 'La France s'apprête à ne reconnaître que la Slovénie', *Le Monde*, 16 January 1992.
[106] 'L'Allemagne a engagé la procédure de reconnaissance de la Slovénie et la Croatie', *Le Monde*, 21 December 1991.

of Croatia satisfied the conditions for recognition by the Member States of the European Community set out in the joint statement on Yugoslavia and the Guidelines on the recognition of new states in Eastern Europe and in the Soviet Union adopted by the Council on 16 December 1991', adding that '[t]he Arbitration Commission did, however, have a reservation about the compatibility of the Constitutional Law of 4 December 1991 with the draft Convention of 4 November 1991, notably the provisions of Article 2(c) of Chapter II regarding "Special status"'.[107] The shift in emphasis was subtle but significant. And while the commission found that even the amended legislation failed to satisfy fully the EC's criteria, it offered this surprising commentary: '[T]he Arbitration Commission finds that, although it must be implemented by all republics, the draft Convention proposed on 4 November 1991 at the Conference on Yugoslavia does not define in detail the concept of autonomy . . .', and furthermore, 'the Arbitration Commission finds that even if the Constitutional Law in question does sometimes fall short of the obligations assumed by Croatia when it accepted the draft Convention of 4 November 1991, it nonetheless satisfies the requirements of general international law regarding the protection of minorities'.[108]

Notwithstanding the uneven application of EC policy, the influence of the Community's recognition criteria on the legislation of minority rights guarantees is evident throughout the region. Croatia's Constitutional Act of 4 December 2001, we have seen, was achieved largely as a consequence of EC pressures on Zagreb to uphold its human rights obligations. The Slovene constitution of 23 December 1991, too, was framed in such a way as to give effect to the relevant minority rights provisions of the EC's draft Convention.[109] The 1991 Macedonian constitution also contains a number of special provisions for the protection of minority rights, including provisions for local self-government,[110] and Chapter II of the Carrington draft Convention

[107] Comments on the Republic of Croatia's Constitutional Law of 4 December 1991, as last amended on 8 May 1992. Dated 4 July 1992. Reprinted in 31 *International Legal Materials* (1992), 1506.

[108] *Ibid.*, 1507.

[109] See, in particular, Article 64 of the constitution, which establishes special rights for the Italian and Hungarian ethnic communities in Slovenia. *Constitution of the Republic of Slovenia* (Ljubljana: Uradni list Republike Slovenije, 1993). In its 1998 report, Minority Rights Group International judged the rights for 'traditional' minorities in Slovenia to be 'excellent'. However, newer minorities – those from other former republics of Yugoslavia in particular – have not fared as well. See Minority Rights Group (Hugh Poulton), 'Minorities in Southeast Europe: Inclusion and Exclusion' (London: Minority Rights Group, 1998), p. 31.

[110] *Constitution of the Republic of Macedonia*, esp. Article 48 (rights of nationalities), Article 78 (Council for Inter-Ethnic Relations), and Articles 114–117 (local self-government).

would continue to serve as a common point of reference in negotiations between the Macedonian government and its ethnic Albanian population in subsequent years.[111] (These provisions are in addition to the constitutional amendments mentioned above that Macedonia adopted with respect to its relations with neighbouring states, i.e., Greece.) The fact that many of these guarantees are merely 'formal' commitments does not diminish their value even if, in the cases of Croatia and Macedonia especially, minorities would suffer discrimination – sometimes very severe – under the new regimes.[112] For one thing, formal commitments establish a domestic standard that both international authorities and local interest groups can then invoke in support of reforms, as indeed these organisations have done. Moreover, they can serve as the basis for further conditionality – in trade relations and aid giving, for instance. Finally, these commitments help to reinforce a gradual but distinct shift that has been taking place since the end of the Cold War from the treatment of minorities as a matter of domestic politics to a view of minority rights as a legitimate subject for international concern.[113]

The German Question

In view of the central and controversial role that Germany played in the events discussed in this chapter, a closer examination of the thinking behind Bonn's actions is warranted. Why did Germany promote recognition so vigorously, even at the risk of creating a serious rift among the Twelve on the eve of the signing of the Maastricht Treaty? And why, having achieved EC consensus in favour of recognition on 16 December, did Germany then break ranks and extend recognition ahead of the other member states?

---

[111] See, for instance, International Conference on the Former Yugoslavia, Working Group on Ethnic and National Communities and Minorities, Sub-Group on Macedonia, 'Present State of the Talks with Representatives of the Macedonian Government and of the Albanians from Macedonia' (c. July 1993), where both the government and the Albanian representatives predicate their claims and/or demands on Chapter II of the draft convention.

[112] See Minority Rights Group International, 'Minorities in Croatia', September 2003, available at http://www.minorityrights.org; and International Crisis Group, 'Macedonia: No Time for Complacency', *Europe Report No. 149*, 23 October 2003, available at http://www.crisisweb.org.

[113] For a discussion of normative shifts on the question of minority rights in Europe since the end of the Cold War, see Jennifer Jackson Preece, 'Minority Rights in Europe: From Westphalia to Helsinki', 23 *Review of International Studies* (1997), 88–92.

Various explanations have been put forward to account for Germany's behaviour. These explanations tend to emphasise one or several of three possible sources of German conduct: expansionist aims, domestic pressures and strategic considerations.

The least compelling of the three is the suggestion that Germany was motivated principally or at all by an interest in expanding its economic, political and even military influence in the Balkan region. This view is embraced, not surprisingly, by many among the Serbian and federal Yugoslav elite. It figures prominently, for instance, in the memoirs of Veljko Kadijević, the former Yugoslav secretary of national defence and chief of staff of the Yugoslav armed forces from 1988 to 1992. Kadijević describes a new Germany, emboldened by unification, acting 'on all fronts' to achieve its goal of gaining 'economic, political and later if need be military control of the Balkans as a region for direct German expansion. . .'[114] To achieve this goal, Kadijević maintains, 'it was necessary [for Germany] to break Yugoslavia into statelets while ensuring against any scaled-down version of Yugoslavia or the creation of an integral Serb state which would embrace all Serbs from the Yugoslav region, for even such a state in the Balkans would pose an insurmountable obstacle to its global, imperialistic objectives'.[115] Similar claims were made by Marko Negovanović, Yugoslavia's deputy defence minister, and by Milan Martić, the Croatian Serb leader.[116]

Echoes of this view can also be heard within the European Union, including, among others, the senior French general Pierre Gallois. Writing in Le Monde in June 1993, Gallois warned against a 'German predominance' in Europe. Germany, he argued, had sought to 'dismantle' Yugoslavia in order to 'tie the Croats and Slovenes more closely to the German economy'.[117] It was a strategy designed, moreover, 'to emancipate the populations once allied with the Central European empires and with the Third Reich, to punish the Serbs stubbornly attached to the victors of the two world wars . . . and to efface the last

---

[114] General Veljko Kadijević, *Moje Vidjenje Raspada: Vojska Bez Države* [My View of the Break-up: An Army Without a State] (Belgrade: Politika, 1993). The reference is to p. 13 of an unofficial English-language translation of the text submitted as evidence to the International Criminal Tribunal for the Former Yugoslavia and provided to the author by Dr James Gow, King's College London.

[115] *Ibid.*

[116] See report by Negovanović excerpted in *Narodna Armija* (Belgrade), 22 December 1991, in Foreign Broadcast Information Service, *Daily Report: Eastern Europe*, FBIS-EEU-92-007, 10 January 1992, 29. For Martić's views, see Carl Bildt, *Peace Journey: The Struggle for Peace in Bosnia* (London: Weidenfeld & Nicolson, 1998), p. 47.

[117] Pierre M. Gallois, 'Vers une prédominance allemande', *Le Monde*, 16 July 1993 (my translation).

vestiges of the treaties sanctioning the two German defeats'.[118] Exaggerated though some of these claims may seem, they bespeak the generalised anxiety – and for some confirm the fears – arising from the unification of Germany.[119] Kohl did little to assuage these concerns when in his address to the party congress of his Christian Democratic Union on 17 December, only one day after the EC Council of Ministers meeting, he referred to EC recognition as 'a great victory for *German foreign policy*'.[120]

There are several reasons why this explanation, despite its resonance in some quarters, is an unsatisfactory one. For one thing, German economic interests in the region were negligible. Germany may have been the largest EC investor in Croatia and Slovenia – as it was throughout most of East-Central Europe – but German trade with these republics was of relatively little importance to the German economy: in 1991, German imports from all of Yugoslavia amounted to 7.73 million Deutschmarks (DM) while German exports were valued at 5.13 million DM – a volume that represented only 1.7 per cent and 1.1 per cent respectively of Germany's total imports from and exports to the EC, not to speak of its global trade.[121] It is not evident that a fractured Yugoslavia would have created greater economic advantages for Germany; indeed, Germany stood to lose from the dissolution of Yugoslavia because Yugoslavia was heavily indebted to Germany and it was not clear how the debt question would be resolved.[122] The timing of Germany's actions, moreover, does not support an expansionist interpretation. If Germany had hegemonic aims, why did it wait until the summer of 1991 – long after Slovenia and Croatia had embarked on the road to independence – to begin to pursue these aims? More than just wait, we have seen, Germany actively supported the continued unity of Yugoslavia through June.

The expansionist view is also contradicted by the basic orientation of post-war German foreign policy, which, with the end of the Cold War, German behaviour seemed only to reaffirm. Mindful of the concerns

---

[118] *Ibid.* Roland Dumas, in more muted tones, warned in July 1991: 'It is imperative to avoid that certain regions too openly become subject to foreign influence.' Cited in Peter Viggo Jakobsen, 'Myth-making and Germany's Unilateral Recognition of Croatia and Slovenia', 4 *European Security* (1995), 400–1.

[119] For evidence of French and British anxieties about the new Germany, see Jacques Attali, *Verbatim* (Paris: Fayard, 1995), vol. III, p. 333; and Margaret Thatcher, *The Downing Street Years* (London: HarperCollins, 1993), p. 792.

[120] Cited in 'US Backs Yugoslavia Compromise', *Financial Times*, 18 December 1991 (emphasis added).

[121] Figures from *Statistisches Jahrbuch für die Bundesrepublik Deutschland* (Wiesbaden: Statistisches Bundesamt, 1995), p. 300.

[122] Hans W. Maull, 'Germany in the Yugoslav Crisis', 37(4) *Survival* (1995–6), 118.

generated by unification, Bonn, for instance, played a leading role in efforts to accelerate the process of European political integration and to strengthen the capacity of European multilateral organisations to cope more effectively with regional security challenges, precisely so that member states did not feel impelled to respond to these challenges unilaterally. Bonn's promotion of a common foreign and security policy in the intergovernmental conferences leading up to Maastricht and its attempts to reinvigorate the WEU and to expand the functions of the CSCE all attest to what Harald Müller has referred to as a policy of 'self-containment by integration'.[123] It makes little sense that Germany would have opted for a course of action tantamount to a repudiation of a foreign policy that was seen by the political elite to have oriented the country successfully for nearly forty years and that was expected to guide the ship of state through the uncertain waters of the post-Cold War period as well. There could be no doubt, however, that Germany's bold and precipitate steps towards recognition of Slovenia and Croatia threatened to jeopardise these foreign policy goals, as the harsh reaction of the media and numerous EC government officials to Bonn's actions soon made clear.[124]

If Germany was putting its foreign policy objectives at risk, it was because of domestic pressures and strategic considerations and not because the German leadership had chosen to sacrifice multilateralism for expansionist aims. The timing of Germany's actions is again key here. Within a week of the outbreak of hostilities in Yugoslavia, all of the major German political parties, which as recently as 19 June had declared their support for Yugoslav unity,[125] were calling for the recognition of Slovenia and Croatia. First Kohl's Christian Democratic Union (CDU), on 27 June, then the opposition Social Democratic Party (SPD) on 1 July, and finally Genscher's Free Democratic Party (FDP)

---

[123] Harald Müller, 'German Foreign Policy after Unification', in Paul B. Stares (ed.), *The New Germany in the New Europe* (Washington, DC: The Brookings Institution, 1992), p. 130. See also Jeffrey J. Anderson and John B. Goodman, 'Mars or Minerva? A United Germany in a Post-Cold War Europe', in Robert O. Keohane, Joseph S. Nye and Stanley Hoffmann (eds.), *After the Cold War: International Institutions and State Strategies in Europe, 1989–1991* (Cambridge, MA: Harvard University Press, 1993), pp. 23–62.

[124] See, for instance, 'Germany Flexes its Muscles on Croatia's Behalf', *The Independent*, 19 December 1991; 'Le retour de la "question allemande"', *Le Monde*, 23 December 1991; 'No More Mr. Nice Guy, Germany's Neighbors Find', *International Herald Tribune*, 23/24 December 1991; and 'Vance kritisiert Deutschland wegen Anerkennung Sloweniens und Kroatiens', *Frankfurter Allgemeine Zeitung*, 28 December 1991.

[125] On 16 June 1991 all the German political parties in the Bundestag signed a common declaration in favour of the continued unity of Yugoslavia. See Beverly Crawford, 'Explaining Defection from International Cooperation: Germany's Unilateral Recognition of Croatia', 48 *World Politics* (1996), 493.

on 9 July announced that they favoured recognition of the break-away republics, although no party was urging unilateral recognition.[126] This consensus in support of recognition can be explained in part by the importance that Germany's political elite attached to the principle of self-determination, especially now that Belgrade was seeking the reassertion of its authority using violent means. 'We won our unity through the right of self-determination', Volker Rühe, the secretary-general of the CDU declared in early July 1991. 'If we Germans think everything else in Europe can follow a status quo policy and do not recognise the right of self-determination in Slovenia and Croatia, then we have no moral or political credibility.'[127] (Within the CDU and especially within its coalition partner, the Christian Social Union, the Catholic Church's support for the two republics also carried some weight.)[128] Important, too, was the 'bandwagoning' effect that the CDU's policy reversal had on the other parties. The SPD in particular, having gambled before and lost when it came out in support of a gradualist approach to German unification in the 1990 all-German elections, did not want to risk misjudging the public mood again.[129]

As the fighting intensified throughout the autumn, so too did the parties' calls for recognition. On 14 November, the four principal political parties – the CDU, SPD, FDP and the Greens – published a joint statement on the situation in Yugoslavia in which they expressed their support for the efforts of the Federal government to gain recognition of those republics seeking independence.[130] The following day the Bundestag unanimously adopted a resolution that singled out the Serbian leadership as 'chiefly responsible' for the fighting and called for recognition of the break-away republics.[131] These pressures could

---

[126] *Ibid.*, 493–4.
[127] Cited in 'Diplomacy Tested by Territorial Integrity', *Financial Times*, 4 July 1991. Similarly Kohl declared at that time, 'The peoples of Yugoslavia must be free to choose their own future. Free Europe must stand beside them . . . The importance of the principle of self-determination is that much more evident for Germans because by means of self-determination our nation was able to regain its unity.' Cited in 'Republics Gain Kohl's Backing Before EC Talks', *The Independent*, 5 July 1991. See also Hans-Dietrich Genscher, 'Für Recht auf Selbstbestimmung', *Das Parlament* Nr. 47–48 (15/22 November 1991), p. 7.
[128] Maull, 'Germany in the Yugoslav Crisis', p. 122 .
[129] Beverly Crawford, 'German Foreign Policy and European Political Cooperation: The Diplomatic Recognition of Croatia in 1991', 13(2) *German Politics and Society* (1995), 10–17.
[130] *Verhandlungen des deutschen Bundestages*, 12.Wahlperiode. Drucksache 12/1591 (14.11.91). See also the Bundestag debates as reported in *Das Parlament* Nr. 47–48 (15/22 November 1991) and Nr. 50 (6 December 1991).
[131] Wolfgang Krieger, 'Toward a Gaullist Germany? Some Lessons from the Yugoslav Crisis', 11(1) *World Policy Journal* (1994), 32.

not have been easily resisted by the German leadership; it would have been politically suicidal for Kohl and Genscher to ignore them.

It would be wrong, however, to think that the chancellor and foreign minister were simply bowing to political pressures. Both were also acutely sensitive to the security risks for Germany of instability in East-Central Europe. As a 'frontline' state with relatively liberal immigration policies, Germany was especially vulnerable to the influx of economic migrants and refugees.[132] Germany had already invested billions of Deutschmarks – roughly half of all G-7 aid to the region – in an effort to foster conditions for growth and prosperity that might forestall mass migration. Unless the escalation of violence in Yugoslavia were halted, Kohl and Genscher concluded, the EC – and Germany above all – would suffer the destabilising effects. (Among EC member states, in fact, Germany would take the largest number of refugees from the region as the warring continued.) Moreover, the German leadership feared that the failure to prevent Milošević from achieving his aims through the use of force would send the wrong signal to other leaders in the region who might be inclined to deal with communal conflict in the same manner. And, finally, the fighting in Yugoslavia threatened to undermine the credibility and effectiveness of the European Community just as it was seeking to assume increased responsibility for the management of regional security.[133] Frustrated by the paucity of effective multilateral instruments, Bonn felt that recognition was the only available option as the crisis grew more acute. 'What can end the bloodshed, I asked myself repeatedly', Genscher recalls in his memoirs. 'Increasingly the recognition of Slovenia and Croatia, and the internationalisation of the conflict that followed from this seemed to be the only remaining political instrument.'[134]

These may not have been the only reasons why Germany inclined towards recognition. Germany was host to a large community of Croatian *Gastarbeiter*, especially in Bavaria, who lobbied the Christian Social Union in support of Croatian interests. Few of these expatriates enjoyed the right to vote, however, and their influence therefore should not be exaggerated. Media coverage of the conflict was also generating public support for Croatian and Slovene self-determination, especially as the JNA's campaign became more violent, although elite consensus on recognition had by then already been achieved.[135] There may also have

---

[132] *Ibid.*, 28.
[133] Müller, 'German Foreign Policy after Unification', pp. 150–4.
[134] Genscher, *Erinnerungen*, p. 956.
[135] Lucarelli, *Europe and the Breakup of Yugoslavia*, p. 139.

been personal reasons for Germany's volte-face. Genscher travelled to the region soon after the outbreak of fighting and was evidently affected by the experience. In Belgrade he was struck by the defiance of President Milošević and moved by the urgency of the situation when confronted with the impossibility of flying to Ljubljana because of heavy fighting.[136] These events were a 'turning point in . . . German policy' towards the region, Slovene Foreign Minister Dimitrij Rupel, who met with Genscher in Austria instead, would later maintain.[137] But it was strategic considerations above all that were to dominate German thinking as Bonn became persuaded that EC insistence on recognition in the context of a political settlement meant that Milošević could continue to refuse a deal, prevent recognition and thereby prosecute the war with virtual impunity.[138]

What is less clear is why Germany broke ranks after the 16 December meeting and extended recognition ahead of the other EC member states. As was suggested earlier, Germany may have feared the findings of the Badinter Commission, which were not expected to be entirely favourable in respect of Croatia. Moreover, Kohl, at the 17 December CDU party congress, had promised that the two republics would be recognised before Christmas – a pledge that he could not easily retract one week later. Beverly Crawford has suggested that pre-emptive moves by France and Britain may also have hardened Genscher's position. On 13 December the two countries sought to block German recognition with a UN Security Council resolution admonishing states not to take unilateral actions that might disturb the political balance in Yugoslavia. Although Britain and France, under pressure from Germany, abandoned the initiative on the eve of the Council of Ministers meeting, a 'spiral of mistrust', as Crawford describes it, may have led Genscher to fear the prospect of other eleventh-hour efforts to impede recognition.[139]

It would be an exaggeration to suggest that when the EC adopted its recognition policy, its sole interest was to mitigate the conflict in Yugoslavia. Advocates of recognition, Germany foremost among them, were motivated by a variety of concerns, some of which had as much to

[136] Genscher describes Milošević as having 'left no doubt as to his determination to realise his plans for Yugoslavia as he saw it'. Genscher, *Erinnerungen*, pp. 939–40.
[137] Rupel interview for 'The Death of Yugoslavia', LHCMA, undated, Box 18, File 4, p. 3.
[138] See transcript of Genscher interview for 'The Death of Yugoslavia', LHCMA, undated, Box 18, File 1, p. 4, where Genscher observes, 'It was obvious that they [the Serbs] wanted to use the negotiations only to enhance their situation by military forces.'
[139] Crawford, 'Explaining Defection from International Cooperation', pp. 484–5; Libal, *Limits of Persuasion*, p. 82.

do with domestic politics as with regional unrest. Others supported recognition, less enthusiastically, out of a desire to maintain cohesion among the Twelve, particularly now that the Community had signalled its determination at Maastricht to work towards a common foreign and security policy. Yet even these states – the majority, clearly – accepted that recognition was inevitable, not simply because the German 'bulldozer' could not be stopped but, more important, because the desire for independence on the part of some Yugoslav republics was too strong to be countered indefinitely. At this stage of the crisis, the EC was faced with what many of its leaders regarded as a poor set of options – what Carrington described at the time as 'a choice of evils'[140] – and recognition appeared to them to represent the lesser of those evils. Yet even poor options may leave room for positive initiative, and the conditions that the EC attached to recognition need to be seen in this light. Clearly the architects of that policy had in mind to lay the foundations for a more secure peace in the region, however imperfectly the policy may have been implemented. Their use of recognition represented a distinctive approach to conflict management – an approach that reflected the EC's belief that its security environment could be managed, in part, with a judicious mixture of diplomatic carrots and sticks.

This chapter has discussed the strategic and, to a lesser extent, the political considerations behind the EC's recognition of new states in Yugoslavia. More than just a policy instrument, however, the recognition of states also occupies an important place in international legal doctrine and historic state practice. While extra-legal considerations, it has been seen, had considerable bearing on the EC's recognition policy, legal norms were by no means irrelevant even if the EC appeared to many observers to be acting with little regard for these norms. But what function did legal norms actually perform in the recognition episode? The next two chapters examine the law and practice of recognition and their relevance to the EC's actions.

[140] Cited in 'US Backs Yugoslavia Compromise', *Financial Times*, 18 December 1991.

2 Recognition of states: legal thinking and historic practice

From the time of the Treaty of Westphalia (1648), the state has been the foundation of the international order.[1] It is hardly surprising, then, that there should exist a vast body of legal thinking and state practice concerned with regulating the emergence of new states within that order. Yet one may wonder just how relevant this legal tradition was to the EC's decision to recognise the constituent republics of Yugoslavia as independent states in 1991. The EC's actions would seem to have been motivated largely, if not entirely, by political and strategic considerations, as we saw in Chapter 1. Any use of the law, critics maintain, served merely to justify what at bottom was a policy governed by extra-legal concerns. As one observer put it, the EC chose to 'mask a selective political choice behind an appeal to general rights and principles of international law'.[2]

Yet while it would be wrong to elevate the importance of legal thinking and precedent above all other factors, it is also incorrect to disparage the legal aspects altogether. There are two reasons for this. First, however liberally West European officials may have interpreted the legal tradition in their response to developments in the region, they nonetheless constructed their policy squarely within that tradition. When it became apparent that the recognition of Slovenia and Croatia could probably not be avoided, the EC turned to the commission of jurists it had established in August 1991 (the Badinter Commission) to advise it, thus ensuring the salience of legal argument. Second, the legal framework, once invoked, both facilitated and constrained EC actions; that is, it provided legal rationalisation for prior and subsequent state practice

---

[1] Although states gradually came into being (in Europe) from 1100, the Treaty of Westphalia is generally credited with having established the international system based on a plurality of independent states. See Antonio Cassese, *International Law in a Divided World* (Oxford: Clarendon Press, 1991), pp. 34–7.

[2] Mario Zucconi, 'The European Union in the Former Yugoslavia', in Abram Chayes and Antonia Handler Chayes (eds.), *Preventing Conflict in the Post-Communist World* (Washington, DC: The Brookings Institution, 1996), p. 269.

while at the same time it defined the parameters of permissible action. The legal principle of *uti possidetis juris* (respect for the territorial status quo), for instance, was used to justify the EC's decision to recognise the boundaries of the former Yugoslav republics as the frontiers of newly established states, while Badinter's reading of the right to self-determination would have made it difficult to extend recognition to any of the sub-republic claimants, such as the Croatian Serb Krajina.

Of course, the legal constraints the EC was operating under were not 'hard' constraints – few if any international legal norms are – and one may question how meaningful they were in practical terms since they were neither determinative of state action (witness the non-recognition of Macedonia despite Badinter's favourable judgement), nor do they appear to have influenced member states to abandon any preferred course of action (for example, the recognition of Croatia in light of Badinter's reservation). It is fair to say, however, that the legal framework helped both to reinforce existing norms and to modify them – in either case circumscribing, if at times only weakly, the range of allowable state behaviour.

If, for the reasons outlined above, one can acknowledge the importance of taking legal thinking and state practice into consideration, a number of fundamental questions arise. To begin with, when is a state a state? Why, for instance, was Croatia, a federal republic of Yugoslavia, recognised as a state whereas Chechnya, an autonomous republic of Russia seeking independence at the same time, was not? What purpose does recognition serve and what are the implications for international relations of non-recognition? Did Macedonia, for example, enjoy any rights and duties normally reserved for states prior to its recognition? When are states considered to have ceased to exist and what consequences follow from such a determination? Specifically, why was Yugoslavia judged to have dissolved when its central authorities exercised greater effective control over its territory than, say, Somalia, at the height of the civil war there? These are not merely 'academic' questions, as the associated illustrations should make clear, and international law, it will be shown, bears on these questions in important, albeit imprecise, ways.

What follows is a brief, critical survey of legal thinking and historic practice with respect to the recognition of states in the period before and after the end of the Cold War and an examination of how this tradition relates to the Yugoslav case. Prior to the collapse of communism in Europe, it will be shown, the tendency among the international community had been to recognise states on the basis of essentially factual criteria. With the dissolution of Yugoslavia, all of that seemed to change.

'No element of international policy has gone more askew in the break-up of Yugoslavia than recognition – whether, when, how, under what conditions – of the emerging parts', an editorial in the *Washington Post* noted a short time after the war in Bosnia and Herzegovina had begun.[3] As a result of these events, recognition would appear to be more of a discretionary political act today than it has been for decades.

Traditional criteria for statehood

While there is no more fundamental unit in public international law and in the international system than the state, the very meaning of statehood, and the function of recognition in relation to it, are shrouded in ambiguity.[4] The Vatican City, with a population of roughly 1,000 permanent inhabitants living on 0.44 square kilometres of territory and relying on the protection of the Italian police, is widely recognised to be a state,[5] whereas Taiwan, with a substantially larger population and land mass, ruled and defended by an independent government and defence force, is not. Rhodesia, which was governed by a white minority regime, was not considered to be a state and yet Zimbabwe, the self-same entity, is. Bangladesh, established in part as a consequence of India's intervention in Pakistan's civil war in 1971, enjoys recognition whereas the Turkish Republic of Northern Cyprus, established three years later due to Turkey's intervention on the island republic, does not. Although it might seem from these examples that statehood has long been a matter of political discretion and even arbitrary judgement as opposed to uniform legal criteria, in fact a fairly consistent set of legal norms has governed these and most other cases until recently.

James Crawford, acknowledging that 'there is no generally accepted and satisfactory modern legal definition of statehood', defines statehood as 'a claim of right [and, one might add, obligation] based on a certain factual and legal situation'.[6] The 'factual situation' to which he is

---

[3] 'The Macedonian Question', *Washington Post*, 16 May 1992.

[4] Legal scholars are virtually unanimous in treating the state as the principal, if not sole, subject of international law. For a classic statement see Ian Brownlie, *Principles of Public International Law*, 2nd edn (Oxford: Oxford University Press, 1973), p. 60. International relations theorists are divided over the primacy of the state, although the dominant tradition (Realism) favours this view. For a discussion of the role of the state and contemporary international relations theory, see Fred Halliday, *Rethinking International Relations* (Basingstoke: Macmillan, 1994), ch. 4.

[5] For a dissenting view see M. H. Mendelson, 'Diminutive States in the United Nations', 21 *International and Comparative Law Quarterly* (1972), 609–30.

[6] James Crawford, *The Creation of States in International Law* (Oxford: Clarendon Press, 1979), pp. 31, 119.

referring is codified in the 1933 Convention on Rights and Duties of States, known as the Montevideo Convention – the most widely accepted formulation of the principal criteria of statehood in international law and an explicit point of reference for current state practice. The Convention asserts that an entity must exhibit the following characteristics to satisfy the requirements for statehood: '(a) a permanent population; (b) a defined territory; (c) government; and (d) capacity to enter into relations with other states'.[7] This list is not exhaustive; other factors, we will see shortly, have since become relevant too. Yet one can readily appreciate from these requirements the fundamentally *factual* basis of statehood: that there must exist, on a given territory, a reasonably stable political community in effective control of that territory claiming the rights of statehood.[8] No longer relevant, by these criteria, would be the 'degree of civilisation' a territorial entity exhibits, or other such overtly political requirements applicable in earlier times.[9] The reason for this is clear: in a pluralistic international system, any specific political, cultural or other basis of statehood would be unlikely to enjoy wide support and, moreover, would risk leaving many territorial entities outside the system, thus threatening the very maintenance of the international order. The danger represented by large numbers of unrecognised entities is reflected in the remarks of George Canning, Britain's representative in Madrid in 1824, with respect to Spain's newly independent Latin American colonies:

It appears manifest to the British government that if so large a portion of the globe should remain much longer without recognized political existence or any definite political connexion with the established Governments of Europe, the consequences of such a state of things must be at once most embarrassing to those Governments, and most injurious to the interests of all European nations. For this reason, and not from mere views of selfish policy, the British Government is decidedly of the opinion that the Recognition of such of the New States as have established, *de facto*, their separate independence, cannot be much longer delayed.[10]

---

[7] Convention on Rights and Duties of States, Article 1. *League of Nations Treaty Series*, vol. 165, no. 3802 (1936), p. 25.

[8] It is in part because it has made no such claim (yet) that Taiwan is not a state.

[9] Lorimer, in *The Institutes of the Law of Nations* (1883), and in characteristic fashion for his time, divided humanity into three groups – civilised, barbarous and savage peoples – and excluded the last two from possible recognition as states. See Hersch Lauterpacht, *Recognition in International Law* (Cambridge: Cambridge University Press, 1947), p. 31. For a discussion of the Western standards used to evaluate non-Western polities, see Gerrit W. Gong, *The Standard of 'Civilization' in International Society* (Oxford: Clarendon Press, 1984).

[10] Cited in C. K. Webster, *Britain and the Independence of Latin America, 1812–1830* (Oxford: Oxford University Press, 1938), vol. II, p. 414.

Requirements as broad as those of the Montevideo Convention will, of course, admit a wide range of possibilities – as again they must if the international system is not to be so rigid as to be unable to accommodate variation and thus function effectively. So while territory is a requirement of statehood, clearly defined frontiers are not.[11] Albania was recognised by a number of states in 1913 despite a lack of settled frontiers, and Israel was admitted to the United Nations in 1948 while its borders remained in dispute.[12] In the latter instance the United States justified its vote by arguing that 'both reason and history demonstrate that the concept of territory does not necessarily include precise delimitation of that territory', only that there should be 'some portion of the earth's surface which its people inhabit and over which its Government exercises authority'.[13]

Historically, allowance has also been made for ineffective government control of territory. The Congolese government, at the time of independence in 1960, did not enjoy control over the whole of its territory. Yet the former Belgian colony was widely recognised as a new state and admitted to the United Nations on that basis. One reason may have been the uncontested transfer of sovereignty from Belgium to Congo as a result of Belgium's decision to relinquish the colony. But still more important was the weight that the principle of self-determination carried.

The significance attached to self-determination by the international community, especially since the onset of decolonisation, has arguably resulted in a relaxation of the Montevideo criteria for statehood.[14] So fundamental is the principle that state entities established in violation of it are likely to be denied recognition. Thus were states enjoined by the United Nations from 1965 not to recognise Rhodesia – an entity which, however effective, was deemed to have been established in breach of the

---

[11] The classic legal case cited in support of the legitimacy of ill-defined borders is *Deutsche Continental Gas Gesellschaft* v *Polish State* (1929) in which the German–Polish Mixed Arbitral Tribunal decided, '[I]t is enough that the territory has a sufficient consistency, even though its boundaries have not yet been accurately delimited, and that the State actually exercises independent public authority over that territory.' *Annual Digest of Public International Law Cases* (London: Longmans, Green & Co., 1935), vol. V (1929–30), case no. 5(c), p. 15.

[12] Crawford, *The Creation of States in International Law*, p. 75.

[13] UN Security Council, *Official Records*, 383rd meeting, 2 December 1948, p. 11. While support for a state's admission to the United Nations is considered to imply recognition, the United States had already recognised Israel when the latter declared its independence on 14 May 1948.

[14] Frederic L. Kirgis, Jr, 'The Degrees of Self-Determination in the United Nations Era', 88 *American Journal of International Law* (1994), 304–10. See also Robert H. Jackson, *Quasi-states: Sovereignty, International Relations and the Third World* (Cambridge: Cambridge University Press, 1990).

right to self-determination of the majority population, constituting, in effect, a form of 'internal colonisation'.[15] Similarly, the British foreign secretary, explaining why Bophuthatswana, the South African *bantustans*, did not qualify for recognition, stated in 1988, 'The very existence of Bophuthatswana is a consequence of apartheid, and I think that is the principal reason why recognition has not been forthcoming.'[16]

Although it may be tempting to view consideration for the norm of self-determination as representing the introduction of political criteria alongside the factual requirements for statehood, this is not an accurate characterisation. International law prohibits any acts committed in violation of *jus cogens*, or peremptory, norms. A peremptory norm is defined by the Vienna Convention on the Law of Treaties as 'accepted and recognized by the international community of States as a whole as a norm from which no derogation is permitted and which can be modified only by a subsequent norm of general international law having the same character'.[17] While there is no consensus as to what constitutes the corpus of *jus cogens* norms (the Vienna Convention does not specify them), in light of state practice many legal scholars agree that they include the prohibition against slavery, piracy, genocide, and the use of force (except in self-defence) and, more controversially, the right to self-determination.[18] To be lawful, then, recognition cannot be extended in violation of peremptory norms, including arguably the right to self-determination.

Whether or not one accepts that the right to self-determination is a peremptory norm, one problem with the exercise of the right is that it can be at odds with another peremptory norm: respect for the territorial integrity of states. Although international law does not recognise that the right to self-determination entails a right to secession, it does not prohibit the emergence of new states as a consequence of secession, as the establishment of Singapore (1965), Bangladesh (1971) and Eritrea (1993) indicate (Bangladesh being the only case of a successful *unilateral*

---

[15] UN SC Res 217 (12 November 1965) called on states not to recognise Rhodesia or to entertain 'any diplomatic or other relations with this illegal authority'. For a discussion of the Rhodesian case, see Brad R. Roth, *Governmental Illegitimacy in International Law* (Oxford: Clarendon Press, 1999), pp. 235–40.

[16] *Parliamentary Debates* (Hansard), House of Commons, vol. 126, cols. 760–61, 3 February 1988.

[17] Article 53, Vienna Convention on the Law of Treaties (1969). For a discussion of *jus cogens*, see Alfred Verdross, '*Jus Dispositivum* and *Jus Cogens* in International Law', 60 *American Journal of International Law* (1966), 55–63.

[18] For a discussion of self-determination as *jus cogens*, see Antonio Cassese, *Self-Determination of Peoples: A Legal Reappraisal* (Cambridge: Cambridge University Press, 1995), pp. 133–40.

secession).[19] International law does, however, proscribe any actions by states aimed at the dismemberment of another state, including support for non-consensual secession.[20] Article 2(4) of the UN Charter prohibits 'the threat or use of force against the territorial integrity or political independence of any state', while Article 2(7) prohibits intervention 'in matters that are essentially within the domestic jurisdiction of any state'. Yet here, too, there may be allowance for derogation from the rule. In the case of Bangladesh (East Pakistan), for instance, the presumed illegality of India's use of force – a violation of *jus cogens*, arguably, which facilitated the establishment of Bangladesh's statehood – was mitigated by humanitarian concerns prompted by the Pakistani government's campaign of violence against the Bangladeshi people and, some maintain, by the latter's right to self-determination. [21] The tension between the peremptory norms of self-determination and territorial integrity, we will see below, has particular relevance for the EC's recognition of new states in Yugoslavia.

The function of recognition

For the past fifty years, then, the criteria for statehood, however problematic in some instances, have been fairly economical, consisting essentially of the Montevideo requirements and the non-violation of *jus cogens* norms. Yet the mere satisfaction of statehood criteria would not seem to be sufficient for a state to come into existence. Were that the case, recognition would be superfluous, and it would render meaningless any injunction against extending recognition to illegal entities. On the other hand, if recognition is granted any significant role at all, what is to

---

[19] James Crawford, 'State Practice and International Law in Relation to Secession', 69 *British Year Book of International Law* (1998), 92–3.

[20] Thus did the Security Council deprecate 'the secessionist activities illegally carried out by the provincial administration of Katanga' in Congo (Res 169, 15 November 1961) and the General Assembly condemn the attempted unilateral secession of Mayotte as a 'violation of the national unity, territorial integrity and sovereignty of the Republic of Comoros' (Res 31/4, 21 October 1976).

[21] The International Commission of Jurists found, in relation to Bangladesh, 'If one of the constituent peoples of a State is denied equal rights and is discriminated against, it is submitted that their full right of self-determination will revive' (self-determination here understood to mean the right to independence). International Commission of Jurists, 'The Events in East Pakistan, 1971' (Geneva: ICJ, 1972), p. 69. India, while it claimed at the time that its intervention was undertaken in self-defence, also observed that Bangladesh satisfied the criteria for a 'non-self-governing territory' and, by implication, was deserving of independence. See the UN provisional verbatim record of the Security Council debate, UN Doc. S/PV. 1606, 4 December 1971 at 86.

ensure the integrity of the process of state creation – that is, to protect it from 'corruption' by political considerations?

The tension between these two understandings of the function of recognition is reflected in a longstanding debate among legal scholars that divides the 'declaratory school' from the 'constitutive school'. The issue, seemingly scholastic, in fact has broad significance since how one views the function of recognition may have implications for states' policies. The EC's Badinter Commission obviously appreciated the importance of this debate. It felt it necessary to assert, in its first opinion, that 'the effects of recognition by other States are purely declaratory',[22] although the Commission's very function, we will see shortly, would seem to belie this view.

Declaratory theorists maintain that the role of recognition is simply to acknowledge the fact that a territorial entity has satisfied the criteria for statehood; recognition itself cannot and does not create states. The classic statement of this view is contained in *Deutsche Continental Gas Gesellschaft* v *Polish State* (1929), in which the German–Polish Mixed Arbitral Tribunal noted: '[T]he recognition of a State is not constitutive but merely declaratory. The State exists by itself (*par lui même*) and the recognition is nothing else than a declaration of this existence, recognised by the States from which it emanates.'[23]

The Montevideo Convention also adopts the declaratory view. Article 3 of the Convention states:

The political existence of the State is independent of recognition by the other States. Even before recognition the State has the right to defend its integrity and independence, to provide for its conservation and prosperity, and consequently to organize itself as it sees fit, to legislate upon its interests, administer its services and to define the jurisdiction and competence of its courts.

Similarly, Article 6 states: 'The recognition of a State merely signifies that the State which recognizes it accepts the personality of the other with all the rights and duties determined by international law.' What might seem peculiar about Badinter's embrace of the declaratory view, then, is that if statehood is merely a matter of fact, as the Commission claims, and recognition an acknowledgement of that fact, on what basis did Badinter accept the further political requirements for the recognition of new states in Yugoslavia that the EC stipulated? Matthew Craven argues that the Commission was not attempting to interpret or apply

---

[22] Opinion No. 1, 29 November 1991 (published on 7 December 1991), 31 *International Legal Materials* (1992), 1495.

[23] *Annual Digest of Public International Law Cases*, vol. V (1929–30), case no. 5(a), p. 13.

general principles of international law in this particular instance but, rather, was acting as a fact-finding body to determine whether the candidate republics met the EC's conditions for recognition.[24] And yet, as we have seen in Chapter 1, Badinter departed from the EC's criteria when it added the further requirement, based on the principle of self-determination, that Bosnia and Herzegovina provide evidence (in the form of a referendum) of 'the will of the peoples . . . to constitute [the republic] as a sovereign and independent State' (Opinion No. 4).

Badinter offered its own defence several months later when, in another opinion, it stated:

[W]hile recognition is not a prerequisite for the foundation of a State and is purely declaratory in its impact, it is nonetheless a discretionary act that other States may perform when they choose *and in a manner of their own choosing*, subject only to compliance with the imperatives of general international law, and particularly those prohibiting the use of force in dealings with other States or guaranteeing the rights of ethnic, religious or linguistic minorities.[25]

The Badinter Commission's view of its own legal assumptions notwithstanding, the difficulty with the declaratory view is that it ignores the inescapably political and normative dimensions of state creation in two critical respects. First, because recognition remains the prerogative of states – there being no suprastate entity that can make such determinations for the international community – and because states are at the same time the guardians of their own interests, there exists the possibility that political expedience will prevail over strictly legal judgement. When, for instance, the facts of a territorial entity's situation are unclear, recognition serves to clarify them. But states cannot always be expected to evaluate the circumstances with complete disinterest, and even if they could they would likely differ in their evaluation of the evidence. Second, state creation is partly norm governed. As we have seen, where some feature of illegality is present in the establishment of a state (e.g., Rhodesia), non-recognition serves to sanction the offence. Indeed, it is only by virtue of non-recognition that a 'state' so conceived does not enjoy the rights of statehood. Yet there would seem to be no logical place for such a function in the declaratory view of recognition.

The constitutive view openly acknowledges a political role for recognition. As Ian Brownlie puts it, 'the political act of recognition on the

---

[24] Matthew C. R. Craven, 'The European Community Arbitration Commission on Yugoslavia', 66 *British Year Book of International Law* (1995), 353.

[25] Opinion No. 10 (4 July 1992), 31 *International Legal Materials* (1992), 1526 (emphasis added).

part of other States is a precondition of the existence of legal rights'.[26] In the more extreme expression of this view, the very existence of a state would depend on the political decision of other states. The reality, of course, is otherwise: even unrecognised states historically have been seen to possess certain rights and duties, as more moderate versions of this view allow. Israel, for instance, has not required recognition by the Arab states to enjoy international legal protections against aggression from them.[27] Nor did non-recognition of Macedonia from 1991 to 1993 mean that the former Yugoslav republic enjoyed no rights associated with statehood. As Marc Weller observes:

> Nonrecognition did not imply that Macedonia had failed to fulfill the requirements of statehood; it merely derived from the initial unwillingness of the Community, or rather Greece, to establish diplomatic relations with that entity. Recognition was therefore a matter of process, in the sense that without recognition the former republics had no international standing – both bilaterally and in international forums – but recognition was not necessary to create fundamental substantive rights associated with statehood.[28]

Macedonia is, in fact, a relatively easy case. What about instances of fiercely contested independence, such as the former Spanish colony of Western Sahara, whose survival as an emergent state (the Sahrawi Arab Democratic Republic) since 1976 has been threatened by Mauritania's and Morocco's efforts to seize the territory?[29] Do these entities also enjoy the rights associated with statehood prior to recognition? The difficulty we run up against here is what one might call the 'existence–recognition paradox': if the legal existence of an entity is in question, then how can states be expected to treat that entity as a state until it has established itself unambiguously as a state? Often only after the fact of recognition can it be said that an entity whose existence is uncertain existed as a state. Recognition, in other words, provides the very evidence of statehood (and acknowledgement of the rights associated with statehood) that may be needed to attract recognition in the first place.[30]

---

[26] Brownlie, *Principles of Public International Law*, p. 206.

[27] Indeed, these same states have regarded Israel as having obligations under international law, which would seem to confirm its existence as a state. See D. J. Harris, *Cases and Materials on International Law*, 5th edn (London: Sweet & Maxwell, 1998), p. 146, fn. 64.

[28] Marc Weller, 'The International Response to the Dissolution of the Socialist Federal Republic of Yugoslavia', 86 *American Journal of International Law* (1992), 604.

[29] On the Western Sahara conflict, see Toby Shelley, *Endgame in the Western Sahara: What Future for Africa's Last Colony?* (London: Zed Books, 2004).

[30] As the US government noted in a statement of its recognition policy in 1976: 'In reaching this judgment [about whether an entity merits recognition as a state], the

If the declaratory view is insufficiently attentive to the political dimension of recognition, the problem for any version of the constitutive view is that it leaves too much to the discretion of existing states, which, as a result, means that recognition may be liable to abuse and arbitrariness. What, for instance, is to prevent states from withholding recognition for political reasons? Legal scholars are acutely uneasy with this conundrum and have gone to great lengths to resolve it. Hersch Lauterpacht, for instance, posits a legal 'duty' to recognise a state when it has met the requirements: 'To recognize a political community as a State is to declare that it fulfils the conditions of statehood as required by international law. If these conditions are present, the existing States are under the duty to grant recognition.'[31] But this is more an aspiration than a description of state practice: it is as good as saying that all states ought to act in conformity with the law.

To some extent, however, it seems necessary to admit something of a quasi-constitutive role for recognition. First, in practical terms, recognition may be seen to be constitutive of specific legal rights deriving uniquely from statehood. For example, only a recognised state has legal standing in the English courts.[32] Recognition may also be a condition for the establishment of formal and bilateral relations, including diplomatic and treaty relations, or even the delivery of economic assistance. Thus did US Congressman Lee Hamilton argue against the allocation of US aid to Macedonia in 1992: 'It seems highly unusual to me for the United States to begin programs designed to promote economic and political reform in a country whose existence and government the United States does not yet recognize', he wrote to Lawrence Eagleburger, the acting US secretary of state.[33]

Second, when at its inception a state's existence is in doubt, recognition may help to consolidate it. As Rein Müllerson observes:

More often than not the recognition of new states takes place in a situation where newly born entities have not yet consolidated their independence and are rather

---

United States has traditionally looked to the establishment of certain facts. These facts include effective control over a clearly-defined territory and population; an organized governmental administration of that territory; and capacity to act effectively to conduct foreign relations and to fulfill international obligations. *The United States has also taken into account whether the entity in question has attracted the recognition of the international community of states.' Digest of United States Practice in International Law 1976* (Washington, DC: US Government Printing Office, 1977), pp. 19–20 (emphasis added).

[31] Lauterpacht, *Recognition in International Law*, p. 6.

[32] *The City of Berne Bank v Bank of England* (1804), cited in M. N. Shaw, *International Law*, 3rd edn (Cambridge: Cambridge University Press, 1994), p. 263.

[33] Letter from Hamilton to Eagleburger, 22 October 1992 (copy on file with author).

feeble and unstable. Therefore, recognition of most newly born entities by the world community of states always contributes to the strengthening of their legal and political status, not only externally but also internally.[34]

Such was the case, Müllerson maintains, with the recognition of the Baltic states in 1991 (Müllerson was Estonia's deputy foreign minister at the time). Even though the independence of these states seemed imminent, he observes, their recognition by other states 'contributed to the objective process already well under way and helped to avert a reactionary backlash'.[35] Similar considerations, Christian Hillgruber argues, were behind the international recognition of Bosnia and Herzegovina: 'Recognition did not function merely as a refutable assumption that the criteria of statehood were met; it actually served as a substitute for these features, which were obviously missing.'[36]

Historic state practice

Until the assertion of statehood claims by the former Soviet and Yugoslav republics, the member states of the European Community – and the international community more generally – had been moving steadily towards the practice of extending recognition to states on the basis of the criteria outlined above. In 1980, for instance, Britain stated publicly that its policy of recognition was 'in accordance with common international doctrine' – that is, that it would ordinarily recognise an entity that satisfied the Montevideo criteria and whose creation did not violate international law.[37] Four years later, the British government reaffirmed this position:

The criteria which normally apply for the recognition of a state are that it should have, and seem likely to continue to have, a clearly defined territory with a population, a Government who are able of themselves to exercise effective

---

[34] Rein Müllerson, *International Law, Rights and Politics* (London: LSE/Routledge, 1994), pp. 123–4.

[35] *Ibid.*, p. 122.

[36] Christian Hillgruber, 'The Admission of New States to the International Community', 9 *European Journal of International Law* (1998), 493. See also the Dissenting Opinion of Judge *ad hoc* Kreca, International Court of Justice, *Case Concerning Application of the Convention on the Prevention and Punishment of the Crime of Genocide (Bosnia-Herzegovina v Yugoslavia)*, Preliminary Objections, 11 July 1996, ICJ Reports (1996).

[37] *Parliamentary Debates* (Hansard), House of Commons, vol. 983, col. 278, 25 April 1980 (written answers).

control of that territory and independence in their external relations. There are, however, exceptional cases when other factors, including relevant United Nations resolutions, may have to be taken into account.[38]

Indeed, on 6 November 1991, only one month before the EC's adoption of its guidelines on the recognition of new states in Eastern Europe and the Soviet Union, Douglas Hogg, the British minister of state for foreign affairs, responding to questions in Parliament about linking recognition of the Soviet republics to their acceptance of human rights treaties, argued against such an approach:

When we are talking about recognition of states we have our tests, and the traditional tests are whether there is a defined territorial area and whether the government has effective control within those territorial frontiers, and whether that government has effective management over its external forces. Those are historical tests of recognition of states, and therefore their adherence to treaties is not a condition of recognition.[39]

Jurists, not surprisingly, tend to look askance at conditional recognition, regarding it as a corruption of international law. 'If recognition is withheld because . . . the new authorities are unable or unwilling to give international guarantees this is an exercise of discretion, not deference to requirement of law', D. P. O'Connell observes.[40] Similarly, Robert Jennings and Arthur Watts maintain that 'it is improper to make [recognition] subject to conditions other than the existence . . . of the requirements which qualify a community for recognition as an independent state'.[41] The attachment of political conditions to recognition, while unwelcome, is generally not, however, considered to be unlawful.

Although a departure from recent state practice, conditional recognition is not without precedent. In fact, the EC's modified 'Helsinki' conditions for the recognition of new states in its region can be said to represent a return to an approach that the leading European powers employed a century earlier. In a manner strikingly similar to the present case, the contracting parties to the 1878 Treaty of Berlin (Austria, France, Germany, Great Britain, Italy, Russia and Turkey) linked their

[38] *Parliamentary Debates* (Hansard), House of Commons, vol. 55, col. 226, 29 February 1984 (written answers). US policy is essentially the same: see note 30 above.

[39] House of Commons, Foreign Affairs Committee, First Report, *Central and Eastern Europe: Problems of the Post-Communist Era* (HC 21–II), vol. II, Minutes of Evidence, HC Session 1991–2, p. 52.

[40] D. P. O'Connell, *International Law*, 2nd edn (London: Stevens & Sons, 1970), vol. I, p. 165.

[41] Sir Robert Jennings and Sir Arthur Watts (eds.), *Oppenheim's International Law*, 9th edn (Harlow: Longman, 1992), vol. I, p. 175.

recognition of Bulgaria, Montenegro, Serbia and Romania to respect for minority rights, then narrowly defined in religious terms, on the part of the newly established states. 'The difference of religious creeds and confessions shall not be alleged against any person as a ground for exclusion or incapacity in matters relating to the enjoyment of civil and political rights, admission to public employment, functions and honours, or the exercise of various professions and industries in any locality whatsoever', the treaty read.[42]

Even more extensive were the minority rights provisions that the Entente Powers established as a condition for their recognition of the new states created after the First World War – Poland; Czechoslovakia; and the Kingdom of Serbs, Croats and Slovenes (later Yugoslavia) – and included in their treaties with many of the defeated and enlarged states. The Polish Minorities Treaty, which served as a model for the others, extended full rights of citizenship to all national minorities habitually resident in the territory or born of parents domiciled there at the time of their birth; guaranteed the free exercise of any creed, religion or belief 'whose practices are not inconsistent with public order or public morals'; guaranteed equality before the law and the same civil and political rights without distinction as to race, language or religion; and even allowed for instruction in minority languages in the primary schools.[43] (Some of the treaties also granted special rights to particular minorities, notably Jews, Vlachs, Muslims, Szeklers, Saxons and Ruthenians.) Unlike the Treaty of Berlin, moreover, which had no meaningful provisions for enforcement, the minorities treaties empowered the Council of the League of Nations to take such action 'as it may deem proper and effective' in response to any infraction of the treaties.[44] Although the authors of these treaties were motivated in part by humanitarian considerations, they were concerned primarily about the threat to European stability posed by unalleviated minority grievances. 'Nothing, I venture to say, is more likely to disturb the peace of the world than the treatment which might, in certain cases, be meted out to minorities', US President Woodrow Wilson intoned in defence of the League's minorities system.[45] Resented by treaty-bound states because of its non-universal scope and abused by kin-states with irredentist aims (notably Germany), the system, however,

---

[42] Treaty of Berlin, 13 July 1878, Articles V, XXVII, XXXV, XLIV in W. N. Medlicott, *The Congress of Berlin and After: A Diplomatic History of the Near Eastern Settlement 1878–1880* (London: Methuen & Co., 1938), Appendix II.
[43] Polish Minorities Treaty in C. A. Macartney, *National States and National Minorities* (London: Oxford University Press, 1934), Appendix I.
[44] Polish Minorities Treaty, Article 12.
[45] Cited in Macartney, *National States and National Minorities*, p. 232.

achieved only limited success and did not survive the Second World War.[46]

A more common practice than conditional recognition, at least until recently, was the recognition of governments as distinct from states. A state, once recognised, need not and cannot be recognised again; nor can it be de-recognised. This is one of the limitations of the use of recognition as an instrument of leverage – a point that we return to in Chapter 5. Governments, on the other hand, may be recognised or, less commonly, de-recognised. With the coming to power in Cambodia of the Vietnamese-backed Heng Samrin–Hun Sen government in 1979, for instance, Australia announced on 14 February 1981 that it no longer recognised the Government of Democratic Kampuchea (the Pol Pot regime).[47] By the late 1980s, however, most countries had abandoned the practice of according formal recognition to governments, in part so as not to appear to be bestowing legitimacy on regimes that were responsible for gross violations of human rights. France was the first European state to abandon this practice, shortly after the overthrow of the Diem government of South Vietnam in 1963.[48] The United Kingdom changed its policy in 1980. Following 'a re-examination of British policy . . . [and] a comparison with the practice of our partners and allies . . . we have decided that we shall no longer accord recognition to Governments', Lord Carrington, then the British foreign minister, announced in the House of Lords on 28 April 1980.[49] Consequently the British government no longer makes a distinction between *de facto* and *de jure* governments, choosing simply to have dealings with one regime and not another.

Collective recognition, which the EC's actions can be said to have approximated, is also not without precedent.[50] The recognition of Greece by the Treaty of London in 1830, of Belgium by the same treaty in 1831, of some of the Balkan states by the Treaty of Berlin, and of

---

[46] The system effectively came to an end when Poland renounced its treaty obligations on 13 September 1934. For a discussion of the system's successes and failures, see Jennifer Jackson Preece, *National Minorities and the European Nation-States System* (Oxford: Clarendon Press, 1998), ch. 5.

[47] Cassese, *Self-Determination of Peoples*, p. 97. Australia, however, also refused to recognise the Samrin–Sen government.

[48] Joe Verhoeven, 'La reconnaissance internationale: declin ou renouveau?', 39 *Annuaire français de droit international* (1993), 16.

[49] *Parliamentary Debates* (Hansard), House of Lords, vol. 408, cols. 1121–1122, 28 April 1980.

[50] The EC sought only to harmonise the positions of its member states. Ultimately it was the individual member states, rather than the Community itself, that extended recognition to new states in Eastern Europe and the Soviet Union.

Albania by the Conference of London of 1913 are all instances of collective recognition.[51] And admission to the United Nations, which for many states is evidence of an entity having achieved the status of statehood and therefore represents an implicit form of recognition, is regulated by the General Assembly and thus also a collective enterprise.[52] As opposed to conditional recognition, however, there are no significant political or strategic implications that follow from collective recognition.

EC recognition of the Yugoslav republics

The EC's recognition of new states in Yugoslavia exhibits both continuity and discontinuity with the legal thinking and historic state practice outlined above. Several features of the EC's policy have already been noted in the course of this survey. This final section will examine additional elements of EC recognition in relation to historic conventions. Not only are the EC's December 1991 policy guidelines relevant for this purpose but also the opinions of the Badinter Commission, whose interpretations of international law and whose reading of unfolding events were used selectively by the Community to underpin its policy.

Of fundamental importance to the EC's actions was its characterisation of the factual situation in Yugoslavia. The disintegration of the Soviet Union, which was occurring at the same time, ultimately posed no serious difficulty for the Community since the independence of the Soviet republics, excepting that of the Baltic republics initially, was uncontested by the central authorities.[53] By contrast, Belgrade challenged Slovenia's and Croatia's declarations of independence, which the federal and Serbian authorities viewed as attempts at unlawful secession,[54] thus raising the stakes considerably for the EC member states, which were confronted with the choice of either supporting Yugoslavia's continued unity or helping to effect the peaceful disintegration of that state.

Historically there has been little support for unilateral secession within the international community if only because states wish to ensure against

---

[51] Lauterpacht, *Recognition in International Law*, pp. 68–9.
[52] John Dugard, *Recognition and the United Nations* (Cambridge: Grotius Publications, 1987).
[53] A. V. Lowe and Colin Warbrick, 'Recognition of States', 41 *International and Comparative Law Quarterly* (1992), 473–82.
[54] See 'Address of Dr Borisav Jović in the Assembly of the Socialist Federal Republic of Yugoslavia' of 19 March 1992, reprinted in *Review of International Affairs* (Belgrade), 1 April 1992, pp. 11–12.

the emergence of legal principles and practices that might facilitate the fragmentation of states – including, possibly, their own.[55] Thus have the traditional requirements for statehood generally been applied more stringently in the case of secessionist entities – a factor that contributed to the failure of Katanga and Biafra to achieve widespread recognition notwithstanding the fact that both entities exercised significant control over the territories they claimed. As UN Secretary-General U Thant stated at the time of Biafra's bid for independence: 'The United Nations' attitude is unequivocal. As an international organisation, the United Nations has never accepted and does not accept and I do not believe it will ever accept the principle of [unilateral] secession of a part of its Member State.'[56] Indeed, as noted earlier, recognition of a secessionist entity could be construed to violate the principle of respect for the territorial integrity of a country as well as the prohibition against intervention in the domestic affairs of a state.[57] And yet, although many states acknowledged the absence of effective government in the case of Croatia because of its loss of control over nearly one-third of its territory,[58] this was not thought to be an obstacle to its statehood given the Badinter Commission's view that the crisis in Yugoslavia was so acute that the state's legal personality was actually being extinguished.

[55] Morton H. Halperin and David J. Scheffer, *Self-Determination in the New World Order* (Washington, DC: Carnegie Endowment for International Peace, 1992), ch. 1. It is interesting to note in this regard that Austria refrained from addressing the question of South Tyrol/Alto Adige (see ch. 1) as a self-determination issue, which might have raised the spectre of secession, treating it instead as a matter of minority protection. The Austrian foreign minister, in his statement to the UN General Assembly Special Political Committee in November 1961, observed that 'any attempt to settle the problem on that basis [self-determination] would seriously disturb democratic Europe and be harmful to the interests of all concerned', adding that the Austrian government should therefore 'not be accused of pursuing revisionist aims or seeking frontier changes'. 'The Status of the German-speaking Element of Bolzano (Bozen)', UN General Assembly, 16th Session, Special Political Committee, 289th Meeting, UN Doc. A/SPC/SR.289, 15 November 1961, para. 3.

[56] Press Conference in Accra, Ghana on 9 January 1970. 'Secretary-General's Press Conferences', *UN Monthly Chronicle*, February 1970, p. 36.

[57] Brownlie uses the term 'premature recognition' in relation to the recognition of 'an unsuccessful attempt at a secession', and views such recognition as a 'classical example of a breach of the principle of non-intervention'. See his 'Recognition in Theory and Practice', in R. St. J. Macdonald and Douglas M. Johnston (eds.), *The Structure and Process of International Law: Modern Essays in Legal Philosophy, Doctrine and Theory* (The Hague: Martinus Nijhoff, 1983), p. 633.

[58] On the eve of EC recognition of Slovenia and Croatia, Douglas Hogg, the British minister of state, observed, 'The traditional criteria that we adopt for the recognition of states probably apply to Slovenia. They do not apply in the case of Croatia in the same way, but . . . one of the reasons why . . . is that Croatian territory has been invaded by the JNA and Serbian irregulars.' *Parliamentary Debates* (Hansard), House of Commons, vol. 200, col. 1166, 12 December 1991.

When Lord Carrington, in his capacity as chairman of the EC peace conference, sought clarification from the Commission in November 1991 about the legal status of Yugoslavia, the Commission responded that 'the Socialist Federal Republic of Yugoslavia is in the process of dissolution'.[59] The Commission's judgement thus made it possible for the EC to extend recognition without contravening international law – or at least without contributing to the promotion of secessionist norms. Indeed, Badinter's characterisation of the situation allowed the EC to maintain that Slovenia and Croatia were not seceding from Yugoslavia because the federal state's continuing existence was in question, even though Croatia had employed the language of secession to describe its actions initially. (Article II of Croatia's Constitutional Resolution in support of independence proclaims that Croatia thus 'begins the process of disassociation from the other republics of the SFRY'.)[60] Germany echoed the Commission's view. In its *ex-post facto* explication of Germany's recognition policy, the Foreign Office stated: '[W]e are not concerned with a secession of peripheral areas from a centre but with the disintegration of a federal State into its individual components.'[61]

The situation, as Badinter described it, is generally thought to be unique. 'There are no previous cases where the predecessor state has dissolved into a number of independent states, with none of these states being considered the continuing state and all of the emerging states considered as equal heirs to the rights and obligations of the predecessor state', Paul Williams has observed.[62] Yet even under these circumstances, it is surprising that the Twelve were so quick to extend recognition. For one thing, the language that the Commission used to describe the situation ('in the process of dissolution') suggested that by December 1991 the disintegration of the Yugoslav state was still incomplete; indeed it would not be until some seven months later that the Commission would conclude that 'the process of dissolution . . . is now complete [and] the SFRY no longer exists'.[63] Moreover, even though Belgrade had lost effective control over Slovenia and most of Croatia – two of its six constituent republics – the historic presumption in favour of

---

[59] Opinion No. 1.

[60] Cited in Roland Rich, 'Recognition of States: The Collapse of Yugoslavia and the Soviet Union', 4 *European Journal of International Law* (1993), 39.

[61] German Foreign Office, Bonn, Position Paper on Recognition (March 1993), mimeo, p. 5.

[62] Paul R. Williams, 'The Treaty Obligations of the Successor States of the Former Soviet Union, Yugoslavia, and Czechoslovakia: Do They Continue in Force?', 23 *Denver Journal of International Law and Policy* (1994), 16.

[63] Opinion No. 8 (4 July 1992), 31 *International Legal Materials* (1992), 1523.

the continuity of an established state subject to disintegrating pressures would seem to argue against such a judgement. As Crawford explains, 'Extinction is thus, within broad limits, not affected by more or less prolonged anarchy within the State.'[64] Somalia, *circa* 1992, is a case in point; despite the virtual absence of any effective government at the time, states continued to treat it as having legal personality.[65] By December 1991, however, with Macedonia and Bosnia and Herzegovina joining Slovenia and Croatia in the assertion of their sovereign rights, the majority of republics now no longer supported the Yugoslav federation.

The Yugoslav constitution (1974) might appear to be an authoritative source as to the rights and obligations of the republics that would thus help to clarify the situation, particularly since the constitution contained language specific to secession.[66] Indeed, Germany, in offering its support for the break-away republics, cited the 'already strong status of the republics in the Yugoslav constitution then still in force'.[67] But, in fact, the authority of the Yugoslav constitution is really of little significance from the standpoint of international law since it represents the embodiment of municipal law. If the provisions of national constitutions were determinative of international law, there would be virtually no uniform criteria with respect to the legality of state practices. And yet, despite the claim to be basing its judgements on 'the principles of international law',[68] Badinter took the Yugoslav constitution into consideration on two occasions. First, the Commission examined the constitution to determine the nature of the state structure, which, although acknowledging this to be 'mere facts', nonetheless thought it relevant to the question of effective control and, by extension, the continuity of the Yugoslav state.[69] Second, the Commission invoked Article 5 of the

---

[64] Crawford, *The Creation of States in International Law*, p. 417.
[65] Acknowledgement of Somalia's continued existence as a state can be found in *Republic of Somalia* v *Woodhouse Drake & Carey (Suisse) SA* (1992).
[66] The 1974 Constitution asserts 'the right of every nation to self-determination, including the right to secession'. *The Constitution of the Socialist Federal Republic of Yugoslavia*, Basic Principles (Belgrade: The Secretariat of the Federal Assembly Information Service, 1974).
[67] German Position Paper on Recognition, p. 1.
[68] Opinion No. 1.
[69] From Opinion No. 1:

(1) The Committee considers:
. . . .
(c) that, for the purpose of applying these criteria [of statehood], the form of internal political organization and the constitutional provisions are mere facts, although it is necessary to take them into consideration in order to determine the Government's way over the population and the territory;

Yugoslav constitution, which stipulates that the republics' boundaries cannot be altered without their consent, in support of the principle of *uti possidetis juris* (respect for existing borders).[70] Not only was the Commission's invocation of the Yugoslav constitution curious because of the document's questionable relevance to international law but also because, having elected to examine the constitution, Badinter then chose to ignore what it said about secession.

The Commission's particular concern with the nature of the Yugoslav state structure would seem to suggest that the test of effectiveness differs depending on the type of government.[71] Federal-type states, according to this reasoning, need to satisfy more stringent criteria for effectiveness than centrally controlled states, since the former are characterised, in part, by a high degree of representativeness, which, the Commission observed, '[t]he composition and workings of the essential organs of the Federation . . . no longer meet. . .'[72] Yet, as Craven points out, this approach contradicts the opinion of the International Court of Justice (ICJ) in the *Western Sahara Case*, where the ICJ stated that 'no rule of international law, in the view of the Court, requires the structure of the State to follow any particular pattern, as is evident from the diversity of the forms of State found in the world today'.[73] A different and, admittedly, more radical claim in support of the 'breakaway' republics might have been made by the Commission on the basis of Belgrade's failure to conduct itself in conformity with the principle of equal rights and self-determination of peoples.[74] But while the EC affirmed the principle of self-determination in its guidelines on recognition, the Commission did not invoke the principle in support of the republics' independence claims.[75] Germany, by contrast, justified its recognition of the Yugoslav

---

(d) that in the case of a federal-type state, which embraces communities that possess a degree of autonomy and, moreover, participate in the exercise of political power within the framework of institutions common to the Federation, the existence of the state implies that the federal organs represent the components of the Federation and wield effective power.

[70] 'The principle applies all the more readily to the Republics since the second and fourth paragraphs of Article 5 of the Constitution of the SFRY stipulated that the Republics' territories and boundaries could not be altered without their consent.' Opinion No. 3 (11 January 1992), 31 *International Legal Materials* (1992), 1500.

[71] Craven, 'The European Community Arbitration Commission on Yugoslavia', p. 366.

[72] Opinion No. 1.

[73] Cited in Craven, 'The European Community Arbitration Commission on Yugoslavia', p. 366.

[74] See Kirgis, 'The Degrees of Self-Determination', for an argument supporting the right of peoples to secede from an established state that does not have a fully representative form of government.

[75] The Guidelines read: 'The Community and its Member States confirm their attachment to the principles of the Helsinki Final Act and the Charter of Paris, in particular the

republics on the basis of self-determination. 'That limited right to self-determination', Bonn argued, 'logically followed from the recognition that the triumph of Serbian nationalism under Milosevic and his readiness to use violence against non-Serbian nations had rendered inevitable the demise of the former Yugoslav State, thus leaving the individual republics as the only bodies wherein political objectives could be formulated in a legitimate democratic way.'[76]

Badinter, in fact, invoked the principle of self-determination not to support but to restrict the emergence of new states in the region. If it was largely on the basis of Badinter's finding of Yugoslavia's dissolution that the EC was able to extend recognition to Slovenia, Croatia and later Bosnia and Herzegovina and Macedonia, it was the Commission's reading of the right to self-determination that sought to ensure that the disintegration of Yugoslavia would be limited to that state's federal units (republics), thus guarding against the establishment of a legal precedent that could conceivably apply to other parts of Yugoslavia. In its second opinion, delivered on 11 January 1992, the Commission acknowledged the right to self-determination of the constituent peoples of Yugoslavia (notably the Serbian population of Croatia and Bosnia and Herzegovina) but argued that the exercise of that right must not involve changes to existing frontiers (*uti possidetis juris*).[77] The Commission, therefore, did not support the unilateral establishment of a separate state by the Croatian and Bosnian Serb communities.

In one sense Badinter's approach was consistent with the thinking that has essentially prevailed since the Commission of Rapporteurs on the Aaland Islands question reported to the League of Nations in 1921 on the demand of the Swedish-speaking majority population of the Islands to leave Finland and join with Sweden. As the League Commission concluded then:

To concede to minorities, either of language or religion, or to any fractions of a population the right of withdrawing from the community to which they belong, because it is their wish or their good pleasure, would be to destroy order and

principle of self-determination.' Declaration on the 'Guidelines on the Recognition of New States in Eastern Europe and in the Soviet Union', Extraordinary EPC Ministerial Meeting (Brussels), EPC Press Release P. 128/91, 16 December 1991.

[76] German Position Paper on Recognition, p. 2.

[77] Opinion No. 2 reads: 'The Committee considers that . . . whatever the circumstances, the right to self-determination must not involve changes to existing frontiers at the time of independence (*uti possidetis juris*) except where the States concerned agree otherwise.'

stability within States and to inaugurate anarchy in international life; it would be to uphold a theory incompatible with the very idea of the State as a territorial and political unity.[78]

This view was echoed more recently by Geoffrey Howe, the British foreign minister, in 1983 when he declared, 'It is widely accepted in the United Nations that the right of self-determination does not give every distinct group or territory subdivision within a state the right to secede from it and thereby dismember the territorial integrity or political unity of sovereign independent states.'[79]

In another sense, however, Badinter was clearly innovating. In novel fashion – the distinction is nowhere codified in international law – Badinter was suggesting that federal-type units enjoy a privileged status over sub-federal entities for purposes of recognition. On this basis the statehood claims of the Albanian community in Kosovo, in addition to those of the Serbian communities in Croatia and Bosnia and Herzegovina, were all rejected. This same reasoning would later facilitate the European Union's decision to reject Chechnya's appeals for recognition in January 1995 at the time of the Russian assault on that territory.[80] Müllerson underscores the difficulties implicit in this distinction:

Such a conclusion would mean that those minorities which already enjoy certain administrative autonomy in clearly defined administrative borders have stronger claims to independence, and that those who do not enjoy autonomy at all are in this sense disadvantaged . . . It seems illogical that haphazard facts such as this should play an important role in resolving crucial issues of the existence of states.[81]

Indeed, had Kosovo been granted republic status under Tito, as many Kosovo Albanians would have liked, Kosovo would presumably be an independent state today.

Badinter's application of the principle of *uti possidetis juris* to the Yugoslav situation was also novel. *Uti possidetis juris* was associated previously with the experience of decolonisation after the Second World War. The principle was interpreted at the time to mean that a newly

---

[78] League of Nations, 'The Aaland Islands Question', Report submitted to the Council of the League of Nations by the Commission of Rapporteurs, Doc. B.7.21/68/106 (1921), p. 28.

[79] *Parliamentary Debates* (Hansard), House of Lords, vol. 446, cols. 93–4, 12 December 1983.

[80] The EU instead called for 'a peaceful settlement to the conflict which respects the territorial integrity of the Russian Federation'. See 'Declaration by the Presidency on Behalf of the European Union Concerning Chechnya', Council of the European Union, General Secretariat, Press Release 4215/95 (presse 11), 17 January 1995.

[81] Müllerson, *International Law, Rights and Politics*, pp. 78–9.

independent state's claim to territory cannot extend beyond the territory of the former colony.[82] Badinter in fact cites the ICJ's judgement, *Frontier Dispute Case (Burkina Faso v Republic of Mali)*, which established that the existing administrative boundaries of the colonies were to serve as the international boundaries of the new states. It is the universal character of the language used by the ICJ that appealed to Badinter, which, in the Commission's third opinion, cites the Court's judgement that *uti possidetis juris* 'is a general principle, which is logically connected with the phenomenon of the obtaining of independence, wherever it occurs. Its obvious purpose is to prevent the independence and stability of new States being endangered by fratricidal struggles. . .'[83] But what the Court seems to have meant by 'a general principle' was that, although originating with Spanish colonial law, it did not pertain solely to that system of law. It is less clear that the Court had anything but colonial situations in mind, as the clause that Badinter omitted suggests: 'provoked by the challenging of frontiers following the withdrawal of the administering power'.[84] This reading is reinforced by ICJ Judge Luchaire's separate opinion. 'In legal discourse', he wrote, 'the term "decolonization" should be used only with great caution and must above all not be confused with accession to independence.'[85]

For hundreds of years the international community has devised and observed practices to regulate the admission of new members to the community, foremost among these practices being the recognition of states. Recognition has always been something of a discretionary political act and has exhibited considerable variation. In the past century, however, recognition has become codified around the requirements for statehood specified in the Montevideo Convention and the additional condition that no state be created in violation of *jus cogens* norms. As we have seen, the EC, in its recognition of new states in Yugoslavia, demonstrated broad continuity with historic convention but it also departed from prevailing state practice in a number of important respects. The EC's innovations are likely to have far-reaching implications

---

[82] Santiago Torres Bernádez, 'The "Uti Possidetis Juris Principle" in Historical Perspective', in Konrad Ginther *et al.* (eds.), *Völkerrecht zwischen normativen Anspruch und politischer Realität* (Berlin: Duncker & Humblot, 1994), p. 433.

[83] Opinion No. 3.

[84] *Frontier Dispute Case (Burkina Faso v Republic of Mali)* in Martin Dixon and Robert McCorquodale (eds.), *Cases and Materials on International Law* (London: Blackstone, 1991), p. 253.

[85] Cited in Craven, 'The European Community Arbitration Commission on Yugoslavia', p. 388.

for the development of human rights, self-determination, secession and statehood, among other aspects of substantive law well beyond the immediate region, in addition to the actual effects of the EC's actions on the Yugoslav crisis, which are discussed in Chapter 4.

Law 'is a major force in international relations and a major determinant in national politics', Louis Henkin argues in his classic study, *How Nations Behave*. '" Realists" who do not recognize the uses and force of law are not realistic. "Idealists" who do not recognize the law's limitations are largely irrelevant to the world that is', he contends.[86] Yet to argue for the relevance of legal norms to the EC's recognition policy, as this chapter has done, is not to explain the precise nature of the relationship between international law and international politics. In the end, how much does international law really matter for state practice? And what were the implications of the 'legal effect' for the EC's recognition of new states in Yugoslavia? These questions are examined more closely in Chapter 3.

---

[86] Louis Henkin, *How Nations Behave: Law and Foreign Policy*, 2nd edn (New York: Council on Foreign Relations/Columbia University Press, 1979), p. 47.

3 International law, international relations and the recognition of states

Chapter 2 examined the tradition of legal thinking and historic practice with respect to the recognition of states. The rationale for that exercise was the claim, in part, that if the EC's recognition of Yugoslav republics was driven primarily by political and strategic considerations, one could not dismiss the relevance of international law altogether. The claim rested on two observations: first, that the EC consciously and deliberately considered the question of recognition within a legal framework, evident most notably in its establishment of the Badinter Commission; and second, that the legal framework, once invoked, both facilitated and constrained the EC in some of its actions.

This chapter returns to the latter point. For to suggest that the EC's response was at all moulded by international law would not only seem to contradict the views of legal scholars and political analysts alike who maintain that the Community's actions were motivated largely, if not entirely, by extra-legal considerations; it also begs a number of fundamental questions about the relationship between international law and politics in general and the bearing that both have on the recognition of states in particular. For instance, how does one distinguish conformity to law from the fortuitous coincidence of law and politics? And if international law at times does indeed facilitate and constrain international behaviour, how does it achieve that effect? Why do states respect international laws and legal norms, when they do, in view of the fact that there exists no central authority capable of enforcing compliance with law in the international order? And what are the implications of non-compliance for any claims about the salience of international law?

Admittedly these are very large questions that, moreover, have occupied legal and political minds for generations. The purpose here is to draw from this body of understanding to make a point about the function of international law that has been obscured by the tendency to see it as a primitive, and therefore deficient, form of law, rather than as an institution in some ways governed by a distinct logic and to which a different measure of effectiveness sometimes pertains. This tendency, characteristic particularly of Realist thinking since the Second World War but shared also by some legal scholars, has arguably contributed to the notion that international law ultimately had little bearing on the EC's recognition of new states in Yugoslavia, just as it is thought to have little bearing on so many other aspects of international society – 'an attorney's mantle artfully displayed on the shoulders of arbitrary power', as Sir Alfred Zimmern once put it.[1]

If, however, one accepts that states' interests may not in all respects be divergent and fluctuating but instead may sometimes be shared and constant (the view held, interestingly, by the pre-eminent Realist, Hans J. Morgenthau),[2] a very different conception of international law begins to emerge – one that has a place for notions of 'rules' and 'cooperation' in numerous areas of international relations, of which one can include the admission of new states to the international order. The relevance of rules and cooperation to international behaviour has long been familiar to students of international regimes, and yet for years international legal scholars and international relations scholars have been engaged in what Louis Henkin has called a *dialogue de sourds*.[3] Only fairly recently have the two begun to appreciate the complementarity of their respective disciplines.[4]

This chapter will explore the relationship between international law and international politics in the light of this interdisciplinary dialogue.[5] It will first examine the alienation of international relations from international law, identifying features of the two disciplines that have resulted in their mutual disregard. It will then discuss developments in both fields that have created opportunities for mutual enrichment, and seek to apply

---

[1] Quoted in J. R. Brierly, *The Outlook for International Law* (Oxford: Clarendon Press, 1944), p. 13.

[2] See Morgenthau, 'Positivism, Functionalism, and International Law', 34 *American Journal of International Law* (1940), 278.

[3] Louis Henkin, *How Nations Behave: Law and Foreign Policy*, 2nd edn (New York: Council on Foreign Relations/Columbia University Press, 1979), p. 4. Henkin actually has diplomats, not political scientists, in mind. He consequently makes scant reference to the scholarly literature on international relations in this study.

[4] Kenneth W. Abbott was one of the first international legal scholars to take an interest in regime theory. See his 'Modern International Relations Theory: A Prospectus for International Lawyers', 14 *Yale Journal of International Law* (1989), 335–411. For an overview of recent interdisciplinary scholarship, see Anne-Marie Slaughter, Andrew S. Tulumello and Stepan Wood, 'International Law and International Relations Theory: A New Generation of Interdisciplinary Scholarship', 92 *American Journal of International Law* (1998), 367–97.

[5] Various schools of contemporary legal and political thought inform this discourse; not all of them, however, are denominated here. For a discussion of the relevant approaches, see Harold Hongju Koh, 'Review Essay: Why Do Nations Obey International Law?' 106 *Yale Law Journal* (1997), 2599–659.

aspects of these approaches to the recognition of states. One can borrow usefully from the work that has been produced on legitimacy in international law and on cooperation in international relations to talk about recognition as an informal regime governed by its own set of norms (legal as well as political) that contribute to the maintenance of a stable order in the state-based international community. One can still argue, as is done here, that the EC departed from state practice and international law in its recognition of Yugoslav states. Yet it also becomes apparent, in this and other cases, that international law circumscribes the range of allowable state behaviour and that the exercise of power is not, as Zimmern would have it, as arbitrary as it might appear.

Two cultures

For more than 300 years, since at least the time of Hugo Grotius (1583–1642), scholars commonly regarded international law as an integral part of political reality. Of course many of these scholars, like Grotius himself, were jurists, and so it would seem only natural that in their efforts to explain interstate relations they would take international law into account. The devastating experience of the Second World War, however, which the League of Nations, the Kellogg–Briand Pact, and other law-based international initiatives were powerless to forestall, alienated even legally minded students of international relations from the study of law. Hans Morgenthau, among others, whose work had an enormous influence on the post-war study of international relations, was profoundly disillusioned by the war. Although trained as an international lawyer, he became less sanguine about its broad utility. In 1946 he wrote: '[T]he questions which the law and the lawyer can answer are largely irrelevant to the fundamental issues upon which the peace and welfare of nations depend. . .'[6] Morgenthau's writings – along with those of E. H. Carr before him and Stanley Hoffmann after him – contributed significantly to the erosion of interest in international law among students of international relations. Indeed, some thirty years later Hedley Bull observed: '[T]he tradition of positive international law [is] regarded with something approaching contempt by students of international politics. . .'[7]

Several features of international law account for its declining significance from the standpoint of international relations. To begin with, the work of legal scholars themselves, aiming ironically to strengthen the

---

[6] Hans J. Morgenthau, 'Diplomacy', 55 *Yale Law Journal* (1946), 1080.
[7] Hedley Bull, 'Recapturing the Just War for Political Theory', 31 *World Politics* (1979), 588.

intellectual foundations of international law, has actually diminished its appeal. It was the efforts of legal positivists to eradicate the metaphysical underpinnings of international law – by grounding it in state consent as opposed to natural law – that helped to fashion the perception of international law as a lesser form of law. John Austin, insisting that law 'properly so called' must proceed from a 'precisely determined party capable of issuing a command' – a sovereign with enforcement capability, in other words – and observing that the international legal order lacked such a capability, classified it as a form of 'positive international morality'. Whereas a proper law must be 'armed with a sanction' and 'impose a duty', international morality in his view relied for its force, rather weakly, on the 'opinions or sentiments current among nations'.[8] Hans Kelsen, another leading positivist, also emphasised the importance of punitive sanctions. '[L]aw is a coercive order', he argued, and international law, because of its lack of 'special organs [charged with] the creation and application of its norms', was merely a 'primitive' form of law.[9] These characterisations found resonance with Morgenthau, who was well acquainted with them. In his classic *Politics Among Nations* (1948), he wrote disparagingly: 'International law is a primitive type of law resembling the kind of law that prevails in certain preliterate societies, such as the Australian aborigines and the Yurok of northern California.'[10]

If international law is seen as a weak form of law it is also because scholars of international law and international politics alike tend to take as their model of a proper legal order the municipal system, where a central agent (the state) is both authorised and empowered to enforce the law. By this standard, international law does indeed seem primitive. In an effort, therefore, to rescue international law from its harsher critics, some legal scholars have sought to recast the domestic arena so that it appears to share more in common with international society. For instance, they may point out that municipal legal orders, too, often suffer

---

[8] John Austin, *The Province of Jurisprudence Determined*, 5th edn (London: John Murray, 1885), Lecture V, pp. 173, 184, 185.

[9] Hans Kelsen, *Pure Theory of Law* (Berkeley: University of California Press, 1967), pp. 34 and 323. At other times Kelsen suggests that international law is a coercive order that relies on decentralised sanctions (i.e., reprisals and war). See, for instance, *ibid.*, pp. 320–2.

[10] Hans J. Morgenthau, *Politics Among Nations*, revised by Kenneth W. Thompson (New York: McGraw-Hill, 1993), p. 255. It bears noting that for all his criticism of international law, Morgenthau was also mindful of its force and value. In the same volume he writes: 'The great majority of the rules of international law are generally observed by all nations without actual compulsion, for it is generally in the interest of all nations concerned to honor their obligations under international law' (p. 267).

from inadequate compliance. 'When one examines the domestic incidence of murder or rebellion in the best-ordered society', Richard Falk observes in this vein, 'the record discloses a frequency of violation that would disappoint any legal perfectionist'.[11] Similarly, they may argue that municipal courts apply law when in fact there is often no real means available to enforce it, as when the US Supreme Court declares a presidential act unconstitutional.[12] Alternatively they may argue that international law has its own enforcement capability that resides in the moral and diplomatic pressures that states exert on one another, or, as a last resort, in self-help.[13] But none of these explanations rings true. However widespread domestic violations of the law may be, nonetheless the capacity for greater enforcement always exists, while structural and even legal constraints (in the form of the UN Security Council veto) militate against the possibility at the global level. Moral and political suasion, on the other hand, appear to be far more effective within states – democratic states at least – than among states. In some respects, as we will see, it is more constructive to view international law not as a pale imitation of municipal law but as an institution characterised by its own distinctive features.

Another reason why international law has suffered is because the methodological principles governing the discipline are significantly different from those of international relations. Whereas international relations is oriented towards explanation – including the formulation of generalisations and, in some instances, the construction of models – international law is principally concerned with the analysis of formal rules and their application to particular cases.[14] Moreover, legal reasoning relies on a very narrow conception of the sources of international law as the basis for those rules.[15] International law is thus vulnerable to the charge that it takes normative claims about the law at

---

[11] Richard A. Falk, *The Status of Law in International Society* (Princeton: Princeton University Press, 1970), p. 50.

[12] Anthony D'Amato, *Jurisprudence: A Descriptive and Normative Analysis of Law* (Dordrecht: Martinus Nijhoff Publishers, 1984), p. 185.

[13] On moral and diplomatic pressures, see Anthony D'Amato, *International Law: Process and Prospect* (Dobbs Ferry, NY: Transactional Publishers, 1987), pp. 1–26; on self-help, see Hans Kelsen, *Law and Peace in International Relations* (Cambridge, MA: Harvard University Press, 1942), Lecture 2.

[14] Kenneth W. Abbott, 'International Law and International Relations Theory: Building Bridges – Elements of a Joint Discipline', 86 *Proceedings of the American Society of International Law* (1992), 168.

[15] The sources of international law are taken to be those listed in Article 38 of the Statute of the International Court of Justice. They are, principally: international conventions, international custom, the general principles of law 'recognized by civilised nations'; and, secondarily: judicial decisions and the teachings of highly qualified publicists.

face value and is indifferent to the broader social and political context. As Stanley Hoffmann has written, 'Social scientists are impatient with a discipline that seems to emphasize exclusively . . . a closed universe of norms – their logical consequences, their hierarchy, their interconnections – divorced from the political and social universe in which they are born and which they try to regulate.'[16]

Of course Realists have also maintained that if international law is not a reliable lens through which to understand international behaviour, nor is it a sound foundation for the management of international affairs. Hence the well-known attack on the 'legalistic-moralistic' approach to international relations made by Morgenthau, and echoed in the writings of some of the most influential scholar-practitioners of the Cold War generation: George Kennan, Dean Acheson and Henry Kissinger.[17] Crucial to any accurate analysis of interstate relations, in their view, are the dynamics of power politics, not considerations of international law, because, as Acheson put it starkly, 'The survival of states is not a matter of law.'[18]

Yet as Acheson's remark suggests, very often what the critics of international law have in mind when they speak of its weaknesses is its lack of effectiveness in the most extreme situations – in particular, when a state's vital interests are thought to be at stake. (Acheson, in fact, was speaking about international law, US actions and the Cuban missile crisis.) This tendency can be likened to evaluating an automobile's efficiency on the basis of how well it performs at top speed rather than under conditions more representative of the typical stresses to which it will be subjected. In times of international crisis, states may be no more inclined to yield their vital national interests to international law than individuals are likely to respect municipal laws when faced with emergency conditions at home. For that matter, in moments of crisis states generally do not have an interest in repudiating the international legal system altogether. South Africa, although ostracised by the international community because of its apartheid policies, nonetheless maintained a 'scrupulously

---

[16] Stanley Hoffmann, 'The Study of International Law and the Theory of International Relations', 57 *Proceedings of the American Society of International Law* (1963), 26. Some legal scholars are sensitive to this criticism. See, for instance, Richard A. Falk, 'The Relevance of Political Context to the Nature and Functioning of International Law: An Intermediate View', in Karl W. Deutsch and Stanley Hoffmann (eds.), *The Relevance of International Law* (Cambridge, MA: Schenkman, 1968), pp. 133–52.

[17] See, for instance, George F. Kennan, *American Diplomacy*, expanded edn (Chicago: University of Chicago Press, 1984), p. 95; Dean Acheson, 'Remarks', 57 *Proceedings of the American Society of International Law* (1963), 13–15; and Henry A. Kissinger, *American Foreign Policy* (New York: W. W. Norton & Co., 1969), p. 34.

[18] Acheson, 'Remarks', 14.

correct' attitude towards international law in almost all other respects.[19] Even Nazi Germany did not take the position that it was above all international law.[20] If pariah and rogue states seek and require a modicum of cooperation from the international system, what does that tell us about the vast number of states that, for all their frustrations and aspirations, are determined nevertheless to realise their ambitions in peaceful ways? By focusing on moments of extreme crisis, as Realists do, they ignore large areas of international life where cooperation is thought by states to be both necessary and desirable.

To generalise in this fashion about international law is not to overlook the fact that there have been notable exceptions to the tendencies described above. For instance, Myres McDougal and associates (the 'New Haven School'), conceding to Realists that the international legal order cannot achieve the same measure of constraint as the municipal legal order, have sought to include within the ambit of legal analysis factors of power and interest that legal scholars have typically excluded. This approach led McDougal to acknowledge that there were values underlying law that were not in all cases shared (McDougal was writing at the height of the Cold War) and to criticise, therefore, 'false conceptions of the universality of international law'.[21] The flip-side of this criticism, however, is the implicit acknowledgement that common interests, and therefore an effective legal system, at least can exist: 'The effective authority of any legal system depends in the long run upon the underlying common interests of the participants in the system and their recognition of such common interests, reflected in continuing predispositions to support the prescriptions and the procedures that comprise the system.'[22]

A legal system built on common interests, however, is very different from one that seeks to restrain states from the Realist 'will to power'. The latter requires rules and norms that, to be effective, are backed by a coercive agency. And as critics of international law have pointed out, few if any effective rules of this sort exist. A global order predicated on common interests also requires rules and norms but their function, in

---

[19] D'Amato, *Jurisprudence*, pp. 199–200.

[20] Thomas Franck recounts how, after German agents kidnapped a refugee from Swiss territory, the Nazi regime repatriated him and apologised for its 'regrettable' violation of the law. See Thomas M. Franck, *The Power of Legitimacy Among Nations* (New York: Oxford University Press, 1990), p. 251, fn. 44.

[21] Myres S. McDougal and Harold D. Lasswell, 'The Identification and Appraisal of Diverse Systems of Public Order', in Richard A. Falk and Saul H. Mendlovitz (eds.), *The Strategy of World Order* (New York: World Law Fund, 1966), vol. II, p. 48.

[22] *Ibid.*, p. 49.

contrast, is to facilitate rather than to constrain. Among legal scholars, H. L. A. Hart deserves credit for highlighting the distinction between laws that constrain and laws that enable, although he does not appear necessarily to have had international law in mind:

> [T]here are important classes of law where this analogy with orders backed by threats altogether fails, since they perform a quite different function. Legal rules defining the ways in which valid contracts or wills or marriages are made do not require persons to act in certain ways whether they wish to or not . . . Instead, they provide individuals with *facilities* for realizing their wishes, by conferring legal powers upon them to create, by certain specified procedures and subject to certain conditions, structures of rights and duties within the coercive framework of the law.[23]

More than a decade would pass before international relations scholars – notably Robert O. Keohane and Joseph S. Nye in the 1970s – would arrive at a similar observation about rules, norms and principles in the context of their studies of interdependency and global institutionalised cooperation (regimes).[24] And yet to judge by the discourse in both fields, especially international relations, the relevance of international law to international politics is only gradually coming to be appreciated.

Cooperation and international regimes

To emphasise the cooperative basis of interstate relations is to take an approach to the global order that would seem to be at variance with the basic tenor of Realism, still the dominant school of thought in the field of international relations. Structural Realism – the more systematic formulation of the theory – argues that a condition of anarchy prevails in the international system that militates against anything but incidental cooperation among states.[25] In the absence of a central agency with system-wide authority, states rely on their own capabilities to protect and further their interests. They 'develop their own strategies, chart their own courses, [and] make their own decisions', in Kenneth Waltz's words.[26] The absence of a central authority does not mean that there are no common structures and procedures in international relations. '[W]orld politics, although not formally organized, is not entirely

---

[23] H. L. A. Hart, *The Concept of Law*, 2nd edn (Oxford: Clarendon Press, 1994), pp. 27–8.
[24] One of the earlier works on this subject is Robert O. Keohane and Joseph S. Nye, *Power and Interdependence: World Politics in Transition* (Boston: Little, Brown, 1977).
[25] The 'classic' structural (or neo-) realist text is Kenneth N. Waltz, *Theory of International Politics* (New York: McGraw-Hill, 1979).
[26] *Ibid*, p. 96.

without institutions and orderly procedures', Waltz acknowledges.[27] But it does mean that cooperation takes place only at the margins of the international system.

Regime theorists start from the same premises as Realists; that is, they accept that the international system is a non-hierarchical one and that states are rational actors within that system. But they differ from Realists in one critical respect: they treat the incidence of formalised cooperation – institutions, codified rules – as an integral, rather than an accidental, feature of international relations. 'Although [Realism] provides a valuable starting point for analysis', Robert Keohane, a leading regime theorist, writes, 'it overlooks the fact that world politics at any given time is to some extent institutionalized.'[28] If Realism offered an accurate model of international behaviour, Keohane argues in one of his early studies, one would have expected that as America's relative power declined in the 1970s there would have occurred a concomitant decline in the strength of global institutions, such as the International Monetary Fund (IMF) or the General Agreement on Tariffs and Trade (GATT), which Realists had taken to be corollaries of the hegemonic dominance of the United States in the world arena. The continuing strength of these and other international institutions, Keohane maintains, is a testament to the intrinsic value of cooperative arrangements in the global system.[29]

Stephen Krasner, in a widely accepted formulation, defines regimes as 'principles, norms, rules, and decision-making procedures around which actor expectations converge in a given issue-area'.[30] The concept is a fairly elastic one. In the narrow sense it is used to refer to formal international organisations, such as the IMF and the World Trade Organisation (WTO), that operate on the basis of explicit rules, agreed upon by states, pertaining to the management or regulation of a particular set of international issues. In the broad sense the term is used to refer simply to 'patterns of regularized cooperative behavior in world politics'[31] – a use of the term that has some relevance to the practice of state recognition, as does Jack Donnelly's typology of regimes, among which

---

[27] *Ibid.*, p. 114.

[28] Robert O. Keohane, *International Institutions and State Power: Essays in International Relations Theory* (Boulder, CO: Westview, 1989), p. vii.

[29] Keohane, 'The Theory of Hegemonic Stability and Changes in International Economic Regimes, 1967–1977', in Ole R. Holsti, Randolph M. Silverson and Alexander L. George (eds.), *Change in the International System* (Boulder, CO: Westview, 1980), pp. 131–62.

[30] Stephen D. Krasner, 'Structural Causes and Regime Consequences: Regimes as Intervening Variables', 36 *International Organization* (1982), 185.

[31] Keohane, *International Institutions and State Power*, p. 76.

he includes 'international standards that are not binding but are nonetheless commended by states'.[32]

Regimes differ from one another in other ways as well. There are multi-issue regimes, such as those that regulate the activities of states in the polar regions of the globe, and single-issue regimes, including those established by numerous commodity agreements (coffee, tin, etc.). Their geographic scope may be universal (the international postal regime) or entail the participation of as few as two states (various river management regimes). Some regimes are arguably more effective than others (the international monetary regime as opposed to the international human rights regime). And some regimes rely on punitive sanctions for enforcement (international whaling) while others may not (arms control).

The attraction of regimes, from the standpoint of the participating states, is that they permit actors to avoid the costs that would otherwise arise from uncoordinated national actions – 'the collective suboptimality that can emerge from individual behavior', in Arthur Stein's words.[33] For instance, in the absence of any interstate coordination many of the world's fisheries could easily become depleted, at great cost, ultimately, to all future possible beneficiaries.[34] The potential danger to human lives as a consequence of unregulated air traffic, similarly, has led to the establishment of the ICAO/IATA air transport system. It is easy to see how the perceived benefits of such a regime lead states to comply with its requirements willingly – that is, in the absence of a power compelling coercion. (Even the submission to any punitive sanction in this and other cases is effectively voluntary.) It is also easy to see that the Realist framework is of limited utility for the purpose of understanding this behaviour. Realists maintain that intrastructural shifts in the global distribution of capabilities – from, say, a bipolar to a multipolar world – will affect the propensity for cooperation among states.[35] That may be true for certain security issues but bearing in mind the limitations of generalising on the basis of extreme situations discussed above, the degree of cooperation that states will achieve in various other issue areas

---

[32] Jack Donnelly, 'International Human Rights: A Regime Analysis', 40 *International Organization* (1986), 603.

[33] Arthur A. Stein, 'Coordination and Collaboration: Regimes in an Anarchic World', 36 *International Organization* (1982), 307.

[34] Oran R. Young, *International Cooperation: Building Regimes for Natural Resources and the Environment* (Ithaca, NY: Cornell University Press, 1989), ch. 5.

[35] Bipolarity, it is argued, encourages small states to cooperate (ally) with one of the two superpowers whereas multiple poles of power create an incentive for shifting allegiances. See Kenneth Waltz, 'The Stability of a Bipolar World', 93 *Daedalus* (1964), 881–909.

appears very often to be independent of the intrastructural features of the international system.

This is not to suggest, assuming the Realist framework, that the constraining influence of regimes is as great as the structural constraints of the international system itself. This is why regime theorists talk about regimes as '*intervening* variables between state behavior and deeper structural forces such as power or interest'.[36] One may recognise in this a language similar to that which was used in Chapter 2 to describe the force of international legal norms relevant to the EC's recognition of Yugoslav states: a 'soft' constraint. And one can thus also appreciate the basis of the interest that regime theorists and international legal scholars have begun to take in one another's work in recent years.[37] International lawyers stand to learn from regime theorists about the importance of taking national (political) interests into account, while regime theorists stand to gain a greater appreciation of the role of law in clarifying the rules of the game and in helping to legitimate (and therefore reinforce) rule-governed behaviour, about which more will be said below.

The two disciplines, for that matter, share not only a common virtue but are also prone to a common weakness. For just as international law can suffer from formalism, so too is there the temptation among international relations scholars to treat nominal agreements as regimes. 'The futile and empty Kellogg–Briand Pact of 1927, to "outlaw war", could on a formalistic definition be considered an international regime', Keohane observes, even though one would not say that there were any obvious behavioural implications of the agreement.[38] Yet to put the emphasis only on the behaviour of states is to lose sight of the salience, if any, of the rules at work. After all, patterns of restrained behaviour are evident even in limited wars but one must be careful not to confuse a structural constraint (interests and power) with a regime constraint (laws and tacit rules).[39] Moreover, some agreements may be effective at some moments but not at others, which does not mean one ought to ignore them altogether.

[36] Donnelly, 'International Human Rights', 602 (emphasis added).
[37] See, in this regard, Robert O. Keohane, 'Compliance with International Commitments: Politics within a Framework of Law', 86 *Proceedings of the American Society of International Law* (1992), 176–80; and Anne-Marie Slaughter Burley, 'International Law and International Relations Theory: A Dual Agenda', 87 *American Journal of International Law* (1993), 205–39.
[38] Robert O. Keohane, 'The Analysis of International Regimes: Towards a European–American Research Programme', in Volker Rittberger (ed.), *Regime Theory and International Relations* (Oxford: Clarendon Press, 1995), p. 27.
[39] Krasner, in 'Structural Causes and Regime Consequences' (187), makes a similar point but does not consider any possible role for law in limited wars.

These difficulties have led regime theorists to respond in two very different ways. The first is to adopt more restrictive criteria for regimes, suggesting, for instance, that a regime must embody explicit rules and decision-making procedures[40] or, more restrictive still, that a regime requires a high degree of 'institutionalization'.[41] The second response is to accept a weaker notion of regime that takes the attitudes of states (similar to what in law is known as *opinio juris*) into account. '[A] regime is an attitudinal phenomenon', Donald Puchala and Raymond Hopkins write. '[R]egimes themselves are subjective: they exist primarily as participants' understandings, expectations or convictions about legitimate, appropriate or moral behaviour.'[42] Keohane concedes that this definition has 'thin' substantive content, but, he maintains, 'a set of rules need not be "effective" to qualify as a regime, [instead] it must be recognized as continuing to exist. Using this definition, regimes can be identified by the existence of explicit rules that are referred to in an affirmative manner by governments, even if they are not necessarily observed.'[43]

If one accepts the weaker notion of a regime – Keohane's 'patterns of regularized cooperative behavior', Donnelly's non-binding 'international guidelines', Puchala's and Hopkins's 'informal regimes' – it is possible to view the recognition of states as a regime or, at the very least, as sharing key features in common with a regime. Like many regimes, it is characterised by a set of guidelines (the Montevideo Convention and subsequent customary and treaty law) that, while not a body of explicit and precise rules or procedures governing the behaviour of states, nonetheless provide considerable guidance with respect to states' admission of new polities to the international order. Moreover, there is broad and deliberate conformity to these guidelines, notwithstanding some notable exceptions, including features of the EC's recognition of Yugoslav republics. (As noted above, and also as shown by John Ruggie in his study of the GATT, regimes can survive even if certain practices are inconsistent with prescribed behaviour.[44] Moreover, norms can withstand violations

---

[40] Robert O. Keohane, 'The Demand for International Regimes', 36 *International Organization* (1982), 341–2.

[41] Hayward R. Alker, Jr, 'A Methodology for Design Research on Interdependence Alternatives', 31 *International Organization* (1977), 37–8.

[42] Donald J. Puchala and Raymond F. Hopkins, 'International Regimes: Lessons from Inductive Analysis', 36 *International Organization* (1982), 246.

[43] Keohane, 'The Analysis of International Regimes', p. 28. Keohane has, at different moments, employed both strict and relaxed notions of regime. Contrast the view here, for instance, with his 'The Demand for International Regimes'.

[44] John G. Ruggie, 'International Regimes, Transactions and Change: Embedded Liberalism in the Postwar Economic Order', 36 *International Organization* (1982), 379–415.

below a certain threshold of frequency and severity.)[45] Finally, regimes typically reflect and uphold particular principles,[46] such as free trade (WTO), sustainable growth (the ozone accords) or democratic rule (Council of Europe). The recognition regime, similarly, reinforces the fundamental principles of the Westphalian system: the centrality of the state (as the principal entity possessing international legal personality), the sovereignty of the state and the inviolability of states' borders.

Indeed, if and when the recognition regime works effectively, it is precisely because it serves to protect the interests of states that are embodied in these principles. This explains why, divided though the international community was during the Cold War, the superpower confrontation did not undermine the general consensus favouring the use of recognition in support of these principles. Neither the United States nor the Soviet Union, for instance, sought to exploit the opportunities for recognition presented by the claims of Katanga (Congo), Biafra (Nigeria) or Eritrea (Ethiopia) to statehood, to name only some of the more prominent cases.[47] (Their aversion to secession, however, did not prevent the superpowers from lending support to separatist movements when they perceived that there were short-term tactical advantages to be gained from such patronage.)[48] Because of Cold War tensions, recognition on the part of Washington or Moscow would not only likely have been supported by the allies of each – or at least not strenuously opposed – but would also arguably have allowed one or the other superpower to gain the allegiance of a new state. Yet while the superpower competition on the African continent was at times fierce, this contest extended at most to support for regime changes and not for the creation of new states, except in the case of decolonisation – a process governed by consensus. To support the fragmentation of states would have been too threatening, it was assumed, not only to stability in Africa but to the state-based international system more generally.[49] This

---

[45] Peter J. Katzenstein, 'Introduction: Alternative Perspectives on National Security', in Peter J. Katzenstein (ed.), *The Culture of National Security: Norms and Identity in World Politics* (New York: Columbia University Press, 1996), p. 20.

[46] Puchala and Hopkins, 'International Regimes', 246.

[47] Tom Farer, 'A Paradigm of Legitimate Intervention', in Lori Fisler Damrosch (ed.), *Enforcing Restraint: Collective Intervention in Internal Conflicts* (New York: Council on Foreign Relations, 1993), p. 323.

[48] James Mayall, *Nationalism and International Society* (Cambridge: Cambridge University Press, 1990), pp. 66–7.

[49] The use of (non-)recognition in support of territorial integrity is widespread but not universal. Five states (Ivory Coast, Gabon, Haiti, Tanzania and Zambia), recognised Biafra's independence during the rebellion although not one of these states established

same reasoning is evident in the thinking of post-Cold War statesmen. '[C]rucial to any common international progress', UN Secretary-General Boutros Boutros-Ghali wrote in 1992, is respect for 'the fundamental sovereignty and integrity' of the state. '[I]f every ethnic, religious or linguistic group claimed statehood, there would be no limit to fragmentation, and peace, security and economic well-being for all would become ever more difficult to achieve.'[50]

It is not only the benefits from cooperation that may induce states to comply with the laws that regulate regimes. States may also observe rules, as Thomas Franck has noted, because they perceive the rule and its associated institutions to have a high degree of legitimacy. 'States' perceptions of the extent to which a rule is legitimate determines in part their sense of an obligation to adhere, and secure the adherence of others, to the rule.'[51] Legitimacy, Franck argues, is derived from four sources: a rule's pedigree ('the depth of the rule's roots in a historical process'); its determinacy (the clarity of a rule's content); its coherence (the consistent application of a rule and its compatibility with other legitimate norms or rules); and its adherence ('the rule's vertical connectedness to a normative hierarchy, culminating in an ultimate rule of recognition, which embodies the principled purposes and values that define the community of states').[52]

All four of Franck's sources have relevance to the norms and practices associated with the recognition of states. The deep-rootedness of the practice – its progressive institutionalisation since the middle of the eighteenth century – confers on it considerable legitimacy. Reliance on the practice of recognition for more than 200 years has helped give it a legitimacy that is essentially unchallenged. No one today questions the right or obligation of states to recognise other states, as they would have, say, in Pufendorf's time.[53] Recognition also exhibits determinacy, even if

formal diplomatic relations with Biafra. See 'Why We Recognized Biafra', *The Observer*, 26 April 1968.

[50] *An Agenda for Peace: Preventive Diplomacy, Peacemaking and Peacekeeping*, UN Doc. A/47/277 (1992), para. 17.

[51] Franck, *The Power of Legitimacy Among Nations*, p. 174.

[52] *Ibid.*, passim, and Thomas M. Franck, 'The Emerging Right to Democratic Governance', 86 *American Journal of International Law* (1992), 51.

[53] Indeed, in Pufendorf's time, recognition would have been considered an affront to the sovereignty of a ruler. As Pufendorf writes in *De Iure Naturae et Gentium* (1672), 'just as a king owes his sovereignty and majesty to no one outside his realm, so he need not obtain the consent and approval of other kings or states, before he may carry himself like a king and be regarded as such . . . [I]t would be an injury for the sovereignty of such a king to be called into question by a foreigner.' Cited in James Crawford, *The Creation of States in International Law* (Oxford: Clarendon Press, 1979), pp. 10–11.

the criteria for statehood are open to varying interpretations. International rules, however, generally permit some degree of elasticity (it would be difficult to apply them to new circumstances otherwise), although if they are too elastic they lend themselves to abuse that weakens their force and undermines what Franck calls their 'compliance pull'. Certainly in comparison with the rules governing the use of force, especially in relation to humanitarian emergencies, recognition exhibits strong determinacy.[54] As for recognition's coherence, until the EC's guidelines it can be said that the norms governing the practice were applied with general consistency, notwithstanding some tension between the right of self-determination and the principle of territorial integrity. And, finally, recognition's adherence – the connection between a rule, norm or practice and the fundamental principles of an order – can be seen in the way recognition affirms the very cornerstone of the international order: the state itself. Bull has written, 'The first function of international law has been to identify, as the supreme normative principle of the political organisation of mankind, the idea of a society of states.'[55] Recognition helps to achieve just that.

The function of international law

Returning now to the question of the relevance of international law to international politics, in view of the foregoing discussion it is easier to see that there is room for an alternate conception of international law to exist alongside the conventional characterisation. One must say 'alongside' rather than 'instead of' because it has to be accepted that states have had in mind to achieve at least a limited coercive effect with some of the covenants and treaties that they have adopted (the Covenant of the League of Nations and the Charter of the United Nations, among others), however imperfectly these laws have been put into effect.[56] And it is their imperfect implementation, whether for structural reasons or for lack of will, that permits us to talk, not altogether unfairly, about the weaknesses of the international legal order.

---

[54] On the indeterminacy of international law with respect to the use of force and humanitarian emergencies, especially in relation to NATO and Kosovo, see Catherine Guicherd, 'International Law and the War in Kosovo', 41(2) *Survival* (1999), 19–34; and Adam Roberts, 'NATO's "Humanitarian War" over Kosovo', 41(3) *Survival* (1999), 102–23.

[55] Hedley Bull, *The Anarchical Society: A Study of Order in World Politics* (London: Macmillan, 1977), p. 140.

[56] See, especially, Article 15 of the Covenant and Chapter VII of the Charter, which both sanction the use of force in response to breaches of the peace. That the enforcement

But if it is possible to distinguish between the constraining and enabling functions of international law, as we have done, it is because there are, broadly speaking, two corresponding sets of circumstances to which laws and legal norms apply: there are those circumstances that are thought to threaten a state's particular interests (e.g., aggression, terrorism, drug trafficking) and there are those circumstances that contribute towards the maintenance of a stable international order and thus serve a more general interest. Morgenthau had a similar distinction in mind, we may recall, when he referred to the 'temporary and fluctuating interests' of states as opposed to their 'permanent and stable' ones. To both, he observed, there correspond 'two obviously different types of international law'.[57] The latter set of rules constitutes, for Morgenthau, 'non-political international law, originating in the permanent interests of states to put their normal relations upon a stable basis. . .'[58] It is what Bull has in mind when he refers to the 'basic rules of coexistence'.[59] These would include the laws and norms that govern diplomatic privileges, extradition, various aspects of maritime law and, arguably, the establishment of new states.

This is not to say that states' interests are never at odds with one another within the sphere of 'permanent and stable' interests, or that states never violate the rules that reflect these common interests. (Witness Iran's seizure of the US embassy in Teheran in 1979 – a violation of the principle of diplomatic immunity.) What it does mean is that states see themselves as having a long-term stake in maintaining an orderly interstate system, and that the shared awareness of mutual gain to be derived from this orderliness induces a large degree of *voluntary* compliance with the rules and norms required for that purpose. Law, in this view, is not Austin's order backed by the threat of sanctions but, rather, a system sustained in large part by the willing respect for rules that are seen by states to safeguard their common interests.[60] Order is not always paramount among states' shared concerns; it may at times be outweighed by other values, such as justice. But it is important

---

provisions of the UN Charter, at least, are not mere paper provisions is evident from the many occasions on which they have already been used.

[57] Morgenthau, 'Positivism, Functionalism, and International Law', 278.

[58] *Ibid.*, 279.

[59] Bull, *The Anarchical Society*, p. 141.

[60] Andrew Hurrell distinguishes between laws of coordination and laws of subordination in this regard. See his 'International Society and the Study of Regimes: A Reflective Approach', in Robert J. Beck, Anthony Clark Arend and Robert D. Vander Lugt (eds.), *International Rules: Approaches from International Law and International Relations* (New York: Oxford University Press, 1996), p. 214.

enough to explain why powerful states will often defer to rules even when there are short-term tactical benefits to be gained from violating them.

This suggests something else about the relationship between international politics and international law. That relationship is not a simple marriage of convenience that states are only too willing to abandon at the moment their interests are no longer served. Rather, the rules of international law are the creation of states, and states subscribe to them precisely because they are designed to serve their interests. '[S]tates do not adopt useless, impractical, or dangerous rules to regulate their relations in the first place', Francis Boyle argues. 'Therefore, the requirements of international law should substantially, albeit imperfectly, coincide with the dictates of vital national interests and vice versa.'[61] To a large extent, then, international law must be rooted in the actual behaviour of states. To be effective, law cannot be expected to achieve objectives that states themselves do not desire. This is the weakness of the 'world peace through world law' approach and similar initiatives that seek to legislate good conduct without taking national interests into account.[62] While it may also be true that some laws reflect the values and the interests of the most powerful nations as against the weaker ones, other laws are based on varying degrees of consensus and mutual interest.

To better appreciate the relevance of international law to the functioning of international society, one can ask what would be the effect if there were no guidelines governing the recognition of states at all. There have been times when the 'global' order has been characterised by multiple polities (ancient Greece) or multiple principalities (seventeenth-century Europe), and relations among them, too, were informed by rules, having their basis, however, in morality, religion and custom as opposed to any positivist legal doctrines. But because the notion of the rights and obligations of these units was not as fully developed and formalised as they were to become with states, there was no need to establish the status of these units with the same precision as there is now. '[T]he idea of an international order founded on or revealed by recognition is crucial only within the Westphalian conception', David Strang observes.[63] Today,

---

[61] Francis Anthony Boyle, *World Politics and International Law* (Durham, NC: Duke University Press, 1985), p. 80.

[62] See Grenville Clark and Louis B. Sohn, *World Peace Through World Law* (Cambridge, MA: Harvard University Press, 1958).

[63] David Strang, 'Contested Sovereignty: The Social Construction of Colonial Imperialism', in Thomas J. Biersteker and Cynthia Weber (eds.), *State Sovereignty as Social Construct* (Cambridge: Cambridge University Press, 1996), p. 23. Perhaps it would be more accurate to say 'within the later Westphalian conception', since, as we have seen,

were there to be no generally agreed upon practice and norms of recognition, it is doubtful that any extensive set of rights and duties could survive at all, and one would expect little uniformity in states' reactions to the emergence of new polities. Instead there would likely develop a chaos borne of myriad bilateral relationships, the same entity – one cannot even say 'territorial entity' since there would be no evident territorial requirement – perhaps being accorded formal or informal recognition by some entities and not by others. There would exist, as Charles de Visscher has noted, 'a prolonged legal "vacuum" injurious to individual interests as to interstate relations'.[64] To overcome this chaos, it is not hard to imagine that these entities might gravitate towards a *modus vivendi* not unlike that which exists now. The present state system arose, after all, because of the perceived need to formalise relations between already existing and largely autonomous territorial communities.[65] That need persists so long as the state system does.

The legal norms and practices of recognition, then, are not so evidently irrelevant. But we are left with a fundamental contradiction. It has been argued throughout that the EC's guidelines in certain respects constituted a departure from international law and state practice. How can it also be maintained that a uniform practice of recognition is necessary for the functioning of international society and that, for that reason, states observe the practice?

It may be helpful to approach the question by way of an analogy to how some linguists understand language to function. Ferdinand de Saussure, for instance, writes about the systemic constraints of language – how the general body of rules that comprise a language (*langue*) constrains an individual's use of that language (*parole*). There is room for inventiveness within the rules of a language but one cannot step outside those rules altogether and remain effective: 'The community, as much as the individual, is bound to its language.'[66] One could say that a violation of language ignores its rules whereas an innovation in language pushes at the boundaries of them from within. Lon Fuller, a legal scholar, makes a similar point about the rules of law and, interestingly, also analogises from language. He sees law as not only 'an instrument of constraint' but also 'a framework within which [people] can organize

notions of sovereignty prevalent in Pufendorf's time would not have permitted an explicit practice of recognition.
[64] Charles de Visscher, *Theory and Reality in Public International Law* (Princeton: Princeton University Press, 1957), p. 228.
[65] James Crawford, 'Negotiating Global Security Threats in a World of Nation States', 38 *American Behavioral Scientist* (1995), 870.
[66] F. de Saussure, *Course in General Linguistics* (London: Duckworth, 1983), p. 71.

their relations with one another in such a manner as to make possible a peaceful and profitable coexistence'. The legal framework operates in much the same way as the rules of language do:

Surely, we may say, the primary function of language is to facilitate a particular kind of interaction – that involving a two-way communication of meaning. At the same time, there are rules of grammar and of word-meaning that we must respect – that must, if you will, 'control' our linguistic behavior – if we are to be understood at all . . . At times in the history of a language under the pressure of new conditions the rules of grammar and the existing limitations of vocabulary may undergo drastic change. But a language that imposed no limitations at all on what we may say, or how we may say it, would fail of its function. Effective communication depends upon orderly means of communication; order, of necessity, implies limits and an acceptance of constraints.[67]

That is not to say that states cannot act outside the limits of the law; they can and certainly do. The soft constraint of law works in a more subtle fashion. States want their behaviour to appear legitimate; indeed legitimacy may be useful, even critical, to the realisation of their goals. States therefore will wish their actions to be perceived to comport with, rather than to violate, international law. This is clearly the impression that the EC sought to communicate with the adoption of its recognition policy: 'The Community and its Member States', the ministers declared, 'affirm their readiness to recognize, *subject to normal standards of international practice* and the political realities in each case', those new states that have emerged in Eastern Europe and the Soviet Union.[68] The cynic will dismiss this choice of language as mere rhetoric without stopping to consider that, like Saussure's idea of *parole*, the use of a particular vocabulary to describe one's actions will constrain the political agent because that language does not permit all possible behaviour. The EC, for instance, could not very well announce that it was granting the United Kingdom dominion over the contested regions of Yugoslavia while claiming to be acting in accordance with international law. Quentin Skinner, in a study of the relationship between political theory and political practice, makes a similar observation with respect to Machiavelli's use of the term 'honour' as part of the Florentine writer's own efforts to gain legitimacy for his recommendations:

---

[67] Lon L. Fuller, 'Law as an Instrument of Social Control and Law as a Facilitation of Human Interaction', 8 *Archiv für Rechts- und Sozialphilosophie* (1974), 99–100.

[68] Declaration on the 'Guidelines on the Recognition of New States in Eastern Europe and the Soviet Union', EPC Press Release P. 129/91, 16 December 1991 (emphasis added).

[T]he term [honour] obviously cannot be applied with propriety to describe *any* Machiavellian course of action, but only those which can be claimed with some show of plausibility to meet the pre-existing criteria for the application of the term. It follows that anyone who is anxious to have his behaviour recognised as that of a man of honour will find himself restricted to the performance of only a certain range of actions. Thus the problem facing an agent who wishes to legitimate what he is doing at the same time as gaining what he wants cannot simply be the instrumental problem of tailoring his normative language in order to fit his projects. It must be the problem of tailoring his projects in order to fit the available normative language.[69]

That law can constrain in this fashion and that political behaviour at times may be tailored to fit the law is evident from the behaviour of the United States before the International Court of Justice (ICJ) in the *Nicaragua Case*. Taken to the ICJ in 1984 by Nicaragua for having placed mines in that country's harbours, the United States argued unsuccessfully that the Court did not have the authority to hear the case. The United States put forward many arguments – among them, that it had entered a reservation to ICJ jurisdiction if a dispute concerned a multilateral treaty (in this case the UN Charter) and that the dispute was already before the Organisation of American States (OAS). But as Franck observes, there is one argument that the United States did not invoke, and that was the Connally reservation – a federal law that bars the ICJ from exercising jurisdiction in any case that bears on domestic matters *as determined by the United States*.[70] The last clause is critical because it means that the United States has available to it a protective shield that, by its very nature, allows it, rather than the ICJ, to judge whether it ought to be exempt from the purview of the Court. (Other states have made similar declarations, the validity of which has been questioned by many but not rejected by the Court.)[71] To have invoked the Connally reservation and made the claim that the dispute concerned a domestic matter would likely have put an end to the litigation. But it would also have been to stretch the normative language beyond all credibility. As Franck explains, 'Even the U.S. Government, anxious to do almost anything to stay out of court, was unwilling to subject itself to the shame and ridicule which would have ensued had the Connally shield been deployed to avoid adjudication.'[72]

---

[69] Quentin Skinner, *The Foundations of Modern Political Thought* (Cambridge: Cambridge University Press, 1978), vol. I, pp. xii–xiii.

[70] Franck, *The Power of Legitimacy Among Nations*, pp. 54–5.

[71] Louis Henkin, 'The Connally Reservation Revisited and, Hopefully, Contained', 65 *American Journal of International Law* (1971), 374–7.

[72] Franck, *The Power of Legitimacy Among Nations*, p. 55.

If the United States could not credibly invoke the Connally reservation in this case but the European Community could condition its recognition of Yugoslav states on democratic requirements and maintain that this practice was consistent with public international law, it is in part because the EC's actions are supported by an international trend in support of democratic governance. 'References to democracy, which a generation or even a decade ago would have been regarded as political and extra-legal, are entering into the justification of legal decision-making in a new way', James Crawford observes.[73] There is considerable evidence, prior to the EC's recognition of the Yugoslav republics, to support this view. The International Covenant on Civil and Political Rights, which entered into force in 1976, specifies and prescribes respect for various rights that are constitutive of democratic governance. UN 'peace-building' activities in Cambodia and El Salvador in the late 1980s and early 1990s had as their aim the establishment and consolidation of democratic rule. And in anticipation of what would soon become EU policy with the Copenhagen Declaration, the Netherlands government, on the eve of Slovenia's and Croatia's declarations of independence, signalled that states seeking to join the EC and the Council of Europe, 'must be plural democracies; they must regularly hold free elections by secret ballot; they must respect the rule of law; [and] they must have signed the European Convention on Human Rights and Fundamental Freedoms'.[74]

Even if one accepts that some of these documents and measures are expressive merely of aspirations or are specific, not general, in their aims, it is difficult to deny a political and legal climate conducive to the articulation of the democratic requirements for state recognition adopted by the EC. And the EC, although departing from international law, would appear to have been pushing at the limits of the prevailing normative vocabulary rather than transgressing those limits altogether. If this is true, we may be witnessing the emergence of new law – regionally if not universally. International law is not a static body of rules and norms, and new state practice is one way in which international law develops. State practice, if generalised, creates customary rules, and

---

[73] James Crawford, 'Democracy in International Law', inaugural lecture, University of Cambridge, 5 March 1993 (Cambridge: Cambridge University Press, 1994), pp. 14–15. See also Franck, 'The Emerging Right to Democratic Governance'.

[74] Letter of 20 June 1990 from Hans van den Broek, Netherlands minister for foreign affairs, to the Netherlands Advisory Committee on Human Rights and Foreign Policy, in *Democracy and Human Rights in Eastern Europe*, Advisory Report No. 11 (The Hague: Advisory Committee on Human Rights and Foreign Policy, 12 November 1990), Annex.

international custom is a recognised source of international law.[75] It is therefore conceivable that in time democratic governance may become a broadly accepted legal requirement of statehood.

'[O]ne of the chief defects of our present understanding of world politics', Bull wrote in *The Anarchical Society*, is that 'it does not bring together into common focus those rules of order or coexistence that can be derived from international law and those rules that cannot, but belong rather to the sphere of international politics.'[76] This chapter represents a partial attempt to overcome that 'defect' and to provide greater political grounding for an understanding of international law generally and the legal norms of state recognition in particular. By drawing on the embryonic dialogue between international legal scholars and regime theorists, this chapter has sought to demonstrate that law is relevant to the behaviour of states not because of what the law says, which is the pitfall of legal formalism, but rather because of how it reflects the political forces at work in the world and, yet, at the same time, constrains those forces. The constraints, however, bear little resemblance to the idealised representations of law that some students of international relations have in mind when they disparage its effectiveness. International law does matter, for diplomatic recognition as well as other state behaviour, but its relevance can only be appreciated in the context of international politics.

---

[75] Art. 38(1)(b) of the Statute of the International Court of Justice identifies 'international custom' as a source of international law. See also Michael Akehurst, 'Custom as a Source of International Law', 47 *British Year Book of International Law* (1974–75), 1–53.
[76] Bull, *The Anarchical Society*, p. xiv.

4 EC recognition of new states in Yugoslavia: the strategic consequences

Chapter 3 argued for a view of diplomatic recognition as an informal regime governed by its own set of norms, legal as well as political, that historically have contributed to the maintenance of a stable order in the international system. Because the practice of recognition originates with states and serves to protect their interests, it is an inherently conservative institution. Outside of decolonisation states are reluctant to confer recognition on new claimants unless their claims are undisputed, for in the absence of *terrae nullius* (territories belonging to no one) recognition can only be achieved at the expense of existing states, and the dismemberment of one state is perceived to pose a threat to the integrity of all states as well as to weaken the foundations of the state-based international order. Although the EC's policy with regard to Yugoslavia might seem to contradict this view – to reflect instead an incautious and even subversive use of recognition – the EC, we have seen, sought to contain the disruptive effects of its actions by interpreting them so narrowly as to have limited application to other states. Statehood for Croatia thus would not mean statehood for, say, Spain's Catalonia or Russia's Chechnya.

There is another way in which the practice of recognition, rather than serving to ensure stability, can be disruptive of the established order, and that is in its potential for exacerbating the violence that may accompany the creation of a new state, particularly if the parent state is contesting and seeking to suppress the emergence of the entity. Recognition, in this sense, constitutes a form of intervention that, by altering the political terms of reference, may contribute to the outbreak and/or intensification of hostilities in a struggle being waged over the establishment of new boundaries. Conventional wisdom holds that this is precisely the effect that the EC achieved with its recognition of new states in Yugoslavia, although, as we saw in Chapter 1, the policy was justified partly on the grounds that it would in fact help to mitigate the conflict in the region.

There are a number of different dimensions to this view of the impact of EC recognition on the war in Yugoslavia, each one bearing on a different strategic moment in the conflict. To begin with, there are the presumed anticipatory effects of recognition. Although the EC's recognition of Slovenia and Croatia came long after the fighting there had erupted, the 'external environment' – including the prospect of recognition – is said to have 'led Slovenia and Croatia to expect political (and most likely economic) support for independence from their neighbors and Germany',[1] arguably reinforcing the two republics in their determination to prevail. A related argument is that the imminence of recognition – Germany's unstinting support in particular – 'hardened Zagreb's demands for complete submission by the Serbian minority';[2] it also led to an intensification of the fighting in Croatia, as both parties sought to achieve gains at the eleventh hour.[3] Recognition is faulted, too, for having brought an effective end to the EC peace talks under the direction of Lord Carrington – for having 'torpedo[ed] the conference' in Carrington's own words[4] – thus elevating the importance of the battlefield as the principal arena for resolving political differences. Moreover, EC recognition of Slovenia and Croatia is said to have left Bosnia and Herzegovina (BiH) no real alternative but to seek recognition itself,[5] with consequences, however, far more disastrous. '[L]ike pouring petrol on a smouldering fire',[6] the EC's recognition of BiH is said to have been the triggering event without which this whole tragedy might have been averted.

Broadly speaking, recognition is thought to have contributed more to aggravating and extending the war in Yugoslavia than perhaps any other single factor.[7] This judgement warrants closer examination. Without

---

[1] Susan L. Woodward, *Balkan Tragedy: Chaos and Dissolution after the Cold War* (Washington, DC: The Brookings Institution, 1995), p. 156.

[2] George Kenney, 'Derecognition: Exiting Bosnia', *IGCC Policy Brief No. 5* (La Jolla, CA: Institute on Global Conflict and Cooperation, June 1995), p. 3.

[3] Misha Glenny, 'Bosnia Means More Bad News for Balkans', *New Statesman & Society*, 17 April 1992, p. 27.

[4] Carrington interview for 'The Death of Yugoslavia' television series, Liddell Hart Centre for Military Archives, King's College London (hereafter LHCMA), 4 April 1995, Box 18, File 1, p. 2.

[5] Misha Glenny, *The Fall of Yugoslavia: The Third Balkan War* (London: Penguin, 1992), p. 150.

[6] David Owen, *Balkan Odyssey* (New York: Harcourt Brace & Company, 1995), p. 46.

[7] There are some notable exceptions to the view that recognition is principally or even largely to blame for the violent conflict, including Christopher Bennett, *Yugoslavia's Bloody Collapse: Causes, Course and Consequences* (London: Hurst & Co., 1995), ch. 8; James Gow, 'One Year of War in Bosnia and Herzegovina', *RFE/RL Research Report*, 4 June 1993, pp. 1–13; Richard Holbrooke, *To End a War* (New York: Random House, 1998), pp. 31–2; and Peter Viggo Jakobsen, 'Myth-making and Germany's Unilateral Recognition of Croatia and Slovenia', 4 *European Security* (1995), 409–11.

wishing to deny the strategic importance of recognition or the validity of some of the claims above, this chapter argues that the responsibility that recognition is thought to bear for the violent conflict in the former Yugoslavia is generally overstated. Far more relevant were the measures adopted by the republic governments to secure their independence – measures that were prompted not so much by the prospect of state-hood but in reaction to adverse political trends in Serbia and at the federal level, notably efforts by the Belgrade authorities to recentralise Yugoslavia. Delayed or non-recognition would not likely have meant a greater chance for peace – and in the cases of Macedonia and Kosovo may have had the opposite effect – if only because the forces of vio-lence in the region were to a large degree operating independently of the factor of recognition. It follows from this analysis that in at least one critical respect the debate over recognition is misconceived: for the real relevance of recognition lies with the opportunities for more effective

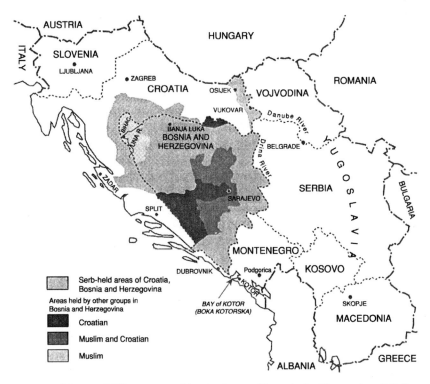

Map 2. Military control in the former Yugoslavia (September 1992).

international action that it created. It was the failure to seize these opportunities, rather than the strategic effects of recognition, that better explains the tragic events that ensued.

Slovenia: against the grain

One of the untold stories of Slovenia's quest for independence is the tremendous uncertainty with which the Slovene leadership laboured in its efforts to attain EC recognition. Indeed, until the fateful EC Council of Ministers meeting on 16 December 1991, when the decision was taken to extend recognition to select republics, the Slovenes perceived the international environment to be generally unpropitious. And yet, looking back over the period since the elections in April 1990 brought independence-minded politicians to power in Slovenia, one might expect, as some have suggested, that the republic's leaders would have been sufficiently encouraged by the various expressions of support they were garnering across Europe.

The signs of support were unmistakable. As early as June 1990, a Slovenian parliamentary delegation visited Vienna at the invitation of the Austrian assembly – a visit that France Bučar, speaker of the Slovene assembly, described at the time as 'very important for Slovenia's state-hood and sovereignty'.[8] The following month, at a congress of Christian Democrats in Budapest, Lojze Peterle, then Slovenia's prime minister, received a sympathetic, although somewhat guarded, reception from German Chancellor Helmut Kohl and Austrian Foreign Minister Alois Mock, among others:

I discussed independent Slovenia with Kohl. I asked his support. He said it was clear that Slovenia was a part of the Western cultural circle but the problem was what to do with the rest of Yugoslavia. He said: 'We can understand your intention but we don't want to ignite the powder keg.' Others made the same point.[9]

Peterle left the conference satisfied that Kohl and others had a 'basic understanding' of Slovenia's predicament and pleased that Slovenia was mentioned in the conference documents, 'not as a state but as a political term alongside other states and not as Yugoslavia'.[10]

---

[8] Cited in *Tanjug* (Belgrade), 27 June 1990, in Foreign Broadcast Information Service, *Daily Report: Eastern Europe*, FBIS-EEU-90-125, 28 June 1990, p. 71.
[9] Author interview with Peterle, Ljubljana, 3 June 1997.
[10] *Ibid.*

In subsequent months there were other positive signs. In December 1990, the same month that Slovenia held its plebiscite on independence, Erhard Busek, the leader of the Austrian People's Party, urged Slovenia to declare its independence and pledged Austria's support for the same.[11] A further boost came on 15 March 1991, when the European Parliament adopted a resolution stating that 'the constituent republics and autonomous provinces of Yugoslavia must have the right freely to determine their own political future in a peaceful and democratic manner and on the basis of recognized external and internal borders'.[12] Soon after, a Slovene delegation travelled to Bonn where it was warmly received in the deputies' club of the Bundestag. 'Practically all the deputies were sympathetic', Bučar recalls. 'They reassured us that eventually, one day, we will be independent.'[13] By early May, Mock was making statements that came close to endorsing the break-up of Yugoslavia,[14] while in Denmark, shortly after, Foreign Minister Uffe Elleman-Jensen was expressing his sympathy for Slovene independence to Rupel.[15]

These developments – and there were others like them – were certainly important, but they did not constitute the critical mass of international encouragement that most Slovene officials thought was necessary to ensure the independence of their aspiring republic. Overall, international reaction to the Slovene drive for independence was perceived to be very discouraging, especially in the early months of the campaign. Janez Janša, Slovenia's defence minister at the time, recalls the response to the December plebiscite: '[S]erious warnings began to arrive from abroad, saying that we were not to rush in our withdrawal from Yugoslavia, for in the case that the YNA [Yugoslav People's Army] responded nobody would offer us protection.'[16] Six months later, when Slovenia declared its independence, Slovene officials were still taking a dim view of the prospects for EC recognition. 'On the day we announced independence', Igor Bavčar, then Slovenia's interior minister, recalls, 'there

---

[11] As reported by Gianni De Michelis, the Italian foreign minister at the time, in his 'Così cercammo di impedire la guerra', 1 *Limes* (1994), 231.
[12] 'Resolution on the Situation in Yugoslavia', *Official Journal of the European Communities*, No. C 106, 22 April 1991, p. 169, Clause 8.
[13] Author interview with Bučar, Ljubljana, 3 June 1997.
[14] James Gow, 'Deconstructing Yugoslavia', 33(4) *Survival* (1991), 304.
[15] Dimitrij Rupel, 'Slovenia's Shift from the Balkans to Central Europe', in Jill Benderly and Evan Kraft (eds.), *Independent Slovenia: Origins, Movements, Prospects* (London: Macmillan, 1994), p. 191.
[16] Janez Janša, *The Making of the Slovenian State, 1988–1992* (Ljubljana: Založba Mladinska knjiga, 1994), p. 91.

were two foreign politicians present in Ljubljana, from Austria and from Italy, and they were both regional politicians. It was a clear sign that there was no will to recognise us at the time. All people from abroad told our ministry that there is no chance for recognition.'[17] Only a few days earlier, on 19 June, the EC member states had voted in favour of a CSCE declaration supporting the 'democratic development, unity, and territorial integrity of Yugoslavia',[18] while on 23 June, the EC foreign ministers meeting in Luxembourg announced that they had agreed 'not to acknowledge' a possible 'unilateral statement of independence by Croatia and Slovenia' and that they would refuse 'any contact' with the leaders of the two republics if they opted for independence.[19] As Janša summed up the moment: '[We knew that] we would be able to depend only on our determination, wits and bravery.'[20]

The fact is that much of the support Slovenia was receiving was not official support; indeed, it could hardly have been otherwise given the interest that EC member states had in maintaining good relations with Belgrade and in discouraging secessionist tendencies in Europe. Peterle, for instance, as leader of the Slovene Christian Democratic Party (SKD), had opportunities to meet many high-ranking officials across Europe, particularly since six out of twelve prime ministers in the EC at the time were Christian Democrats. But the support they were able to offer him was strictly personal or, at best, party denominated. (Christian Democrats embraced the Slovene and Croatian nationalists in part because they viewed them as determined anti-communists.) Thus would Giulio Andreotti, Italy's Christian Democratic prime minister, announce to Peterle in early June 1991: 'When you will proclaim independence, in two minutes we will recognise you',[21] while at the same time Gianni De Michelis, Italy's Socialist foreign minister, would insist to Marko Kosin, Slovenia's ambassador to Rome: 'Don't believe the Christian Democrats, and don't believe Mock.'[22] The Slovenes, for the most part, appreciated the difference. Kosin recalls when De Michelis sought to disabuse him of any illusions he might have had about recognition: 'He was very harsh and very blunt but very sincere. It was good for us

[17] Author interview with Bavčar, Ljubljana, 4 June 1997.

[18] *Agence Europe* (Brussels), No. 5516, 20 June 1991, p. 4.

[19] *Agence Europe*, No. 5519, 24–25 June 1991, pp. 4–5. Quotes are from a statement by Jacques Poos, the Council president, who added that this did not mean that the Twelve would never recognise a republic wishing to leave the Yugoslav federation but that such an action 'must be the result of negotiation and internal agreement'. *Ibid.*, p. 5.

[20] Janša, *The Making of the Slovenian State*, p. 92.

[21] Author interview with Peterle.

[22] Author interview with Kosin, Ljubljana, 4 June 1997.

although we were very discouraged. We believed Andreotti and the others would recognise [us], so it was helpful for De Michelis to make these points.'[23] In fact, when Andreotti met Slovenia's President Milan Kučan a few days after meeting Peterle, he conceded that Italy could not take separate steps and would follow the policy of the EC.

The Slovene government attached particular importance to the thinking in Italy, in part because it was a neighbouring EC country with which there had been difficult relations in the past,[24] but also because Italy, which held the EC presidency in the second half of 1990, had special responsibility for the Yugoslav question within the Community. Yet the Slovenes were frequently rebuffed by the Italians. When, for instance, Kučan sought to meet with the EC ambassadors in Belgrade or to invite them to Ljubljana, the Italian ambassador, on the order of Rome, strongly opposed the initiative. The opening of an Italian consulate in Ljubljana in December 1990 offered some grounds for hope but when De Michelis used the occasion to deliver a strongly worded speech against the dissolution of Yugoslavia, it was very badly received. And when Kosin visited Rome in the early spring of 1991 and met with Bruno Bottai, the secretary-general to the Ministry of Foreign Affairs, to explain the implications of the Slovene plebiscite, Bottai confessed that he could not understand the logic of Slovenia's actions. 'When the rest of Europe is integrating, why do you Slovenes want to break up Yugoslavia?' he asked.[25] As late as May 1991, Italy sent a parliamentary commission to Slovenia to persuade the Slovenes not to seek independence.

Italy had several reasons to prefer a united Yugoslavia. Despite some minor territorial and property disputes in the aftermath of the Second World War, principally concerning Slovenia, there had been good relations with Belgrade since the Osimo agreement was signed in 1975.[26] Moreover, Italy saw in Yugoslavia a kind of *cordon sanitaire* with respect first to the Warsaw Pact and later to a unified Germany.[27] There was also fear that the break-up of Yugoslavia would lead to instability on its borders. The flight of nearly 20,000 Albanians to Italy in March 1991 no doubt heightened Italian sensitivity to this question. Finally, Italy was

---

[23] *Ibid.*

[24] James Gow, 'The First Test Case for Integration', *War Report* No. 30 (December 1994/ January 1995), pp. 25–6.

[25] As recalled by Kosin in interview with the author.

[26] Duncan Wilson, *Tito's Yugoslavia* (Cambridge: Cambridge University Press, 1979), pp. 232–3.

[27] See the interview with the former Italian president Francesco Cossiga, 'Perché contiamo poco', in 3 *Limes* (1995), 18–19.

concerned about a realignment of forces in the region following the collapse of the Eastern bloc, and the possibility that Serbia, effectively still under communist rule, might seek to build closer ties to other communist states in the region and thus threaten Italy. Slovenia and Croatia were seen as a counterbalance to this tendency, provided that they remained in Yugoslavia.[28]

As we saw in Chapter 1, it was not until war broke out *after* the Slovene and Croatian declarations of independence that the tide of European opinion turned dramatically, though not yet decisively, in favour of recognition.[29] The reasons for this shift were two-fold. First, there was shock and dismay at Belgrade's use of force, which was incompatible with the EC's stated concern for human rights and the rule of law. However, much as some European leaders may have sympathised personally with the Slovenes, until that time they had maintained a position of unambiguous support for the unity of Yugoslavia. Now, with the outbreak of fighting, states became sceptical that Yugoslavia could be kept together peacefully. Yet even Genscher, although he would raise the possibility of EC recognition of Slovenia and Croatia to his counterparts on 5 July at a summit in The Hague, would not formally propose recognition until the EC foreign ministers' meeting in Venice on 14–15 September, having by that time concluded that EC mediation efforts could not bring an end to the fighting.[30]

Slovenia's determination was also a factor in the shift in West European opinion. De Michelis, for one, appears to have been impressed that the Slovenes did not intend to back down under the pressure of the JNA. At the second meeting with an EC foreign ministerial troika in Zagreb on 30 June, where the EC negotiators were seeking a restoration of the status quo ante, De Michelis approached Rupel and assured him privately that Slovenia would not be forced to rejoin Yugoslavia: 'You will be an independent state. Croatia, on the other hand is a more complicated issue, since its situation is different from yours. But you'll be free in three months. You just have to be patient and stick to your

---

[28] The latter observation was made to Kosin by Sergio Vento, Italy's ambassador to Yugoslavia at the time. Author interview with Kosin.

[29] The day the war began, the only EC politician to call Peterle to offer support was the former British prime minister, Margaret Thatcher (author interview with Peterle). Meanwhile, Mock, although previously outspoken in support of recognition, was constrained to declare on 26 June that recognition would only be given when the 'necessary preconditions of international law' had been met. Cited in 'A Policy Fixated on Unity Borders on the Absurd', *The Independent*, 27 June 1991.

[30] See Chapter 1 for a discussion of Germany's role in the EC's recognition of Yugoslav republics.

agreements.'[31] The Brioni agreement of 7 July, which was the outcome of these negotiations, put an official imprimatur on this shift of opinion.[32] By requiring the Yugoslav federal government to desist from further attacks on Slovenia and Croatia, the EC in effect made the two republics subjects of international law. But even then recognition was no certainty, in view of the fact that the agreement also required Slovenia and Croatia to suspend implementation of their independence and, more importantly, because no EC member state was willing to recognise the two republics unilaterally. Thus when, in August, Rupel and Kosin travelled to Rome asking for recognition (it was Slovenia's first formal appeal), De Michelis, whose support of Slovenia was by now beyond question, made it clear that recognition was a matter for the EC, not Italy alone, to decide.[33] Genscher, too, told Rupel that, in Rupel's words 'individual recognition by the friendly countries could not be a good solution' and that Germany would prefer 'unanimity in the EC'.[34] Well into the autumn, Belgium, Britain, France and Greece were also insisting that recognition must be a common action of the EC – a requirement that the Slovenes naturally found worrying, given the continued opposition of some member states to recognition.[35]

A further obstacle to achieving recognition of Slovenia was the view that Slovenia could not be treated separately from Croatia, and that as long as Croatia's problems remained unresolved – an ongoing war, an unsettled minority problem – Slovenia would have to wait.[36] This thinking is reflected in Genscher's and De Michelis's remarks to Rupel above. The German government, apprehensive that Slovenia's declining interest in Yugoslavia might encourage the Serbs and Croats to pursue their own agendas, even thought to exploit the Slovenes' dependence on

---

[31] Author interview with Kosin; and Rupel interview for 'The Death of Yugoslavia', LHCMA, undated, Box 18, File 4, p. 2.

[32] The agreement was known formerly as the 'Common Declaration on the Peaceful Resolution of the Yugoslav Crisis'. For a discussion of the agreement, see *Unfinished Peace: Report of the International Commission on the Balkans* (Washington, DC: Carnegie Endowment for International Peace, 1996), p. 43.

[33] Author interview with Kosin.

[34] Rupel, 'Slovenia's Shift from the Balkans to Central Europe', p. 194.

[35] See 'Le Conseil de sécurité approuve à l'unanimité la nouvelle mission de Mr. Cyrus Vance', *Le Monde*, 29 November 1991; 'M. Perez de Cuellar espère régler rapidement les "détails techniques" du déploiement d'une force de paix', *Le Monde*, 30 November 1991; and 'Eyskens: Anerkennung auf "EG-Niveau"', *Frankfurter Allgemeine Zeitung*, 30 November 1991.

[36] Sometimes the problem was generalised to include all the republics. 'A simultaneous recognition of Slovenia, Croatia, Macedonia, and Bosnia-Hercegovina would be the ideal solution – so I heard from American Secretary of State Lawrence Eagleburger', Rupel recalls. See Rupel, 'Slovenia's Shift from the Balkans to Central Europe', p. 194.

international recognition to ensure their continued participation in negotiations.[37] Concerned that recognition might thus elude them, the
Slovenes adopted a strategy that sought not to minimise Croatia's problems but, rather, to emphasise the differences between Croatia and
Slovenia, thereby de-linking one from the other. In this way, it was
thought, Croatia would no longer be an excuse for not recognising
Slovenia. (By stressing their differences with Croatia, the Slovenes
were also able to resist pressures in the Hague negotiations to accept
common institutions with the other republics.)[38] Zvonimir Šeparović,
then Croatia's foreign minister, calls this 'a tricky game' that Ljubljana
played: 'I was told in Budapest and also in China later on that
the foreign minister of Slovenia was arguing *against* the recognition of
Croatia – that is, arguing against rushing to recognise Croatia straight
away because Croatia was not in full control of its territory, which was
true, not a peaceful state [and therefore] not ready to be recognised.' As
Šeparović sees it, the Slovenes seemed to be telling the international
community: 'You may have problems recognising Croatia but you will
have no problems recognising us. We are different.'[39]

To the Slovenes, then, recognition was never a sure thing. Even their
victory in the ten-day war for independence was not a sufficient guarantee for recognition, just as the Turkish military victory in 1974 has still
not brought recognition of the Turkish Republic of Northern Cyprus.[40]
Of course, if one reads the history of this period backwards from its final
denouement, the uncertainty is less apparent. And historians are sometimes prone to this kind of teleological reading of events. Mindful of a
given outcome, they may ascribe to antecedent developments an anticipatory logic that may not have existed at all – some future outcomes
being more uncertain than others – and that in any case may not have
been apparent to the subjects at the time. 'It would be the height of
arrogance for historians to condemn those who made history for not
having availed themselves of histories yet to be written', John Lewis
Gaddis reminds us.[41] As much as the Slovenes may have wished and

---

[37] Michael Libal, *Limits of Persuasion: Germany and the Yugoslav Crisis, 1991–1992*
(Westport, CT: Praeger, 1997), p. 32.
[38] Author interview with Matjaž Šinkovec, Slovenia's ambassador to the United Kingdom, London, 21 May 1997. Šinkovec was a member of the Slovene delegation to the
Hague peace negotiations in 1991.
[39] Author interview with Šeparović, Zagreb, 14 July 1997.
[40] On the refusal of legal recognition of the Turkish Cypriot state, see S. K. N. Blay, 'Self-
determination in Cyprus: The New Dimensions of an Old Conflict', 10 *Australian
Yearbook of International Law* (1987), 67–100.
[41] Gaddis cited in Tony Judt, 'Why the Cold War Worked', *New York Review of Books*,
9 October 1997, p. 41.

hoped for EC recognition, it was really not until the EC Council of Ministers meeting of 16 December that they would be assured of it.[42] And the progress towards that moment was not a steady advance but a fitful one rife with setbacks as well as gains. It is difficult to see, then, how the prospect of recognition could have played a significant role in the Slovene determination to sustain their campaign for independence, and how it bears any responsibility for this first phase of the war.

If Slovenia was not encouraged by the EC's policy on recognition, the Serbian leadership and the JNA, however, were. As James Gow observes:

Although the EC wanted Yugoslavs to sort out an arrangement among themselves, its policy of strongly favouring a single state militated against Yugoslavs who sought independence . . . Secure in the knowledge that the international community, particularly the EC, wanted what only the Serbian government and the army in Yugoslavia wanted, the latter two actors were able to intimidate other Yugoslavs with threats of violence.[43]

EC policy only reinforced the impression that Yugoslavia's political and military elite were forming of European lack of resolve. In the spring and summer of 1991 the Yugoslav military undertook a series of studies of the Yugoslav situation in the context of the post-Cold War order and the 1991 Gulf War in particular. These findings helped to persuade the elite that although the European states might interfere in the crisis, they were most unlikely to intervene militarily in the absence of a US leadership role, which, they concluded rightly, the United States was not inclined to exercise at the time.[44]

The prospect of recognition, then, did not either precipitate or aggravate the war in Slovenia but, once fighting had erupted there, an opportunity was created for the use of recognition as a means of preventing the extension of the war to Croatia. Indeed, several European governments –

---

[42] Genscher recalls in his memoirs: 'As I arrived in Brussels in the afternoon, public opinion did not expect any decision on recognition that day. The reports on the radio and the television – not only in Germany but everywhere in Europe, above all in Slovenia and Croatia – seemed to suggest a further delay.' Hans-Dietrich Genscher, *Erinnerungen* (Berlin: Siedler Verlag, 1995), p. 960 (my translation).

[43] Gow, 'Deconstructing Yugoslavia', pp. 305–6. Viktor Meier, Germany's veteran Balkans correspondent, suggests similarly that Yugoslav Federal Prime Minister Ante Marković felt emboldened by the behaviour of the Western states to call on the army to restore control over Slovenia and Croatia. Witnesses report Marković declaring that he had 'more than just one mandate' – a reference to tacit Western support for his actions. Viktor Meier, *Yugoslavia: A History of its Demise* (London: Routledge, 1999), p. 215.

[44] Patrick J. Garrity, *Why the Gulf War Still Matters: Foreign Perspectives on the War and the Future of International Security*, Report No. 13 (Los Alamos, NM: Center for National Security Studies, July 1993), p. 35.

Germany, Denmark and Austria – now began to argue in favour of the prompt recognition of Slovenia and Croatia for this very reason. As we saw in Chapter 1, the proponents of recognition maintained that it would internationalise the conflict and thereby deter Belgrade from further aggression against what would be two sovereign states entitled to a greater measure of international protection, both military and legal. To be a credible deterrent, however, recognition would arguably need to have been backed by a threat to use force in defence of Slovenia and Croatia – just as the UN Security Council had threatened to use force in response to Iraq's invasion of Kuwait less than one year earlier.[45] Yet the strongest proponent of this approach, Germany, was in the weakest position to implement it because of constitutional constraints and domestic political considerations that made it impossible for Germany to participate in any military operations in Yugoslavia at that time, even as part of a multilateral security initiative.[46] And for all their misgivings about the relatively little diplomatic and military weight that they carried in the post-Cold War period,[47] the leading members of the Community – France and Britain in particular – could not reach agreement at this stage of the conflict on the use of force in Yugoslavia.

Croatia: going to extremes

In the lead-up to independence, Croatia does not seem to have enjoyed any greater encouragement from EC member states than did Slovenia. This did not prevent an overconfident Franjo Tudjman, however, from concluding that the West would stand with him in his fight for Croatian independence. In May 1991, the newly elected president announced that he would not hesitate to call in Western troops to defend Croatia if the republic were attacked.[48] Tudjman appears to have been influenced in his thinking, in the early months at least, not so much by EC member states as by the Croatian émigré community, which was well

---

[45] UN Security Council Res 678, 29 November 1990.

[46] Trevor C. Salmon, 'Testing Times for European Political Cooperation: the Gulf and Yugoslavia, 1990–1992', 68 *International Affairs* (1992), 237–8. Salmon discusses 'tensions' within the German Basic Law in relation to German participation in the Gulf War, but the same constraints pertained to Yugoslavia. It was not until July 1994 that the German constitutional court removed constitutional objections to the deployment of German troops in missions beyond NATO's borders, subject to specified qualifications. See Franz-Josef Meiers, 'Germany: The Reluctant Power', 37(3) *Survival* (1995), 83–5.

[47] See Nicole Gnesotto and John Roper (eds.), *Western Europe and the Gulf* (Paris: Institute for Security Studies of Western European Union, 1992), p. 4.

[48] See 'Yugoslavia Fears Grow as Army Goes on Alert', *The Times*, 8 May 1991.

organised and well connected politically in Germany, the United States, Canada and Australia.

Once the war intensified, support from Germany and other EC member states became more vocal, and Tudjman's expectations rose accordingly. But, even then, Kohl and Genscher, when they met with Tudjman in Bonn on 18 July, gave no specific assurances and pointedly avoided any discussion of recognition, according to Michael Libal, the German Foreign Ministry official responsible for Yugoslav affairs at that time.[49] Similarly, the US ambassador to Yugoslavia, Warren Zimmermann, when he met with Tudjman the following month, emphasised to the Croatian president that he should not count on the United States for military support. To Zimmermann's astonishment, Tudjman challenged him on this point: 'I don't believe you. I know more about your government than you do and you're going to support us', Zimmermann recalls Tudjman insisting.[50] Zimmermann maintains that the Croatian *émigrés* had a completely distorted picture of what the US position was and that they had influenced Tudjman in his thinking.

Yet even Tudjman's confidence would occasionally be shaken, as when on 1 September the EC won Milošević's agreement for the deployment of EC monitors to observe a cease-fire in Croatia. '[Tudjman] was visibly disappointed', Henry Wynaendts, an EC negotiator, recalls. 'It was the end of Croatian hopes of a common action with the European Community against Serbia.'[51] Moreover, Tudjman's confidence was not shared by everyone in his government. At the time of independence, Foreign Minister Šeparović, like his Slovene colleagues, had the impression of being surrounded by 'enemy-like attitudes' on the part of 'all those who had been in love with Yugoslavia'.[52] Even once the war began, official positions were slow to change. 'My diplomacy was not an easy one', Šeparović says. 'The country was at war – attacked, suffering – and we did not have recognition.' Šeparović travelled across Europe to plead for recognition. Where Socialists were in power, these states were not very sympathetic to Croatian aspirations – the legacy, in part, of the European left's historic support for Yugoslavia's 'socialism with a human face'.[53] And those states that were the most sympathetic (Germany,

---

[49] Libal, *Limits of Persuasion*, pp. 25–6.

[50] Author interview with Zimmermann, New York, 20 November 1996.

[51] Henry Wynaendts, *L'engrenage: chroniques yougoslaves, juillet 1991–août 1992* (Paris: Denoël, 1993), p. 77 (my translation).

[52] Author interview with Šeparović.

[53] Ivanka Nedeva, 'Kosovo/a: Different Perspectives', in Thanos Veremis and Evangelos Kofos (eds.), *Kosovo: Avoiding Another Balkan War* (Athens: Hellenic Foundation for European and Foreign Policy, 1998), pp. 126–7.

Austria, Hungary) were not willing to act unilaterally. An unexpected overture came from Iceland in September 1991, when Šeparović was attending the UN General Assembly in New York. Iceland had been the first country to recognise the Baltic states and the fact that it was a NATO country was not lost on Šeparović, who had in mind, among other things, to offer NATO the use of Croatian islands off the Dalmatian coast as bases. It was a desperate move and 'one of my mortal sins', Šeparović now concedes, to attach so much importance to this opening.

Against the backdrop of the debate over recognition, and at the height of the war in Croatia, two major diplomatic initiatives were being pursued – the EC's Hague negotiations and the UN's Vance negotiations – both of whose chances for success, it was argued at the time, were threatened by the prospect of recognition. The two initiatives were closely related. The Hague negotiations, launched on 7 September with the aim of achieving a comprehensive political settlement, had by early November reached a stalemate that the continued fighting in Croatia was making it harder to break. The Vance negotiations, led by UN special envoy Cyrus Vance, thus sought to bring about a permanent cease-fire in Croatia (to be maintained by UN peacekeeping forces) that, it was thought, would improve the climate for negotiations in The Hague.[54] Vance and Carrington maintained that recognition would jeopardise the chances of a settlement because once recognition had been extended there would be no incentive for Croatia (or any other republic granted recognition) to participate further in the Hague negotiations. Nor would there be an incentive for Croatia to respect a cease-fire that left unresolved the precise status of the Serb-occupied territories in the Krajina.

The original concept of the EC negotiations, we saw in Chapter 1, had indeed been that recognition would be granted only in the framework of a general settlement acceptable to all parties. Recognition was thought to be the ultimate weapon in the EC's arsenal of non-military instruments at its disposal to induce the parties to arrive at a new *modus vivendi* – 'the one real instrument to keep the parties engaged in the negotiating process', as Carrington later put it.[55] But the logic of this approach was flawed, as should have become apparent by November. The

---

[54] For an elaboration of the Vance plan's 'basic concepts', see Report of the Secretary-General Pursuant to Security Council Resolution 721 (1991), UN Doc. S/23280, 11 December 1991.

[55] Lord Carrington, 'Turmoil in the Balkans: Developments and Prospects', *RUSI Journal* (October 1992), 2.

approach assumed that the interest all parties had in recognition was
symmetrical when, in fact, it was asymmetrical. If it was in Slovenia's and
Croatia's interest to achieve international recognition, it was in Serbia's
interest to deny them the same while seeking to wring from them,
Croatia in particular, further concessions. (If this meant that Serbia,
too, would be denied recognition, it was a small price for Belgrade to
pay – small, certainly, in comparison with the more punishing battery of
sanctions that Belgrade later proved willing to endure.) And it was
Serbia, more than any other republic, that was responsible for the
stalemate in The Hague. When on 18 October Lord Carrington presented his draft 'Arrangements for a General Settlement', reflecting
principles that had been agreed to by Serbia and Croatia on 4 October,
Serbia alone among the six republics rejected the document. (Under
pressure from Belgrade, Montenegro later retracted its support for the
draft accord.)[56] Not only would Serbia now no longer accept the idea of
a 'loose association or alliance of sovereign or independent republics', as
it had agreed to two weeks earlier, unless the Serbs in Croatia enjoyed
exceptional rights in excess of the large measure of autonomy that the
EC had been proposing, but Serbia also challenged the legality of any
unilateral declaration of independence and opposed recognition in response to such a move. The EC, having threatened on 28 October
to impose sanctions on any party that did not accept the outline agreement, adopted punitive measures against Serbia and Montenegro: the
EC suspended various trade and aid agreements with Yugoslavia on
8 November and then on 2 December restored these benefits to the
'cooperative republics' – that is, to all but Serbia and Montenegro.[57]

The structure of the negotiating process – the requirement for consensus – made it possible for Serbia to impede EC recognition of the
other republics while at the same time Serbian forces were able to
consolidate their control over nearly one-third of Croatia. (The beginning of the most intense phase of fighting in Croatia coincided with the
meeting in The Hague on 4 October, when the JNA withdrew from Istria
and Rijeka and redeployed to eastern Slavonia and the area around

---

[56] For an account of the pressures Montenegro was subjected to by Serbia, see the
interview with Momir Bulatović, then president of Montenegro, for 'The Death of
Yugoslavia', LHCMA, 7 October 1994, Box 18, File 1.
[57] Letter Dated 30 October 1991 from the Permanent Representatives of Belgium, France
and the United Kingdom of Great Britain and Northern Ireland to the United Nations
Addressed to the President of the Security Council, UN Doc. S/23181, 30 October
1991, Annex; 'Declaration on Yugoslavia', Extraordinary EPC Ministerial Meeting
(Rome), EPC Press Release P. 109/91, 8 November 1991; and 'EC Partially Lifts
Yugoslav Sanctions', *International Herald Tribune*, 3 December 1991.

Dubrovnik.) It is difficult to see how, then, the EC's decision to recognise Croatia in December 1991/January 1992 'torpedoed' the Carrington plan, as Carrington would later claim. The Carrington plan was already sunk at the end of October with Milošević's rejection of the terms for an agreement that he had agreed to a few weeks earlier. Nor did recognition necessarily remove an incentive for continued negotiations, notwithstanding the damage done to the design of Carrington's particular efforts. Carrington and his successors would soldier on; indeed, when the Conference on Yugoslavia reconvened on 9 January 1992, Carrington observed that the Serbian delegation was now playing a 'more constructive' role in the proceedings, having obviously 'taken note' of the EC's impending recognition of Croatia.[58] While it is true that henceforth all negotiations would have to exclude from consideration the possibility of a reconstituted Yugoslavia, it was already the case by October that Slovenia and Croatia would not countenance even the loosest association with Serbia. As Janez Janša, then Slovenia's defence minister, recalled four years later, Milošević's determination to re-centralise Yugoslavia under Belgrade's control had left Slovenia (and Croatia) no choice but to seek independence.[59]

The prospect of recognition did not lead to a significant intensification of hostilities in Croatia either, as Vance and Carrington, among others, had warned. By early January, the UN-mediated cease-fire – the thirteenth – was holding reasonably well. Prior to that time the JNA, it is true, had engaged in new offensive operations, but the federal army seems to have been motivated less by a pre-recognition land grab than by a determination to establish the UN cease-fire line as far as possible from the Serbian border.[60] (Other violations the UN attributed largely to irregular armed elements not fully under the control of established military commands.)[61] There seems to be some evidence, in fact, that

[58] Carrington cited in James Gow and James D. D. Smith, *Peacemaking, Peace-keeping: European Security and the Yugoslav Wars*, London Defence Study No. 11 (London: Centre for Defence Studies/Brassey's, 1992), p. 36.

[59] Remarks delivered at the Department of War Studies, King's College London, 1 November 1995. More than a decade earlier, A. Ross Johnson, a Yugoslav expert and Rand analyst, wrote presciently: 'At the turn of the 1970s, Yugoslavia underwent an *irreversible* decentralization; under no circumstances short of civil war and Soviet invasion could it be recentralized – and perhaps not under those circumstances either.' *Impressions of Post-Tito Yugoslavia: A Trip Report*, Rand Note N-1813 (Santa Monica, CA: The Rand Corporation, January 1982), p. 15.

[60] 'L'armeé fédérale a lancé une nouvelle offensive en Croatie', *Le Monde*, 8–9 December 1991.

[61] Further Report of the Secretary-General Pursuant to Security Council Resolution 721 (1991), UN Doc. S/23513, 4 February 1992, para. 7.

the prospect of recognition may in the end have helped to dissuade the Serbs from continuing their military campaign in Croatia, and thus to encourage them to accept the Vance plan. According to Branko Kostić, acting president of rump Yugoslavia in the latter part of 1991, concerns were raised repeatedly in the federal presidency that autumn about the strategic implications of recognition – about 'the possibility', as he put it, that 'Slovenia's and Croatia's international recognition [would mean] that we would have to pull out the JNA from these territories [i.e., the Serb Krajina].' '[O]ur solution', Kostić explains, 'was to use peacekeepers to protect the Serbs in Krajina.'[62] Similarly, Colonel General Zivota Panić, who was soon to become chief of the General Staff of the Yugoslav army, maintains that the JNA had decided to halt its operations in Croatia after the EC 'offered' recognition, having concluded that Belgrade would have to give up any territorial gains 'under international pressure'.[63]

But it appears to have been more the attractiveness of the Vance plan than the implications of recognition that bore on Serb considerations ultimately. By the time EC recognition seemed likely, in mid-November 1991, the Serbs were in control of those territories in Croatia over which they wished to exercise their authority. And a permanent cease-fire in the form of the Vance plan would allow Belgrade to consolidate these gains. (The plan envisioned the establishment of three demilitarised UN 'Protected Areas', or UNPAs, in Serb-majority areas nominally under the sovereign authority of the Croatian government but to be administered by the local Serbs themselves.) Indeed it was Yugoslavia's representative to the United Nations who, on 26 November 1991, made the formal request for a peacekeeping operation in Croatia to the Security Council.[64] The deployment of UN peacekeepers, the Serbs reasoned, would allow them to freeze the situation and then to cement their gains.[65] Confirmation of the effectiveness of this strategy, in the short

---

[62] Kostić interview for 'The Death of Yugoslavia', LHCMA, 8 August 1994, Box 18, File 2, p. 24.

[63] Panić quote from *Vojno Delo*, Nos. 1–2 (January–April 1992) cited in James Gow, 'Coercive Cadences: The Yugoslav War of Dissolution', in Lawrence Freedman (ed.), *Strategic Coercion: Concepts and Cases* (Oxford: Oxford University Press, 1998), p. 282.

[64] Letter Dated 26 November 1991 from the Permanent Representative of Yugoslavia to the United Nations Addressed to the President of the Security Council, UN Doc. S/23240, 26 November 1991.

[65] The Serbs were by no means united in support of the plan and a serious rift occurred between Belgrade and the Knin leadership, who worried (correctly) that the indeterminate status of the Krajina and the fact that Croatia was about to gain international recognition could lead eventually to the restoration of Zagreb's control over the area. See the interview with Milan Babić, the leader of the Krajina Serbs, for 'The Death of Yugoslavia', LHCMA, undated, Box 18, File 1, pp. 18–19.

term at least, can be found in the concerns expressed by UN Secretary-General Boutros Boutros-Ghali who, in his 16 March 1994 report to the Security Council, observed: 'The Serb side has taken advantage of the presence of UNPROFOR in its efforts to freeze the status quo, under UNPROFOR "protection", while establishing a self-proclaimed "State" of the "Republic of Serb Krajina" in UNPROFOR's area of responsibility.'[66] These same concerns led President Tudjman to seek modifications in the UN peacekeeping operation in early 1995, which in turn paved the way for his reconquest of all Serb-held territories later that year.[67]

There is considerable evidence to suggest, moreover, that the JNA had by this time become overstretched and thus was also motivated to accept the Vance plan to alleviate the strain. By mid-December the JNA was facing widespread desertion and was unable to mobilise its forces. Approximately 10,000 draftees had failed to report for duty.[68] Meanwhile, Bosnian President Alija Izetbegović, not wishing to be a party to aggression in Croatia, was refusing to implement mobilisation orders. Borisav Jović, Serbia's representative on the federal presidency at the time, recalls the meeting when the decision was taken to accept the Vance plan: '[The Army] said they couldn't defend the borders forever by waging the war, so they wanted a political solution. They were so categorical that they said we couldn't leave the room until the problem was solved.'[69] For that matter, the deepening crisis in BiH, where in December Izetbegović had announced that his republic would apply for EC recognition, necessitated that the JNA immediately shift its attention. The presence of UN peacekeepers in Croatia were thus welcomed by Belgrade for an additional reason: they allowed the JNA to disengage and redeploy its forces to the next theatre of the war.

EC recognition seems to have had even greater bearing on Croatia's decision to respect a cease-fire and to accept the Vance plan, which Croatia initially agreed to on 2 January. Of course, the attraction of a lasting cease-fire for Croatia at that time was very great. The war had cost Croatia the lives of thousands of people and forced hundreds of thousands more to flee from either the fighting or ethnic cleansing. Some thirty-five settlements had been razed to the ground, including large

---

[66] Report of the Secretary-General Pursuant to Resolution 871 (1993), UN Doc. S/1994/300, 16 March 1994, para 8.

[67] See Anthony Borden and Richard Caplan, 'The Former Yugoslavia: The War and the Peace Process', in *SIPRI Yearbook 1996* (Oxford: SIPRI/Oxford University Press, 1996), pp. 204–10.

[68] Woodward, *Balkan Tragedy*, p. 189.

[69] Jović interview for 'The Death of Yugoslavia', LHCMA, undated, Box 18, File 2, p. 92.

sections of the city of Vukovar, and some 210,000 houses had been destroyed – roughly 12 per cent of the entire housing stock in the country.[70] Publicly, Tudjman argued that the Vance plan was necessary 'to prevent further destruction', including the 'destruction of Zagreb, Split, Sibenik, [and] Zadar . . .'[71] But General Anton Tus, the former JNA general who commanded the Croatian armed forces, maintains that the Croatian army was in fact growing stronger and that given the JNA's need to divert its attention to BiH, Croatia had the capacity to turn the tide. Tus asked that new operations be launched to liberate occupied lands but Tudjman refused his request, largely, Tus believes, because the president thought that acceptance of the Vance plan was an unstated condition for international recognition.[72] Šeparović shares this view of Tudjman's motivations, as does Dražen Budiša, minister without portfolio in Tudjman's wartime 'government of democratic unity', and Slaven Letica, then Tudjman's principal political adviser. Letica says that Tudjman was prepared 'to do anything to get recognition at that time', and interpreted Croatia's acceptance of the Vance plan as one of the requirements.[73]

EC recognition, then, rather than intensifying hostilities in Croatia, may have helped unwittingly to secure the peace. The irony is that where the EC set out consciously to mitigate tensions it did not have the intended effect. The EC, we have seen, had conditioned its recognition of Croatia on Zagreb's acceptance of the provisions of the Carrington plan with respect to ethnic and national rights. These provisions, which would have granted a large measure of autonomy to minority groups throughout Yugoslavia, had been adopted with Croatia's Serb community very much in mind.[74] In fact, the Serbian Democratic Forum (SDF), based in Zagreb, played an important role in advising Carrington on the drafting of these provisions.[75] The EC's guidelines for recognition

---

[70] Figures from Marcus Tanner, *Croatia: A Nation Forged in War* (New Haven, CT: Yale University Press, 1997), p. 278.

[71] Tudjman interview for 'The Death of Yugoslavia', LHCMA, undated, Box 18, File 4, p. 16.

[72] Author interview with Tus, Zagreb, 11 July 1997.

[73] Author interview with Šeparović; author interview with Budiša, Zagreb, 11 July 1997; author interviews with Letica, Zagreb, 12 and 13 July 1997.

[74] Letter to the author from Paul Sizeland, Lord Carrington's assistant at the time, 3 November 1997.

[75] This is apparent if one compares the provisions of the Carrington plan with the contents of two SDF memoranda to Lord Carrington: 'Promemorija o položaju Srpskog naroda u Republici Hrvatskoj' [Memorandum on the Situation of the Serbian Nation in the Croatian Republic] of 25 September 1991 and 'Polazišta za rješenje Srpskog pitanja u Hrvatskoj' [Points for Resolution of the Serbian Question in Croatia], October 1991 (copies on file with the author).

were of course drawn up too late to contribute to preventing war in Croatia but the framers of the document clearly thought that these provisions could be effective in mitigating tensions and thus help to lay the ground for a lasting resolution of the conflict.[76] It is evident, however, that the EC's requirements had neither effect. To the contrary, once the EC had adopted its policy of recognition, the immediate result was not to pacify the Krajina Serbs but to provoke them.

As Milan Babić, then the leader of the rebel Serbs, recalls the moment, 'It was clear to us that Croatia was becoming an independent state and we wanted Srpska Krajina to become [a] republic because Yugoslavia [was leaving] those areas. We wanted to seek international recognition equally with the other states being formed in the territory of former Yugoslavia.'[77] The Krajina Serbs proclaimed the independence of their 'republic' on 19 December 1991, three days after the EC announced its policy.[78]

A simple explanation for this turn of events would be that the EC-mandated national rights guarantees came too late to make any difference; relations between Serbs and Croats were so thoroughly polarised after months of fierce fighting that a voluntary reintegration of the Krajina on almost any basis would have been unlikely. One can find support for an explanation of this kind in other secessionist/self-determination struggles. In the cases of Katanga (Congo), Biafra (Nigeria) and Bougainville (Papua New Guinea) in the twentieth century, for instance, and the Confederacy (United States) in the nineteenth century, reabsorption of the break-away entity was achieved in an involuntary manner – that is, only after the entity had been subdued militarily. But other factors may also be relevant to explaining why a break-away entity will continue to resist reintegration, among them the intervention of external agents who, for their own purposes, have an interest in provoking and/or sustaining a conflict. The roots of conflict, in such a case, may not be entirely domestic but may also have a regional dimension, and measures which are directed only or primarily at the domestic roots of the conflict – as the EC's minority rights guarantees were – may therefore be inadequate.

The Croatian conflict conforms closely to this pattern. There can be no doubt that some of Tudjman's early moves did much to frighten and

---

[76] Author interview with Alain Dejammet, the former French political director, who helped to conceive the guidelines, New York, 21 November 1996.

[77] Babić interview for 'The Death of Yugoslavia', p. 19.

[78] 'New Serbian "Republics" Emerge', *RFE/RL Research Report* ('*Weekly Review*'), 10 January 1992, p. 70.

alienate the Croatian Serb community as well as to threaten their inter-ests.[79] Whereas under communism the Serbs enjoyed the status of a constituent nation in Croatia, soon after taking office Tudjman, in June 1990, prepared a draft of a new constitution that now described Croatia as the sovereign state of the Croatian nation without any reference to the Serbs.[80] Tudjman also revived the *šahovnica* chequered shield as Croa-tia's national symbol, which Serbs associated with the Second World War atrocities of Ante Pavelić's Independent State of Croatia (NDH), whose Ustashe murdered tens or hundreds of thousands of Serbs (the actual figure is still disputed) in genocidal fashion.[81] Although no apolo-gist for the Pavelić regime, which as a presidential candidate Tudjman described as 'a quisling organisation and a Fascist crime', Tudjman ac-knowledged that the NDH was 'an expression of the Croatian nation's historic desire for an independent homeland',[82] thus endowing it with a certain degree of legitimacy. Moreover, Tudjman set about to redress what he considered to be years of discrimination against ethnic Croats under communism, removing large numbers of Serbs from the public administration and the police, where they were disproportionately rep-resented.[83] Most worrying, of course, for the Serbs was the prospect of an independent Croatia severed entirely from Yugoslavia.

Many Croatian Serbs could accept the need for reform of a system that for a number of reasons – historical, socio-economic and

---

[79] Even before the election of Tudjman a large segment of the Serbian population felt discriminated against. For a discussion of relevant pre-election surveys, see Lenard J. Cohen, *Broken Bonds: Yugoslavia's Disintegration and Balkan Politics in Transition*, 2nd edn (Boulder, CO: Westview Press, 1995), p. 99.

[80] *Ibid.*, pp. 130–31. The constitution was further revised and adopted in December 1990. At the suggestion of Tudjman's principal advisor, Slaven Letica, reference was made to the Serbs as members of 'other nations and minorities' in Croatia. Tudjman, however, insisted on adding 'Muslims, Slovenes, Czechs, Slovaks, Italians, Hungarians, Jews and others' alongside the Serbs, thus further diluting the importance of the Serbs. See *The Constitution of the Republic of Croatia*, ch.1. Details concerning Tudjman's intervention provided by Letica, who furnished the author with a copy of his notes for a constitution ['Naputak za izradu Ustava Republike Hrvatske'], which contain hand-written marginalia by Tudjman. For a discussion of the constitution drafting process, see Branko Smerdel, 'The Republic of Croatia: Three Fundamental Constitutional Choices', 1(1) *Croatian Political Science Review* (1992), 60–77.

[81] For a discussion of the figures, see Aleksa Djilas, *The Contested Country: Yugoslav Unity and Communist Revolution, 1919–1953* (Cambridge, MA: Harvard University Press, 1991), pp. 125–7.

[82] Cited in Tanner, *Croatia*, p. 223.

[83] Serbs represented 11.5 per cent of the population of Croatia in 1989 but accounted for 24.8 per cent of the republic-level and 21.4 per cent of the local political posts, held 32 per cent of the positions in the Ministry of Defence, and made up 70 per cent of the police force. Figures from Norman Cigar, 'The Serbo-Croatian War, 1991: Political and Military Dimensions', 16(3) *The Journal of Strategic Studies* (1993), 301.

'ethnic-compensatory' – afforded Serbs a certain measure of privilege. 'This was one of the negative legacies of the communist period', Milorad Pupovac, cofounder of the Serbian Democratic Forum, would admit several years later. 'But', he adds, 'the responsibility lay with the communists, not the Serbs.'[84] More radical Serb nationalists, however, interpreted these and later moves on the part of the Tudjman government as mortal threats to the Serb nation. By September 1990, *Politika*, one of the most authoritative and widely read national newspapers, then firmly under Milošević's control, was publishing article upon article beneath such headlines as: 'The Whole Serb People is Attacked', '1941 Started with Same Methods', 'Genocide Musn't Happen' and 'Mad Policies of Croatian Government'.[85] The US Congress, in its own investigation into the plight of Croatia's Serbs, concluded that '[W]hile there is some evidence of discrimination against Serbs and a general insensitivity to Serbian concerns . . . the situation has more to do with disagreement between Serbs and Croats over the future of Yugoslavia than with human rights violations.' The report observed further:

The recent troubles between Serb and Croat in Croatia, may be instigated in large part by Serbian President Slobodan Milosevic as part of larger arguments between the republics on the future of Yugoslavia . . . *In general, it seems as that the genuine concerns of Serbs in Croatia have been used by the Serbian Government and more militant Serbs in Croatia as a pretext for forcing a showdown with the Croatian Government regarding the future of Yugoslavia as a whole. . .*[86]

It is clear that for all their outrage and concern, Croatia's Serbs, for the most part, were not drawn to nationalist options in response to Tudjman's agenda – not initially, at least. Telling, in this regard, is the fact that in the 1990 elections, the reformed Communist party (SDP) and the Coalition of National Reconciliation – parties that represented a civic, non-nationalist orientation – out-polled the nationalist Serbian Democratic Party (SDS) among Croatian Serbs by nearly three to one.[87] Even then, the SDS, under the leadership of Jovan Rašković,

---

[84] Author interview with Pupovac, Zagreb, 10 July 1997.
[85] Cited in Mark Thompson, *Forging War: The Media in Serbia, Croatia and Bosnia-Hercegovina* (London: Article XIX, 1994), p. 72.
[86] US Commission on Security and Cooperation in Europe, *Minority Rights: Problems, Parameters, and Patterns in the CSCE Context* (Washington, DC: Congressional Information Service, 1991), p. 137 (emphasis added).
[87] Only 23 per cent of Croatia's Serbs – most of the them living in rural regions – voted for the SDS; 46 per cent voted for the SDP and 16 per cent for the coalition. Figures from V. P. Gagnon Jr, 'Ethnic Nationalism and International Conflict: The Case of Serbia', 19(3) *International Security* (1994/95), 155, fn. 78.

was more moderate than it would later become under Babić. Rašković originally wanted to dispense with any nationalist orientation of the SDS when it was formed in February 1990 (he had preferred to call it simply the Democratic Party).[88] And he clearly saw the future of Croatia's Serbs lying with Croatia, not Serbia. 'We are Serbs by birth, but our homeland is in Croatia . . . [W]e do not tie ourselves to Serbia', he told *Borba*, the Belgrade daily, in June 1990.[89] At the same time, Rašković publicly acknowledged the Croatian people's right to a sovereign state, insisting, however, that Croatia's Serbs must enjoy national equality and a large measure of cultural autonomy within that state, notably the right to speak their own language, use their own script, have their own schools and education programmes and publish their own books and newspapers.[90]

Rašković's demands at the time were in fact more modest than the minority rights provisions of the Carrington plan sixteen months later. Yet under pressure from Belgrade and from militants within his party, Rašković quickly upped the ante. He turned down an invitation to join the Tudjman government as a deputy prime minister, and instructed the five SDS parliamentary representatives not to take their seats when the first session of the Sabor opened in July 1990.[91] Then in November 1990, when the Tudjman government undertook to rewrite the constitution once again and invited Rašković to submit his recommendations, Rašković now demanded political and territorial autonomy, including the right of the Serbs to establish their own autonomous provinces or regions on the basis of local plebiscites, and, within those areas, to make their own laws.[92] The Tudjman government promptly dismissed his proposals; as far as it was concerned Rašković's provinces had all the 'prerogatives of a state'.[93]

Yet even these recommendations were deemed too modest for Serb militants. Rašković, it seems, was hopelessly out of step with the ascendant radicals within the SDS and their backers in Belgrade. He resisted

[88] Laura Silber and Allan Little, *The Death of Yugoslavia* (London: Penguin, 1995), p. 101.
[89] Rašković interview with *Borba* (Belgrade), 18 June 1990, in Foreign Broadcast Information Service, *Daily Report: Eastern Europe*, *FBIS-EEU-90-123*, 26 June 1990, p. 57.
[90] Text of speech by Rašković in Petrinja, Croatia, 23 June 1990, in Foreign Broadcast Information Service, *Daily Report: Eastern Europe*, *FBIS-EEU-90-124*, 27 June 1990, p. 83.
[91] Cohen, *Broken Bonds*, p. 131.
[92] 'Primjedbe na nacrt Ustava Republike Hrvatske' [Comments on the Draft Croatian Constitution], memo from Jovan Rašković to Slaven Letica, dated 11 December 1990 (copy on file with the author).
[93] As described by Letica in his interview with the author.

Babić's decision to proclaim the autonomy of the Serb Krajina in July 1990, arguing that it was too early for such a move.[94] And he never did enjoy the favour of Milošević, who met with Babić in August and at the latter's request arranged key meetings between Babić and Jović and Petar Gračanin, the federal interior minister,[95] both of whom, along with the JNA, would later assist in arming the Krajina Serbs and help them to consolidate control in the region.[96] In September, Milošević replaced Rašković with Babić as the head of the SDS.

With Belgrade's assistance Babić set about systematically to eliminate whatever support there was among moderate Croatian Serbs interested in accommodation with Zagreb. In Korenica, for instance, where local Serbs had voted for the SDP and were seeking a dialogue with the Tudjman government to enhance tourism in the area (Plitvice National Park is located nearby), Babić sent forty armed men to pre-empt a mid-summer visit by Slavko Degoricija, Tudjman's minister for local government. In the weeks that followed, the SDS staged a series of rallies and eventually drove the SDP deputies out of office.[97] Similarly, in Baranja, Vojislav Vukčelić, a moderate Serb leader, and his associates came under attack by the state-controlled Radio Belgrade, after which, in April 1991, Serb paramilitaries Vojislav Šešelj and Milan Paroski arrived in the company of Stanko Cvijan, Serbia's minister for Serbs outside of Serbia, to threaten them.[98] Babić's terror extended to selected assassinations of moderate mayors in Serb-majority towns.[99]

It is evident, then, that there existed broad support among Croatia's Serbs for dialogue with the Tudjman government, which the Serb leadership in Belgrade and its allies in the Krajina sought to undermine. (Zagreb, for its part, played the role of unwitting handmaiden in this particular drama through its own efforts to marginalise Rašković.)[100]

---

[94] Babić interview for 'The Death of Yugoslavia', p. 7.

[95] *Ibid.*, p. 10.

[96] For details concerning Yugoslav federal government and JNA arms transfers to the Krajina Serbs, see Paul Williams and Norman Cigar, *A Prima Facie Case for the Indictment of Slobodan Milosevic* (London: Alliance to Defend Bosnia-Herzegovina, 1996).

[97] Silber and Little, *The Death of Yugoslavia*, p. 104.

[98] Vukčelić interview in *Srpska reč* (Belgrade), 15 August 1994, pp. 26–7, cited in Williams and Cigar, *A Prima Facie Case for the Indictment of Slobodan Milosevic*, p. 79, fn. 175.

[99] Woodward, *Balkan Tragedy*, p. 221.

[100] The Tudjman government helped to marginalise Rašković but not with the aim of further radicalising Croatia's Serbs. When on 23 July 1990 Tudjman met privately with Rašković to explore possible autonomy arrangements, the conversation was leaked to *Danas* (Zagreb), a leading weekly, permanently damaging Rašković's standing among his fellow Serbs. In the conversation Rašković urged Tudjman to understand that Serbs

Belgrade's interests were essentially two-fold. By exaggerating the security threats that Croatia's Serbs faced and by eliminating moderate voices among them who were seeking some form of accommodation, Belgrade was able to build support among Croatian Serbs for the establishment of a unitary Serb state ('Greater Serbia').[101] But the threat to Serbs abroad also enabled the Belgrade leadership to strengthen its position at home. By defining political interests in ethnic-security terms and by portraying themselves as the true defenders of those interests, Milošević and his associates were able to bolster their domestic support in much the same way as Milošević had exploited the plight of the Serbs in Kosovo four years earlier to help him gain power.[102]

The EC's recognition policy addressed itself to the objective threats to minority groups in the former Yugoslavia. In view of the preceding, it seems fair to conclude that even if the EC had been able to secure credible guarantees for the Serb population in Croatia at an early stage of the crisis, these guarantees alone might not have succeeded in mitigating the conflict, at least in the short term, because they did not speak to the *external* sources of the conflict. As Alicia Levine observes in her study of separatist struggles, 'External support for separatist regions generally makes violence more likely, conflicts more intense, and compromise more difficult.'[103] Belgrade actively encouraged and armed the Krajina Serbs to reject minority status within Croatia under almost any circumstances. While Zagreb may be justly criticised for provocations

are a 'crazy people' and that he, Rašković, should therefore not be asked to make too many compromises. Letica acknowledges responsibility for having provided *Danas* with the transcript. 'Our intention was to destroy [Rašković's] credibility because he did not have moral or political autonomy', Letica maintains (interview with the author).

[101] This strategy is reflected in a July 1991 interview with Dobrica Ćosić, an influential Serb nationalist writer and later president of rump Yugoslavia. 'The Serb people of Croatia', he explained, 'are threatened to life by revived Croatian fascism . . . [T]he terror against Serbs in Croatia has convinced all Serbs that they must unite and create an integral national identity.' Ćosić interview in *Politika* (Belgrade), 27 July 1991, cited in Reneo Lukic and Allen Lynch, *Europe from the Balkans to the Urals: The Disintegration of Yugoslavia and the Soviet Union* (Oxford: SIPRI/Oxford University Press, 1996), p. 191.

[102] Gagnon, 'Ethnic Nationalism and International Conflict'. See also his 'Ethnic Conflict as an Intra-Group Phenomenon: A Preliminary Framework', 26(1–2) *Revija za sociologiju* (Zagreb) (1995), 81–90. To emphasise Belgrade's role in the radicalisation of the Croatian Serbs is not, however, to argue for a 'dyadic view' that ignores the salience of indigenous fears and grievances, as Rogers Brubaker suggests it does. See his *Nationalism Reframed: Nationhood and the National Question in the New Europe* (Cambridge: Cambridge University Press, 1996), pp. 69–72.

[103] Alicia Levine, 'Political Accommodation and the Prevention of Secessionist Violence', in Michael E. Brown (ed.), *The International Dimensions of Internal Conflict* (Cambridge, MA: CSIA/MIT Press, 1996), p. 312. See also Alexis Heraclides, 'Secessionist Minorities and External Involvement', 44 *International Organization* (1990), 341–78.

and discriminatory acts against its Serb population – policies that inspired genuine fear among the Croatian Serbs – the commitment of the federal army and the Serbian authorities to the use of force with the aim of establishing a new Yugoslavia dominated by Serbia diminished significantly whatever chances there might have been for meaningful compromise.

Bosnia and Herzegovina: 1914 revisited?

It is in BiH that the causal link between EC recognition and armed conflict would appear to be the strongest. Indeed, when in December 1991 UN Secretary-General Javier Pérez de Cuéllar cautioned the EC against the recognition of Slovenia and Croatia, it was principally with BiH in mind: 'I am deeply worried that an early, selective recognition could widen the present conflict and fuel an explosive situation especially in Bosnia-Hercegovina and also Macedonia', the secretary-general wrote to the Dutch Foreign Minister Hans van den Broek in the latter's capacity as president of the European Council.[104] Lord Carrington, Cyrus Vance and other statesmen seeking to negotiate a settlement echoed this view. The EC and its member states chose nonetheless to recognise the two republics in January 1992, followed by BiH as from 7 April 1992. Conforming to predictions, Bosnian Serb gunmen opened fire on the capital city of Sarajevo, soon plunging the entire country into the most violent phase of the Yugoslav war.[105] Commentators could not resist comparisons with the First World War. 'Only the odd-numbered world wars start in Sarajevo', it was observed at the time. But the comparison, though apt, was misplaced – misplaced because the war was effectively contained in the region; apt, however, because one could say that the Bosnian war was no more 'caused' by EC recognition than the First World War was 'caused' by the assassination of Archduke Franz Ferdinand in Sarajevo on 28 August 1914. In both cases a single event served as a trigger, or proximate cause of war, in the absence of which, and assuming no contravening measures, it seems likely that war would have erupted nonetheless.

Indeed, Bosnian Serb preparations for war-fighting were initiated well in advance of any serious consideration of recognition, EC or otherwise.

---

[104] UN Doc. S/23280, Annex III.

[105] The attacks on Sarajevo actually began on 4–5 April after Izetbegović issued a general mobilisation of the Bosnian territorial defence in response to reports of Serb paramilitary attacks on Bijeljina a few days earlier. See Silber and Little, *The Death of Yugoslavia*, pp. 247–50.

These preparations, moreover, were not merely precautionary moves undertaken in anticipation of armed opposition or military intervention. The nature and the extent of the Bosnian Serbs' early moves suggest that they were the first steps towards the establishment of a separate sub-state entity – a Republika Srpska. Seen in this light, EC recognition was less a cause than a pretext for the Bosnian Serbs to accelerate a process that they had already put into motion. It is questionable, therefore, whether delayed recognition or non-recognition of BiH would have meant a better chance for peace. Even Warren Zimmermann, who considered the timing of recognition to have been 'atrocious' and maintained that '[h]ad Izetbegovic pleaded for time to allow the Bosnian parties to work out their mutual relationships . . . he might have avoided a war', felt constrained to qualify his criticism: 'Even this is not certain', he would later write, 'because Milosevic and [Bosnian Serb leader Radovan] Karadzic had made careful plans for a major takeover of Bosnia.'[106]

In fact, with hindsight, it seems more accurate to suggest that the war in BiH did not begin in April 1992 but as many as eight months earlier. 'The practice of "cleansing" [by the JNA and Serbian militia] can be considered to have begun in a major, systematic way in mid-August 1991', James Gow has observed.[107] A number of incidents support this view. On 25 September 1991, JNA units, assisted by Serb volunteers, attacked Ravno, a village in Herzegovina inhabited mostly by ethnic Croats. Using heavy artillery, the JNA 'completely obliterated' the village, in the words of Ejup Ganić, a member of the Bosnian government delegation that subsequently investigated the incident.[108] The JNA claimed at the time that it was responding to provocations by civilians loyal to the Croatian army (HVO) but the nature and extent of the damage would suggest otherwise. According to Jovan Divjak, a Bosnian Serb general who later became deputy commander of the Bosnian army, the real reason was to avenge the death of JNA soldiers who were killed in an ambush near Čepikuće in Croatia, and, more importantly, to push the Croats out of a region that was inhabited largely by Serbs.[109] In

---

[106] Warren Zimmermann, 'A Pavane for Bosnia', 37 *The National Interest* (1994), p. 78.

[107] Gow, 'One Year of War in Bosnia and Herzegovina', p. 1.

[108] Cited in *Tanjug*, 31 October 1991, in Foreign Broadcast Information Service, *Daily Report: Eastern Europe, FBIS-EEU-91–212*, 1 November 1991, p. 26. Ganić recalls that Yugoslav army soldiers he met at the time greeted him with the three-finger Chetnik salutation. When he asked a JNA deputy commander, 'Is this the Yugoslav army or Chetniks I am seeing?' he was told, 'It's up to you, Ganic, to decide what they are.' Ganić interview for 'The Death of Yugoslavia', LHCMA, undated, Box 18, File 1, p. 5.

[109] Author interview with Divjak, Sarajevo, 19 June 1997.

October, one month after the Ravno incident, uniformed Bosnian Serb policemen provoked the flight of several thousand Muslims from the village of Šipovo. The policemen entered the village, killed a Muslim youth and then surrounded the town and fired into its Muslim quarter, causing some 3,000 Muslims to flee to Jajce.[110] Meanwhile Foča, Višegrad, Bratunac, Bijeljina and other eastern Bosnian towns were, from September 1991, the targets of Serbian paramilitary gangs intent on fomenting ethnic conflict, often under the watchful gaze of the JNA.[111]

Many Bosnian Croats and Muslims interpreted these and other similar incidents as a warning that if they did not accept political arrangements on Bosnian Serb terms they would face similar attacks. An actual warning may have come in July 1991 (the evidence is anecdotal), soon after the war in Slovenia had begun. General Nikola Uzelac, the commanding officer of the JNA's 1st army corps based in Banja Luka, gave Stjepan Kljuić, the Croat member of the Bosnian presidency, a copy of a letter that had been written to Uzelac earlier that month by General Blagoje Adžić, the JNA chief of staff. In the letter, Adžić explained that Uzelac must be prepared, when ordered, to detain all leading Croat and Muslim members of the Bosnian government.[112] The thinking behind the letter was consistent with the JNA strategy outlined several months earlier by Borisav Jović, Serbia's representative on the Federal Presidency. In his diary entry for 25 February 1991, Jović wrote:

In the wavering republics (Macedonia and B-H) using combined political means – demonstrations and uprisings – it is necessary to overthrow the leadership or to turn them in a different direction. These actions ought to be combined with some military actions. The entire action should be led by those members of the SFRY Presidency who are in favour of this course of action, and rely on the army.[113]

---

[110] Norman Cigar, *Genocide in Bosnia: The Policy of "Ethnic Cleansing"* (College Station, TX: Texas A&M University Press, 1995), p. 44.

[111] Woodward, *Balkan Tragedy*, p. 276. Izetbegović openly criticised the JNA for its failure to prevent the massacre of twenty-seven people, mostly Muslim, at Bijeljina on 2 April. See 'Yugoslav Army Blamed for Bijeljina Massacre', *RFE/RL Research Report*, '*Weekly Review*', 17 April 1992, p. 71.

[112] Letter from Kljuić to the author, 31 July 1998. Muhamed Filipović, vice-president of the Bosnian Liberal Party, who was shown a copy of the Adžić letter, confirmed the details of it in an interview with the author, Sarajevo, 18 June 1997.

[113] 'U kolebljivim republikama (Makedonija i BiH) kombinovanim političkim merama – demonstracijama i pobunama – treba srušiti rukovodstva ili ih preokrenuti u drugom pravcu. Ove aktivnosti valja kombinovati i sa nekim vojnim aktivnostima. Celu akciju treba da vode oni članovi Predsedništva SFRJ koji se opredele za ovaj kurs, sa osloncem na vojsku.' Borisav Jović, *Poslednji dani SFRJ: izvodi iz dnevnika* [The Last Days of the SFRY: Extracts from a Diary] (Belgrade: Politika, 1995), p. 277.

If Ravno was the first partisan attack by the JNA in BiH, it was not, however, an isolated incident but part of a pattern of activities in BiH in which the JNA was engaged at the time. According to Gow, the JNA had begun manoeuvres the previous month that would later become apparent were preparations for seizing the main communication arteries as well as the surrounding non-Serb population centres – of which Ravno was one. 'It would seem that the war for new borders, which would also be carved from Bosnia, was launched at this stage', Gow observes.[114] One month later JNA arms, which throughout 1990 had been pouring into BiH for deployment in Croatia, began to be distributed to the Bosnian Serbs. Divjak maintains that in the following year the JNA provided arms to Serb paramilitaries throughout BiH – in Vogošća, Ilijaš, Hadžići, Breza, Visiko, Zenica, Doboj, Brčko and Foča (in the latter case, as early as July 1990).[115] The transcript of a telephone conversation between Milošević and Karadžić, leaked by the embittered federal Prime Minister Ante Marković, reveals that Milošević and General Uzelac were working together in September 1991 to supply arms to Karadžić's paramilitaries.[116] Documents seized from the headquarters of the JNA's 2nd army command provide further confirmation of arms deliveries, including 51,900 unspecified weapons (*komada naoružanja*) to Karadžić's men.[117] By September, the JNA was also deploying artillery and digging trenches around Sarajevo – preparations, it is clear in retrospect, for the siege of the capital that would commence in May 1992, although at the time the JNA claimed to be strengthening its defensive fortifications.[118]

These preparations were not undertaken in response to any apparent military threat, nor were they carried out in anticipation of probable EC

[114] James Gow, *Triumph of the Lack of Will: International Diplomacy and the Yugoslav War* (London: C. Hurst & Co., 1997), p. 25.
[115] Jovan Divjak, 'Nastanak, Razvoj i Perspektive Armije RBiH – Vojske Federacije' [The Emergence, Development and the Future of the Army of the Republic of BiH – the Army of the Federation], unpublished manuscript, 1997, p. 4.
[116] Details were published in *Vreme* (Belgrade), 23 September 1991. Transcript entered as evidence with ICTY (Exhibit No. 353.39) and available, together with the transcripts of other intercepted telephone calls between ex-Yugoslav officials, at http://www.domovina.net/php/tribunal/page_006.php.
[117] Memo dated 20 March 1992 from General Milutin Kukanjac, the JNA commander of Sarajevo, to the General Staff of the Armed Forces SFRY, reproduced in Smail Čekić, *Agresija na Bosnu i Genocid nad Bošnjacima 1991–1993* [Aggression against Bosnia and Genocide against the Bosniacs, 1991–1993] (Sarajevo: Ljiljan, 1994), p. 289.
[118] Bennett, *Yugoslavia's Bloody Collapse*, p. 185; and author interview with Zoran Pajić, then a professor of law at the University of Sarajevo and an eye-witness to the JNA's military deployments in the hills surrounding the city, London, 28 April 1997. Pajić recalls that the JNA was engaged in these efforts for at least a year before the war began in BiH.

recognition. Indeed almost all of these developments occurred prior to 15 October 1991, the day the Bosnian Assembly proclaimed BiH to be sovereign (though not yet independent).[119] But it was clear even before that time that Izetbegović was determined to secure Bosnian sovereignty at almost any cost. On 27 February 1991 he told the Bosnian Assembly: 'I would sacrifice peace for a sovereign Bosnia-Herzegovina, but for that peace in Bosnia-Herzegovina I would not sacrifice sovereignty.'[120] The Serbs' military preparations therefore make sense largely in reaction to Izetbegović's moves towards sovereignty/independence. The EC's recognition policy no doubt facilitated these moves. To maintain, however, as Misha Glenny and others do, that 'Izetbegović was thus forced by German-led EC policy' to seek recognition in December, is to ignore the Bosnian government's own efforts on behalf of independence.[121] Indeed, there is some evidence to suggest that by the autumn of 1991 Izetbegović had concluded that Yugoslavia was beyond salvation and that it might be prudent to achieve independence before the Serbs could mobilise to prevent it. This may explain why, when on 22 November Izetbegović met with Genscher in Bonn – a meeting that had been arranged by Zimmermann to provide the Bosnian president with an opportunity to make the case against recognition – Izetbegović chose not to voice objections to recognition.[122] As Zimmermann would later recall: 'You can imagine Genscher's impression. If Izetbegović does not make the argument in a private conversation with Genscher, then he's not strongly against recognition. I think Genscher took this as a green light.'[123]

---

[119] 'Bosnia Declares Sovereignty; Serbia, Croatia Set Peace Talks', *Washington Post*, 16 October 1991.

[120] Cited in Silber and Little, *The Death of Yugoslavia*, p. 233. Izetbegović seems to have been opposed to independence at the time; two months later, on 10 April, he rejected the suggestion that BiH declare its independence along with Croatia and Slovenia, according to Muhamed Filipović, a confidant of Izetbegović at the time. Author interview with Filipović.

[121] Glenny, *The Fall of Yugoslavia*, p. 151.

[122] John Newhouse, 'Dodging the Problem', *The New Yorker*, 24 August 1992, p. 65. Libal writes of the meeting: 'If Izetbegović intended to warn the Germans about recognition, he failed to do so, at least in a direct and unequivocal way.' Libal claims that Izetbegović instead urged that recognition be used to influence Croatia to join a loose association with the other republics. Libal, *Limits of Persuasion*, p. 77.

[123] Author interview with Zimmermann. Izetbegović was anything but consistent on this issue. In Pérez de Cuéllar's letter of 10 December 1991 to Van den Broek, the secretary-general writes: 'Leaders of Bosnia-Hercegovina and Macedonia were among the many political and military figures who last week underscored to Mr. Vance their own strong fears . . . about the possibility of premature recognition of the independence of some of the Yugoslav republics and the effect that such a move might have on the remaining republics.' UN Doc. S/23280, 11 December 1991, Annex IV.

If Serb military preparations made sense principally in response to the Bosnian government's moves towards independence, they also made sense in support of Karadžić's fundamental goal and persistent demand – the partition of BiH[124] – and, towards that end, the progressive establishment of Serbian autonomous regions that gradually took on the characteristics of a state within a state, with their own governmental offices, administrative structures, sources of revenue and military organisation. As early as April 1991 an association of Serb municipalities had been formed in BiH. Although this was originally a loose association whose declared purpose was to promote economic and cultural cooperation, separate police forces and assemblies were created very quickly alongside it.[125] Then on 12 September, Bosnian Serbs proclaimed the first of several Serbian Autonomous Regions (SAOs) in Herzegovina, followed in short succession by the SAO of Bosanska Krajina (16 September), Romanija (17 September) and Northeastern Bosnia (19 September).[126] It was at this moment that the JNA was carrying out the large troop deployments described above, including on one day alone (20 September), a column of 100 military vehicles moving against Čapljina in western Herzegovina; another, larger column taking control of the major communications point at Nevesinje in eastern Herzegovina; and the movement of 5,000 troops westwards out of Sarajevo.[127] Bosnian government officials interpreted these troop and armour movements as an attempt by the JNA to secure Serb-populated areas of BiH.[128] The Canadian Department of Foreign Affairs' own reading of events, in November 1991, led it to conclude that fighting was likely to erupt in BiH without the spark of diplomatic recognition.[129]

---

[124] As Izetbegović recalls, 'We had a score of talks, our delegations, with Karadzic, mainly failures in which they insisted upon the impossible conditions for B&H. Their demands were practically reduced to partition of the country, to dissolution of the country. . .' See Izetbegović's interview for 'The Death of Yugoslavia', LHCMA, undated, Box 18, File 2, p. 4.

[125] International Tribunal for the Prosecution of Persons Responsible for Serious Violations of International Humanitarian Law Committed in the Territory of the Former Yugoslavia since 1991, Case No. IT-94-1-T, *Prosecutor v. Dusko Tadić a/k/a "Dule"*, Opinion and Judgement, 7 May 1997 [hereafter 'Tadić judgement'], para. 97, available at http://www.un.org/icty/tadic/trialc2/judgement/tad-tsj70507JT2-e.pdf.

[126] James Gow, 'The Role of the Military in the Yugoslav War of Dissolution', 9(1) *Storia delle Relazioni Internazionali* (1993), 117.

[127] *Ibid.*

[128] 'Bosnian Leadership Orders Mobilization', *RFE/RL Research Report, 'Weekly Review'*, 4 October 1991, p. 44.

[129] A senior Canadian foreign ministry official speaking on condition of anonymity at the Humanitas conference on former Yugoslavia, Leeds Castle, Kent, 25–27 February

The extent and timing of Bosnian Serb preparations for the take-over of local authority is evident in a number of documents of Karadžić's Serbian Democratic Party (SDS) that have come to light in the course of investigations into the commission of war crimes in BiH. A memo dated 29 October 1991 and issued by Radoslav Brdjanin, vice-president of the Assembly of Autonomous Regions, enumerates the 'Orders of SDS Sarajevo' (*Naredba SDS Sarajevo*), which, the memo states, were made public at a meeting of all presidents of the municipalities under the chairmanship of Karadžić at Banja Luka on 26 October. These 'orders' instruct local agents to 'immediately form a command centre and organise patrols'; 'form units for the front and designate their replacements'; prepare to 'take over the administration of firms, post offices, SDK [Social Accounting Offices, or payment bureaus], banks, courts, and the means of information'; establish a 'war programme scheme' for radio stations; and arrange for the collection of 'war taxes for the bigger success of the complete action'; among other directives.[130] Although some of the measures appear to have been adopted with the war in Croatia in mind, the procedures are consistent with those detailed in a later SDS planning document entitled 'Instructions for the Organisation and Activity of Organs of the Serbian People in Bosnia and Herzegovina in Extraordinary Circumstances'.[131] This document, dated 19 December 1991, one day before Izetbegović would announce his government's decision to seek EC recognition, distinguishes between measures to be carried out in those municipalities where Serbs form a majority ('*Varijanta "A"*') and those where they do not ('*Varijanta "B"*'). But the aim in both cases is the same: to implement 'the results of the plebiscite at which the Serbian people in Bosnia and Herzegovina decided to live in a single state [i.e. Yugoslavia]. . .'[132]

1994. Similarly, the Belgrade daily *Večernje novosti* commented on 27 January 1992 that the break-up of BiH 'looks more likely to happen than recognition of the republic as an independent state'. Cited in Milan Andrejevich, 'Bosnia and Herzegovina: A Precarious Peace', *RFE/RL Research Report*, 28 February 1992, p. 10.

[130] 'Naredba SDS Sarajevo'. The relevant passages read: '1. Odmah formirati komandu mjesta i odrediti stalno dežurstvo; . . . 3. Formirati jedinice za front i odrediti njhove zamjene; . . . 5. Preuzeti vlast ujavnim preduzećima, pošti, SDKa, banci, sudstvu i obavezno sredstva informisanja; 6. Na radio stanicama proglasiti ratnu šemu programa; . . . 13. Odrediti i ratne poreze za veći uspjeh kompletne akcije. . .'. Reproduced in Čekić, *Agresija na Bosnu i Genocid nad Bošnjacima 1991–1993*, pp. 273–4.

[131] My reference is to an unpublished, English translation of the document (Copy No. 096) submitted as evidence at the International Criminal Tribunal for the Former Yugoslavia in Case No. IT-95-18-R61, *The Prosecutor of the Tribunal* v. *Radovan Karadžić and Ratko Mladić*. Copy provided by Dr James Gow, King's College London.

[132] *Ibid.*, p. 2. The reference is to the SDS-organised referendum of 9–10 November 1991.

More significant, these measures conform to the actual practices carried out by the many 'crisis staffs', which the 'Instructions' order the establishment of in each municipality. These bodies were typically made up of SDS leaders, Serb police officials, the Serb Territorial Defence commander and the JNA commander of the area, whose purpose it was to assume government functions and carry out municipal management in time of 'crisis'.[133] The crisis in question could very well be one of the Bosnian Serbs' own making, as was the case in Prijedor on 30 April 1992, when armed Serbs seized control of the town following the transmission on Belgrade TV of a facsimile said to have been orders by the leader of the Bosnian Territorial Defence to obstruct JNA troop movements – a document that the Bosnian government declared to be false and promptly denounced. Despite the appearance of spontaneity, the *de facto* Serbian authorities of Prijedor stated clearly that the takeover was the final stage of a long-standing plan.[134] The UN Secretary-General's Commission of Experts, in its investigation of the incident, concluded that Serbs had begun to arm and make plans for seizing control of Prijedor more than six months before the outbreak of hostilities.[135] Indeed, in July 1991 General Uzelac had requested that Karadžić take 'political action' in 'five or six municipalities': more specifically, that Karadžić (or his associates) 'denounce all calls and acts of treason' over the radio and via the press and then 'introduce a state of emergency in these municipalities'.[136]

With such extensive preparations carried out so well in advance of EC recognition, it is hard to imagine that delayed recognition would have

---

[133] Tadić judgement, para. 103.

[134] *Ibid.*, para. 138.

[135] Final Report of the United Nations Commission of Experts Established Pursuant to Security Council Resolution 780 (1992), UN Doc. S/1994/674, 27 May 1994, paras. 156–8 and 174. See also Annex V (The Prijedor Report), para. 115ff.

[136] Excerpt from intercepted conversation between Karadžić and Uzelac, 9 July 1991, entered as evidence at the ICTY (Office of the Prosecution reference B6599), available at http://www.domovina.net/tribunal/page_006.php:

UZELAC: You know what I'd like to ask you?
KARADŽIĆ: Just say it.
UZELAC: Just political action.
KARADŽIĆ: All right. Yes, yes.
UZELAC: In all municipalities, over the radio, via the press, by every means. Liven up everyone. Denounce all calls and acts of treason. To that effect.
KARADŽIĆ: All right.
UZELAC: To that effect and I'll, you see, I've already arranged this, they'll declare a state of emergency. Introduce a state of emergency in these municipalities, these border/municipalities/, these five or six municipalities, including Banja Luka.
KARADŽIĆ: All right.

improved the strategic environment. In fact, it might even have exacerbated the situation. If the international community had done nothing at all, it would have been that much easier for Belgrade to use violence to suppress the actions of its 'secessionist' Muslims and Croats, just as Moscow would later attempt to do in Chechnya and Belgrade itself in Kosovo. As it was, the delay of nearly three months – from January 1992, when the EC recognised Slovenia and Croatia – allowed Serb forces additional time to make their military preparations, including the transfer of substantial military assets from the JNA to the Bosnian Serb Army.[137] A further delay might also have raised questions about the status of BiH, especially as the entity began to splinter, which would have made it that much more difficult for Sarajevo to assert its claim to statehood. In this sense recognition was to play a constitutive role, as was discussed in Chapter 2. In any event, it seems that the issue for the Serbs was not international recognition of BiH *per se* but rather the control of territory *within* BiH. Milošević made this point to Karadžić with an analogy to the Roman emperor Caligula. As Karadžić recalls:

President Milosevic did not see the international recognition of Bosnia-Herzegovina as an event of crucial importance which would change anything for its people. We even joked about this and he said that although Caligula declared his horse a senator, the horse never became one, and added that the same applied to Izetbegovic. He [would have] international recognition but no state.[138]

Many observers, however, have argued that delayed recognition would have enhanced the possibility for a mutually satisfactory condominium to be arrived at through negotiations, notably the negotiations being conducted by the Portuguese EC mediator José Cutileiro from February 1992. Karadžić, too, says that recognition was detrimental to the negotiating process.[139] Yet it is not clear that these negotiations, if sustained, would have averted war. For at the same time that Karadžić was negotiating with Izetbegović, he was also conferring with the

---

[137] Jović and Milošević began preparations for the transfer of military assets as early as January. See Jović interview for 'The Death of Yugoslavia', pp. 95–6. Boutros-Ghali would refer to these developments in his report of 3 December 1992 to the UN Security Council: 'Though JNA has withdrawn completely from Bosnia and Herzegovina, former members of Bosnian Serb origin have been left behind with their equipment, and constitute the Army of the "Serb Republic".' 'The Situation in Bosnia and Herzegovina', Report of the Secretary-General, UN Doc. A/47/747, 3 December 1992, para. 11.

[138] Karadžić interview for 'The Death of Yugoslavia', LHCMA, undated, Box 18, File 2, p. 3.

[139] *Ibid.*, p. 15.

Croatian leadership from both BiH and Croatia about a territorial division of BiH. (Tudjman and Milošević had had discussions along similar lines as early as March 1991 in Karadjordjevo.)[140] Karadžić speaks openly about these meetings. Of one such meeting, on 26 February 1992, just prior to the third round of EC talks, Karadžić recalls: Josip Manolić, Tudjman's adviser, said that 'the Croats would be prepared to consider territorial exchanges when the Croats in Bosnia regulate their status. I told him then that this would be much easier if the Croats, like the Serbs, formed their own state in Bosnia. So we gave them the idea to create the Republic of Herzeg-Bosnia.'[141]

Over the next three weeks, Cutileiro succeeded in gaining the support of the three main Bosnian political parties for a 'Statement of Principles for New Constitutional Arrangements for Bosnia and Hercegovina'. (Izetbegović, it seems, expected the assistance and protection of the EC in exchange for his support.)[142] The cornerstone of these arrangements was the idea that BiH would be an independent, decentralised state 'composed of three constituent units, based on national principles'.[143] Each constituent unit, in turn, was to be comprised of those municipalities where the respective nationality – Serb, Croat and Muslim – was in an absolute or relative majority. Although the constituent units were not meant to be contiguous, there was a territorial dimension to them, and this arguably gave legitimacy to Karadžić's vision of a BiH divided territorially along ethnic lines. Besides which, Karadžić seemed prepared to use force to adjust the borders anyway, as he had indicated in his discussions with the Croats. Just a few days before the fifth round of EC negotiations began on 16 March, he stated, 'We have 30,000 armed fighters and artillery [in the Sarajevo area]. We now only need a good excuse.'[144] Similarly, just after the Lisbon

---

[140] Tudjman acknowledges these discussions in his interview for 'The Death of Yugoslavia', pp. 11–13.

[141] Karadžić interview for 'The Death of Yugoslavia', p. 5. Nikola Koljević, the Bosnian Serb 'vice president', says that earlier meetings were held in late December between him and the Croatian leadership (including Tudjman) to discuss 'resettlement of the population'. See Koljević interview for 'The Death of Yugoslavia', LHCMA, undated, Box 18, File 2, p. 5.

[142] Author interview with Filipović. Rusmir Mahmutćehajić, one of the Muslim negotiators, says: 'We accepted this proposal because Cutileiro told us it was the only way the EC was willing to protect Bosnia as a sovereign state.' Cited in Tihomir Loza, 'Getting to Dayton', contribution to unpublished edited volume, *Implementing Dayton*, 1997.

[143] 'Statement of Principles for New Constitutional Arrangements for Bosnia and Herzegovina', 18 March 1992, section A1. The statement was signed by Karadžić, Izetbegović and the Bosnian Croat leader Mate Boban.

[144] Karadžić quote from *NIN* (Belgrade), 1 July 1994, cited in Loza, 'Getting to Dayton'.

agreement was signed, Vojo Kuprešanin, a member of the SDS execu-
tive board, declared, 'The document is non-binding, but it is a good
starting point for confederalisation of Bosnia and annexation of the Serb
lands to Yugoslavia.'[145]

In view of the foregoing, recognition would seem only to have provided a pretext for starting a war that the Serbs were disposed to launch
anyway – indeed, a war that arguably had already commenced. Violence
was intrinsic to the political goals of the Bosnian Serb leadership, which
was not only determined to exercise authority over a significant portion
of BiH's territory but also to expel from those territories most of the non-
Serb population. (Brdjanin stated publicly before the war began that
the largest percentage of non-Serbs he would tolerate in the Serb
Autonomous Region of the Banja Luka area was 2 per cent.)[146] The
Bosnian Serbs simply could not achieve their political goals without
resort to violence – unless, of course, the other peoples of BiH would
have agreed to a surrender of their sovereign authority and a massive
transfer of their populations. The international community therefore
had three choices: it could either acquiesce in the Serb demands, induce
the Serbs to accept revised goals compatible with democratic norms and
human rights, or deter the Serbs from seeking to realise their goals.
Delayed or non-recognition could only have worked in support of the
second of the three options – and then assuming a willingness on the part
of the Serbs to compromise their fundamental goals. Given the balance
of forces in their favour, however, the Serbs had no real reason to
consider that option.

If delayed recognition, then, would not necessarily have improved the
chances of avoiding war, recognition created an opportunity for more
effective international engagement, as has been argued with respect to
Croatia. The Bosnian government was certainly mindful of this logic,
although its leaders also thought that intervention, in the form of EC or
UN peacekeepers, need not await recognition – as, indeed, the deployment of EC monitors to Croatia in July would not. Soon after the war
began in Slovenia, the Bosnian government requested the preventive
deployment of EC observers to their republic. The EC, on 29 July,
turned down the request, saying that it had chosen to concentrate on
the situation in Croatia, which it considered to be 'at the heart of the

---

[145] Kuprešanin quote from *NIN* (Belgrade), 27 March 1992, cited in Loza, 'Getting to
Dayton'.
[146] Tadić judgement, para. 89.

Yugoslav crisis'.[147] Its expectation was that its efforts in Croatia, if successful, would reduce tensions in BiH. There was some support within the EC for preventive action, however. Both Belgium and the Netherlands, by mid-September, were in favour of extending the EC monitor missions to BiH.[148]

The Bosnian government then appealed to the United Nations for a peacekeeping contingent. On 12 November 1991 Izetbegović called for the immediate deployment of UN peacekeeping forces to head off the impending violence and, on 20 November 1991, the Sarajevo authorities presented Herbert Okun, Vance's assistant, with a plan that envisaged the deployment of 2,000 UN peacekeeping troops.[149] However, the proposal was essentially ignored. In his report to the Security Council of 5 January, Boutros-Ghali noted that UN peacekeeping arrangements in the region already anticipated the deployment of UN military observers to BiH and that 'for the time being' no modification of the UN's original concept was planned.[150] One reason for the UN's lukewarm reception, Henry Wynaendts, Carrington's deputy, has suggested, was that Vance was concerned not to antagonise Milošević, who opposed the deployment of UN forces in BiH and whose cooperation Vance needed at the time to broker the interim peace plan for Croatia.[151] Shashi Tharoor, UN special assistant for peacekeeping operations, maintains that the secretary-general was also mindful of probable Chinese objections to the plan, given Beijing's sensitivity to dispatching UN troops to what was still, strictly speaking, an internal Yugoslav affair – a problem, of course, that would be circumvented with the recognition of BiH.[152]

[147] Libal, *Limits of Persuasion*, p. 28; and Wynaendts, quoting an unspecified EC document, in *L'engrenage*, p. 63.
[148] Willem van Eekelen, *Debating European Security, 1948–1998* (The Hague and Brussels: Sdu Publishers/Centre for European Policy Studies, 1998), pp. 145–6.
[149] Tanjug, 12 November 1991, cited in Sabrina Petra Ramet, *Balkan Babel: The Disintegration of Yugoslavia from the Death of Tito to the War for Kosovo*, 3rd edn (Boulder, CO: Westview Press, 1999), p. 205; Keesing's *Record of World Events* (November 1991), p. 38559; Ganić interview for 'The Death of Yugoslavia', pp. 2–3.
[150] 'With regard to the request made by President Izetbegovic of Bosnia-Herzegovina that a substantial United Nations peace-keeping presence be deployed immediately in the Republic, the concept paper of 11 December 1991 already envisages a deployment of United Nations military observers in Bosnia-Herzegovina.' Further Report of the Secretary-General Pursuant to Security Council Resolution 721 (1991), UN Doc. S/23363, 5 January 1992, para. 30. The concept paper to which Boutros-Ghali refers, however, envisaged the deployment of UN military observers to BiH only *after* the demilitarisation of the UN Protected Areas (UNPAs) in Croatia had been achieved. Even then their functions were to relate largely to maintaining the peace in the UNPAs. See UN Doc. S/23280, 11 December 1991, para. 13.
[151] Wynaendts, *L'engrenage*, p. 141.
[152] Author interview with Tharoor, New York, 28 April 1994.

Indeed, with recognition came another appeal for the deployment of UN forces – this time by Haris Silajdzić, the Bosnian foreign minister, on 10 April. Again the Bosnians were rebuffed. Boutros-Ghali, in turning down this further request, explained to Silajdzić that the United Nations was not the appropriate party to call upon. As Boutros-Ghali recalled in his report to the Security Council of 24 April:

I once more emphasized [to Silajdzić] the division of labor between the United Nations, whose peacemaking mandate was limited to the situation in the Republic of Croatia, in accordance with the Security Council resolution, and the peacemaking role of the European Community (EC) for Yugoslavia as a whole. Concerning his specific request, I observed that it might be more appropriate for the EC to expand its presence and activities in Bosnia-Hercegovina.[153]

In the same report, Boutros-Ghali offered another explanation for the UN's refusal – this one provided to Izetbegović. The secretary-general told the Bosnian president that 'the limitations on human, material and financial resources, and especially in view of the current widespread violence [make it] impossible to define a workable concept for a United Nations peace-keeping operation'.[154] The situation, in other words, was not suitable and the UN was ill-equipped for a peacekeeping operation in this particular instance, the secretary-general surmised. The Security Council did not challenge this judgement. Moreover, when it met in emergency session that day, the Council chose not to adopt a formal resolution proscribing outside interference in what was now a sovereign state but instead issued a presidential statement that, although strongly worded, had no binding legal authority and thus did not provide a basis for any enforcement actions.[155]

Had UN peacekeeping forces been sent to BiH in early 1992, the initiative might have inhibited the spread of war there.[156] Wynaendts, Carrington and Zimmermann, among other participant-diplomats, all urged that such action be taken at the time for that very reason.[157] The

---

[153] Report of the Secretary-General Pursuant to Security Council Resolution 749 (1992), UN Doc. S/23836, 24 April 1992, para. 2.
[154] *Ibid.*, para. 27.
[155] Marc Weller, 'The International Response to the Dissolution of the Socialist Federal Republic of Yugoslavia', 86 *American Journal of International Law* (1992), 601.
[156] The UN did establish a small presence in Sarajevo but it served only as the headquarters for the Croatian peacekeeping mission and played no effective role in BiH. See Further Report of the Secretary-General Pursuant to Security Council Resolution 749 (1992), UN Doc. S/23844, 24 April 992, para. 2. Most of the UN personnel would be withdrawn on 17 May 1992 as the fighting in BiH intensified. 'UN Peacekeepers Pull Out of Sarajevo', *Financial Times*, 18 May 1992.
[157] Wynaendts, *L'engrenage*, pp. 141–2; Warren Zimmermann, 'The Last Ambassador', 74(2) *Foreign Affairs* (1995), 16.

difficulty is that by early 1992 arms had already been distributed widely throughout the Serb communities of BiH and the JNA had already begun to re-deploy troops there from Croatia. Nonetheless, an international presence might have been a deterrent against some of the more egregious violations of human rights that would later be perpetrated, including ethnic cleansing and the establishment of concentration camps. To the extent that recognition could facilitate an intervention, EU and US recognition of BiH in April only raised expectations that such action would now be forthcoming, especially in view of the fact that recognition alone did nothing to dampen the hostilities. (Nor did recognition exempt BiH from the UN arms embargo imposed on the Socialist Federal Republic of Yugoslavia in September 1991,[158] notwithstanding the fact that as a sovereign state BiH was entitled to take measures in its own defence, as specified by Article 51 of the UN Charter.)[159] The Western powers were thus vulnerable to the criticism that they had failed to deliver on the promise of support implicit in the act of recognition, however much they had always been at pains to discourage expectations of intervention.

Macedonia and Kosovo: the price of equivocation

If in the case of BiH, 'premature' recognition provided the spark that ignited the war there in earnest, in the case of Macedonia it might very well have had the opposite effect. Indeed because of uncertainties surrounding Macedonia's identity, early recognition might have helped to achieve greater definition, and hence stability, for a territory that one journalist aptly described at the time as a 'political no-man's land where Serbian, Albanian, Bulgarian, and Greek ambitions vie with one another and with a nascent Macedonian nationalist movement'.[160] Instead, by withholding recognition for nearly two years, the EC placed Macedonia in a state of political limbo that various interests sought to exploit, thus heightening tensions inside the territory as well as in the wider balkan region.

Already the poorest of the Yugoslav republics, Macedonia was further handicapped at the time of independence in September 1991 by the weakness of its identity. While there has long been a geographic

---

[158] UN Security Council Res 713 (1991), 25 September 1991.
[159] For a discussion of the legality of the arms embargo against BiH, see Marc Weller, 'Peace-Keeping and Peace-Enforcement in the Republic of Bosnia and Herzegovina', 56 (1–2) *Zeitschrift für ausländisches öffentliches Recht und Völkerrecht* (1996), 87–9.
[160] Robert D. Kaplan, 'History's Cauldron', *The Atlantic Monthly*, June 1991, p. 94.

Macedonia, as a national and political entity Macedonia had largely ceased to exist in the aftermath of the Balkan Wars (1911–13), when it was divided and then subsumed by Bulgaria, Greece and Serbia.[161] Tito's creation of the Republic of Macedonia in the context of the second Yugoslavia represented not only the revival but in important respects the construction of a Macedonian nation, endowing these 'western Bulgarians', 'Slavophone Greeks' and 'southern Serbs' with their own officially recognised language, culture and institutions.[162] As a result, many Bulgarians, Greeks and Serbs have been somewhat sceptical about the authenticity of Macedonian nationhood.[163]

Although at the time of Yugoslavia's disintegration no one seriously doubted the existence of a distinctive nation on the territory of the former Socialist Republic of Macedonia, excepting some Serbian and Bulgarian nationalists, the lack of clarity about Macedonia's status pending recognition invited a form of 'land speculation' that arguably would have been more difficult to pursue had Macedonia been promptly and firmly constituted as a new state. Thus in January 1992 Athens and Belgrade conducted talks about the prospect of establishing a 'joint Serbian–Greek border', while in March 1992 Branko Kostić, the vice-president of rump Yugoslavia, spoke more bluntly about the possibility of partitioning Macedonia. A few months later, in October 1992, *Time* magazine reported that 'several European governments have relayed to Washington reports that [Greek Prime Minister] Mitsotakis has secretly discussed the partition of Macedonia with Serbia and perhaps with Albania and Bulgaria as well'.[164] There were also concerns that Serbia might use the plight of the tiny Serbian community in Macedonia, numbering roughly 44,000 or 2 per cent of the population, as a pretext for military actions against the republic. Of course statehood had not been enough to prevent predatory advances against BiH by Croatia and

---

[161] H. R. Wilkinson, *Maps and Politics: A Review of the Ethnographic Cartography of Macedonia* (Liverpool: Liverpool University Press, 1951), ch. 8.

[162] Duncan M. Perry, 'Macedonia: A Balkan Problem and a European Dilemma', *RFE/RL Research Report*, 19 June 1992, p. 36. 'Nation-making' was an important feature of socialist state-building. For a discussion of this process in the Soviet context, see Ronald Grigor Suny, *The Revenge of the Past: Nationalism, Revolution and the Collapse of the Soviet Union* (Stanford, CA: Stanford University Press, 1993), ch. 3.

[163] John B. Allcock, 'The Dilemmas of an Independent Macedonia', *ISIS Briefing* No. 42 (London: International Security Information Service, June 1994), p. 3.

[164] As reported by Radio Belgrade Network (19 January 1992), *Politika* (6 March 1992), and *Time* (12 October 1992) and cited in Sabrina Petra Ramet, 'The Macedonian Enigma', in Sabrina Petra Ramet and Ljubiša S. Adamovich (eds.), *Beyond Yugoslavia: Politics, Economics, and Culture in a Shattered Community* (Boulder, CO: Westview Press, 1995), p. 219.

Serbia but precisely because adjustments to territory were being openly, and not so openly, discussed in the region, Macedonia's position was made even more vulnerable by its indeterminate status. As Kiro Gligorov, Macedonia's president, cautioned in June 1992: 'The EC's tendency to take a wait-and-see attitude regarding recognition . . . encourages all those who are interested in exploiting this unclear situation in that region or even turning to open aggression.'[165] Bulgaria, in particular, seemed to appreciate this logic and, like Germany with respect to Croatia, argued that recognition would discourage the use of force against Macedonia.[166]

As a non-state entity, moreover, Macedonia could not qualify for critically needed international assistance from either the World Bank or the International Monetary Fund at a time when the country was suffering from the loss of its traditional markets to the north, the effects of UN sanctions against Belgrade and an economic boycott by Athens as part of its efforts to force Skopje to renounce any irredentist aspirations.[167] In response to Greek pressures, the Macedonian Assembly on 6 January 1992 adopted two amendments to the constitution, forswearing any 'territorial pretensions towards any neighbouring state' and pledging 'not [to] interfere in the sovereign rights of other states or in their internal affairs'.[168] These changes, while enough to satisfy the Badinter Commission that Macedonia had 'renounced all territorial claims of any kind in unambiguous statements binding in international law',[169] were not enough to placate the Greeks, who continued to insist that Macedonia relinquish the name 'Macedonia'. As Greece would explain in a letter to the UN secretary-general concerning the application of Macedonia for admission to the United Nations:

It is important to note that [the authorities in Skopje] have explicitly adopted the name of a wider geographical region extending over four neighbouring countries . . . This fact by itself clearly undermines the sovereignty of neighbouring states to their respective Macedonian regions . . . There is no doubt that the exclusive

---

[165] Cited in *ibid.*, p. 225.
[166] Patrick Moore, 'Diplomatic Recognition of Croatia and Slovenia', *RFE/RL Research Report*, 24 January 1992, p. 14. Bulgaria was the first state to recognise Macedonia.
[167] Basil Kondis *et al.* (eds.), *Resurgent Irredentism: Documents on Skopje 'Macedonian' Nationalist Aspirations (1934 – 1992)* (Thessaloniki: Institute for Balkan Studies, 1993).
[168] *Constitution of the Republic of Macedonia*, Amendments I and II. The Greeks objected especially to Article 49 of the constitution, which reads: 'The Republic cares for the status and rights of those persons belonging to the Macedonian people in neighbouring countries, as well as Macedonian ex-patriates, assists their cultural development and promotes links with them.'
[169] Opinion No. 6, 11 January 1992, 31 *International Legal Materials* (1992), p. 1511.

use of the Macedonian name in the republic's official denomination would be a stimulus for expansionist claims not only by present nationalist activists in Skopje but by future generations as well.[170]

The reasons for Greece's persistence had as much to do with domestic political imperatives as with genuine security concerns, but the effects of its economic boycott of Macedonia were palpable all the same. By October 1992, the Greek oil embargo had led to sharp fuel price increases, the partial idling of dozens of enterprises, long petrol queues and an anticipated agricultural shortfall, prompting an unofficial US government representative in Skopje (the United States, too, had not yet recognised Macedonia) to warn in an internal memorandum about the prospect of violent unrest in the capital.[171] The irony is that if Greece were truly concerned about the emergence of a hostile, unstable state on its northern border, its actions against Macedonia – which EC non-recognition only encouraged – were doing more to foster than to counter such a development.

Continued non-recognition also aggravated what was, arguably, the more serious threat to Macedonia stability: interethnic tensions within the country. The failure to gain EC recognition contributed to the fall of the moderate government of Prime Minister Nikola Kljusev in July 1992, thus strengthening the hand of Macedonian nationalists, notably the Internal Macedonian Revolutionary Organisation – Democratic Party for Macedonian National Unity (VMRO – DPMNE), which held the largest number of seats in the Assembly.[172] The nationalists had already alienated the country's ethnic Albanian community, comprising roughly one-quarter of the population,[173] with, *inter alia*, their promulgation of a constitution whose preamble defined Macedonia as 'a national state of the Macedonian people' alongside 'other nationalities'; the establishment of Macedonian as the official language; proposed residency requirements for citizenship (twenty-five continuous years),

---

[170] Letter Dated 25 January 1993 from the Permanent Representative of Greece to the United Nations Addressed to the Secretary-General, UN Doc. S/25158, 25 January 1993, Appendix.

[171] 'Post Report for September and October 1992', US Government memorandum, Skopje, 26 October 1992 (copy on file with author).

[172] 'Macedonian Government Falls', *RFE/RL Research Report*, *'Weekly Review'*, 17 July 1992, p. 82.

[173] The Albanians claim to make up 30–40 per cent of the population. An EU-UN census conducted in June–July 1994, which was judged to be free and fair by several international observers, confirmed the lower estimate (26.6 per cent). See Biannual Report of the Co-Chairmen of the Steering Committee on the Activities of the International Conference on the Former Yugoslavia, UN Doc. S/1994/1454, 29 December 1994, Annex, para. 28.

which were seen to disadvantage Albanians who, until the collapse of Yugoslavia, had lived freely between Kosovo and Macedonia;[174] and an unwillingness to provide adequate Albanian-language instruction at institutions of higher learning.[175] Although the Albanians had largely boycotted the referendum on independence in September 1991 and their MPs had abstained from voting on the new constitution one month later, they did not oppose Macedonia's bid for EC recognition in December 1991 and, moreover, chose to participate in successive governments – an expression of their acceptance of the new state. As their frustration grew, however, they saw in EC equivocation an opportunity to exploit the unresolved situation in the interest of improving their status. Thus in November 1992, Sami Ibrahimi, deputy president of the Party for Democratic Prosperity (PDP), the main ethnic Albanian party, called on EC countries to postpone recognition of Macedonia until changes had been made to the constitution acknowledging the Albanians as a 'constituent nation' together with the Slav Macedonians.[176] In the absence of such a change, Ibrahimi said, the PDP would be forced to demand the creation of an autonomous province in the predominantly Albanian region of western Macedonia.[177] The EC was hardly to blame for the country's ethnic polarisation. Indeed, in important respects its recognition policy can be credited with inducing the government to adopt measures to ensure the rights of its national minorities. But at the same time it is fair to say that EC foot-dragging provided the Albanians with a lever that, however justified its use, threatened to undermine the already weak foundations of this new state.

Kosovo deserves mention, finally, for the questions it raises about the EC's differential treatment of the Yugoslav republics as sole candidates for recognition in relation to the other territories of former

---

[174] 'Human Rights in the Former Yugoslav Republic of Macedonia', 6(1) *Helsinki Watch* (1994), 7. In the end a fifteen-year residency requirement was adopted, which the OSCE high commissioner on minorities, Max van der Stoel, found to be still too high. He recommended a reduction to five years. See *The Role of the High Commissioner on National Minorities in OSCE Conflict Prevention: An Introduction* (The Hague: Foundation on Inter-Ethnic Relations, 1997), p. 58.

[175] Hugh Poulton, 'The Albanians of Macedonia', in *The Southern Balkans* (London: Minority Rights Group, 1994), pp. 25–31.

[176] 'Minority Threatens Macedonia Split', *The Guardian*, 17 November 1992.

[177] The Albanians held an unofficial referendum earlier, in January 1992, in which they claimed that more than 90 per cent of all Albanians participated with over 99 per cent voting in favour of territorial and political autonomy. See Minorities Rights Group (Hugh Poulton), 'Minorities in Southeast Europe: Inclusion and Exclusion' (London: Minority Rights Group, 1998), p. 26.

Yugoslavia.[178] Long considered to be one of the Balkans' most dangerous flashpoints, Serbia's Albanian-majority province had for many years
defied the odds and managed to avoid the kind of conflagration that had
engulfed the regions to its north. A combination of repressive measures
by Belgrade and a campaign of non-violent resistance by the Kosovo
Albanian leadership had kept a lid on unrest for nearly eight years since
the break-up of Yugoslavia. That delicate balance was severely upset,
however, when on 28 February 1998 Belgrade launched the first in a
series of large-scale offensives against the ethnic Albanian population
that, in March the following year, prompted a massive NATO air campaign against Yugoslavia that left Kosovo a *de facto* international
protectorate only nominally under Belgrade's sovereign authority.[179]

Because the Badinter Commission had concluded in December 1991
that Yugoslavia's republics alone qualified for recognition, Kosovo was
never a candidate under the EC's guidelines. Until 1989 Kosovo had
been one of two autonomous provinces of Serbia (the other being
Vojvodina) which, however, enjoyed virtually all the prerogatives of a
republic, including its own constitution, government, courts and national bank, and an equal voice within the collective federal presidency.[180] Then in March 1989 Serbia essentially abolished Kosovo's
autonomy, precipitating a crisis that hastened the collapse of Yugoslavia.
Were it not for an arcane constitutional principle Kosovo might very well
have been a republic. The architects of the Yugoslav federal system had
reasoned in 1943, however, that the status of republic should be reserved
for nations (*narodi*) as opposed to nationalities (*narodnosti*) – the former
having their principal homeland inside Yugoslavia and the latter outside
Yugoslavia.[181] The Kosovo Albanians were thus a nationality because
they presumably had their homeland in Albania – a curious policy, it
might seem, given the concerns about irredentism that such an approach
would have seemed to encourage. Although a communist-era distinction, it was one that suited the EC and ultimately the international

---

[178] The following section draws on the author's 'International Diplomacy and the Crisis in
Kosovo', 74 *International Affairs* (1998), 745–61.

[179] For a discussion of the international administration of Kosovo, see Richard Caplan,
International Governance of War-Torn Territories: Rule and Reconstruction (Oxford:
Oxford University Press, 2005).

[180] *The Constitution of the Socialist Federal Republic of Yugoslavia* (Belgrade: The Secretariat
of the Federal Assembly Information Service, 1974).

[181] Frits W. Hondius, *The Yugoslav Community of Nations* (The Hague: Mouton, 1968),
ch. 1. The term 'nationality' was preferred to 'minority', which was considered officially
to be a pejorative denomination. See Zoran Pajic, 'The Former Yugoslavia', in Hugh
Miall (ed.), *Minority Rights in Europe* (London: RIIA/Pinter Publishers, 1994), p. 63.

community well. For it allowed a line to be drawn between entities whose independence would be legitimately recognised and those whose independence would not, at a time when it was thought that some regulation of state fragmentation was necessary lest the 'scourge of tribalism', as *The Economist* put it, be allowed to undermine world order.[182] Yet, as we have seen in Chapter 2, the EC was clearly innovating; there was no precedent for determining statehood on this basis. Nor was it obvious that the republic/province distinction was the most relevant one for the purpose of making such an important determination, particularly since a country's administrative boundaries might be subject to almost arbitrary change.[183] Yet as a consequence of this decision, the EC refused to consider the request for recognition as an independent state that the Kosovo authorities submitted in December 1991 along with the Yugoslav republics.[184]

A further sidelining of Kosovo occurred with the actual mechanics of EC recognition. The Kosovo Albanians, it was seen earlier, were one of the target populations whose status the EC was seeking to enhance with its requirements for the adoption of provisions for minority rights on the part of the republic authorities. In fact, the version of the Carrington draft convention dated 23 October 1991 contained the further requirement that the 'republics shall apply fully and in good faith the provisions existing prior to 1990 for autonomous provinces' – an obvious reference to the autonomy of Kosovo and Vojvodina that Serbia had revoked.[185] But in an effort to gain Milošević's acceptance of the accord, Lord Carrington made an extraordinary concession and eliminated this requirement from the subsequent version of the convention.[186] And when

[182] 'Playing as One?' *The Economist*, 29 June 1991.
[183] Consider Karelia, which was a constituent republic of the Soviet Union from 1940 to 1956 when its status was downgraded to that of an autonomous republic in the Russian Federation. Had this not occurred, Rein Müllerson observes, the Karelians would have had a claim to independent statehood every bit as strong as that of the Ukrainians or Byelorussians at the time of the Soviet Union's collapse in 1991. See Rein Müllerson, *International Law, Rights and Politics* (London: LSE/Routledge, 1994), p. 79.
[184] Letter dated 21 December 1991 by the government of the Republic of Kosovo to the extraordinary EPC ministerial meeting in Brussels, reprinted in Academy of Sciences of the Republic of Albania, Institute of History (ed.), *The Truth on Kosova* (Tirana: Encyclopaedia Publishing House, 1993), pp. 341–3.
[185] Treaty Provisions for the Convention, Article 2.C.6 in Report of the Secretary-General Pursuant to Paragraph 3 of Security Council Resolution 713 (1991), UN Doc. S/23169, 25 October 1991, Annex VII.
[186] Treaty Provisions for the Convention [4 November 1991], ch. 2 in David Owen, *Balkan Odyssey* CD-ROM, academic edition, version 1.1 (London: Apple/electric company, 1995). For a discussion of this point, see Hans-Heinrich Wrede, '"Friendly Concern" – Europe's Decision-making on the Recognition of Croatia and Slovenia', 4(3) *Oxford International Review* (1993), 32.

in April 1996 the EC, now the European Union, decided finally to extend recognition to the Federal Republic of Yugoslavia (FRY), consisting of Serbia and Montenegro, it dispensed with the weaker requirement of a 'special status' for the Kosovo Albanians altogether. The EU merely noted at the time that it 'considers' that improved relations between the FRY and the international community will depend on, among other things, a 'constructive approach' by the FRY to the granting of autonomy for Kosovo.[187]

These concessions were a profound disappointment to the Kosovo Albanians. But the gravest disappointment came with the Dayton negotiations in November 1995, culminating in the signing of the General Framework Agreement for Peace in Bosnia and Herzegovina, which formally ended the war there. It had been evident to many analysts throughout the war that a lasting peace for the region would require a comprehensive approach to the issue of national minorities – one that took account of the problems of minorities across all of the former Yugoslavia. Both the Hague conference and its successor, the London conference, reflected this imperative with their working groups on ethnic and national minorities. Although the peace plans conceived in the interim (Vance–Owen, Owen–Stoltenberg, Contact Group) failed to address wider concerns, it was hoped that some attempt would be made to do so at Dayton. And, indeed, agreements were reached at Dayton concerning regional arms control, regional confidence-building measures, and the status of Eastern Slavonia – the remaining Serb-controlled enclave of Croatia.[188] But Kosovo never made it on to the agenda at Dayton for three reasons. First, it was felt that there was simply too much to negotiate already. Other critical issues for that matter, including the continued influence of indicted war criminals, were hardly addressed at all.[189] Second, no one wanted to alienate Milošević, the 'peacemaker' who had forced the Bosnian Serbs to accept the compromises necessary for the Dayton agreement and whose continued cooperation was thought necessary to ensure successful implementation of the accord.[190] Finally, in the absence of war in Kosovo it was thought that there was no

---

[187] 'Presidency Statement on Behalf of the European Union Concerning the Member States' Recognition of the Federal Republic of Yugoslavia', 9–10 April 1996 (Rome and Brussels), *Bulletin of the European Union* 4–1996, § 1.4.7.

[188] Anthony Borden and Drago Hedl, 'How the Bosnians Were Broken: 21 Days at Dayton', *War Report* No. 39 (February/March 1996), pp. 32–3.

[189] Pauline Neville-Jones, 'Dayton, IFOR and Alliance Relations in Bosnia', 38(4) *Survival* (1996–7), 58–9. Neville-Jones was leader of the British delegation at Dayton.

[190] For a view of Milošević as the linchpin of the diplomatic process, see the reminiscences of Richard Holbrooke, the US envoy and chief architect of Dayton: 'The Road to

urgent need to deal with the question. In this respect Ibrahim Rugova, the Kosovo Albanian leader, had arguably become the victim of his own success.

For more than six years since he first assumed the leadership of Kosovo with overwhelming support in unofficial elections in 1992, Rugova steered the province of nearly 2 million Albanians peacefully through some of its hardest times.[191] The situation in Kosovo – the poorest region of the former Yugoslavia – had always been difficult but under Milošević conditions became dire. New laws passed in 1989 made it a crime for Albanians to buy or sell property without special permission of the authorities – just one in a series of measures designed to shore up the position of the small Serb minority there (numbering less than 200,000 or 10 per cent of the population). Then tens of thousands of Albanians were dismissed from their jobs in state-owned firms. Students were barred from entering university buildings and a new curriculum – using Serbian language and Serbian versions of history – was introduced. Meanwhile, arbitrary arrest and police violence directed towards Albanians became routine practices, earning Kosovo distinction as the region with some of the worst human rights violations in all of Europe.[192] Rugova countered this policy of concerted repression with one of Gandhian non-violent resistance, encouraging the development of a vast parallel society of Albanian-run political, cultural, educational, health and media structures.[193] By eschewing violence Rugova calculated that he would avoid provoking the Serb authorities into open conflict and that he would gradually gain the support of the international community for Kosovo's independence.

Rugova's strategy had indeed been an effective one for keeping the peace. Milošević, who could easily have had Rugova imprisoned at any time for the commission of crimes against the state, tolerated Rugova's non-violent resistance precisely because it kept the Albanians quiet. The strategy also won Rugova plaudits from the international community. But plaudits and support for one's objectives are two very different

Sarajevo', *The New Yorker*, 21 and 28 October 1996, pp. 88–104. Holbrooke maintains that some effort was made at Dayton to persuade Milošević of the need to restore the rights of the Kosovo Albanians. See Holbrooke, *To End a War*, p. 357.

[191] For a discussion of Kosovo under Rugova, see Noel Malcolm, *Kosovo: A Short History* (London: Macmillan, 1998), ch. 17.

[192] Helsinki Watch, *Human Rights Abuses in Kosovo, 1990–1992* (New York: Human Rights Watch, 1992), passim; Minority Rights Group, 'Kosovo: Oppression of Ethnic Albanians' (London: Minority Rights Group, November 1992).

[193] Tihomir Loza, 'Kosovo Albanians: Closing the Ranks', *Transitions*, May 1998, pp. 16–37.

things. And the international community made it very clear that it would not support an independent Kosovo because it would not support secession and a redrawing of international borders that might awaken latent or historical claims elsewhere in the region. 'Rugova should know by now that independence is not an option', Robert Gelbard, Clinton's special envoy, stated emphatically in March 1998 – a view that would be echoed again and again by European officials.[194]

To countless Kosovo Albanians, Dayton had already demonstrated the limits of international support – and, by extension, of Rugova's own effectiveness.[195] Rugova's non-violent approach seemed to be producing no tangible results; it did not even earn him a seat at the table. (The only real achievement would come in September 1996, when Rugova would secure a pledge from Milošević to allow the return of Albanian students to the schools and universities from which they had been ousted – a pledge that Milošević subsequently failed to honour.)[196] Meanwhile, in neighbouring BiH, the Albanians observed, the international community had shown a willingness to ratify the redrawing of boundaries achieved by force. It did not matter that the analogy was an imperfect one: Dayton had established a separate Bosnian Serb entity, Republika Srpska, but it was not allowed actually to secede from BiH.[197] And the international community was committed, in principle at least, to the reintegration of BiH. Nevertheless, the conclusion many Albanians drew from the Dayton proceedings, in the words of Veton Surroi, editor-in-chief of the Pristina daily *Koha Ditore*, was that 'ethnic territories have legitimacy' and that 'international attention can only be obtained through war'.[198] In a manner reminiscent of the commencement of the *intifada* in 1987, when the Palestinians in the Occupied Territories perceived that they, too, were slipping from the agenda of regional and international concerns, Kosovo's Albanians increasingly lost faith in the patient ways of their leadership and gravitated towards armed struggle.

---

[194] Cited in International Crisis Group, 'Kosovo Spring', *ICG Balkans Report* (Brussels: International Crisis Group, 20 March 1998), p. 42.

[195] Fabian Schmidt, 'Teaching the Wrong Lesson in Kosovo', *Transition*, 12 July 1996, pp. 37–9.

[196] Stefan Troebst, *Conflict in Kosovo: Failure of Prevention?* ECMI Working Paper No. 1 (Flensburg, Germany: European Centre for Minority Issues, 1998), pp. 76–8.

[197] Articles I.2 and III.2(a) of the Constitution of Bosnia and Herzegovina. General Framework Agreement for Peace in Bosnia and Herzegovina, Annex 4, in *Bosnia and Herzegovina: Essential Texts*, revised and updated edition (Brussels: Office of the High Representative, May 1997).

[198] Veton Surroi, 'The Albanian National Question: The Post-Dayton Pay-off', *War Report* No. 41 (May 1996), p. 25.

It is this reservoir of disillusionment that explains the growing support among Albanians for the militant separatist Kosovo Liberation Army or UÇK (Ushtria Çlirimtare e Kosovës) from 1997 – not only in the province but in southern Serbia and Macedonia as well. Whereas Rugova's strategy appeared to be yielding no political dividends, the UÇK succeeded in waging a series of attacks on Serbian police stations and Yugoslav army sites that by July 1998 had left the clandestine organisation in 'soft control' of roughly 30 per cent of Kosovo's territory. Serb counterattacks – in many cases resulting in the destruction of entire villages and producing large numbers of civilian casualties – only generated more support for the UÇK. Adem Demaçi, popularly known as Kosovo's Nelson Mandela and head of the second-largest political party in the province at the time, spoke for many of his compatriots in mid-March 1998 when he announced, 'I will not condemn the tactics of the Kosovo Liberation Army because the path of non-violence has gotten us nowhere . . . The Kosovo Liberation Army is fighting for our freedom.'[199]

An important consequence of international diplomacy over the past decade, then, has arguably been to radicalise the Kosovo Albanians. And while the EU, and the international community generally, sought to respond with greater resolve to the upsurge in violence in Kosovo from February 1998, culminating in the NATO air campaign one year later, Milošević was abetted by the fact that, paradoxically, he and the major powers shared some of the same fundamental aims. Like Milošević, the international community has been opposed to independence for Kosovo, although for different reasons. EU member states and the United States – the chief architects of the Dayton agreement – have been concerned that the establishment of an independent Kosovo would make it easier for the forces of separation to triumph over those of integration in BiH and that the fragile peace they have constructed there would be shattered. More serious still, as many states see it, is the danger that an independent Kosovo would destabilise neighbouring Macedonia where the Albanian minority, unhappy with its status, might be encouraged to pursue more radical options – including a unilateral declaration of autonomy or even union with Kosovo. Finally, there is the concern that an independent Kosovo will serve as a positive example for the numerous self-determination movements bent on separation elsewhere in Europe. Milošević and the international community, therefore, had a common interest in defeating the forces of militant separatism in

---

[199] *International Herald Tribune*, 14–15 March 1998.

Kosovo, although they disagreed about the means to be employed and the framework for a possible solution.[200] Yet as a result of these shared interests, the major powers have been reluctant to pursue measures that would weaken Belgrade's hold on Kosovo altogether, even in the wake of the mass atrocities committed by Belgrade against the Kosovo Albanian population during the eleven weeks of NATO bombing. UN Security Council Resolution 1244, which provides the legal basis for an interim settlement of the Kosovo question, was unambiguous in its re-affirmation of 'the commitment of all Member States to the sovereignty and territorial integrity of the Federal Republic of Yugoslavia'.[201]

EC/EU policy to date has been predicated on the assumption that recognition of Kosovo statehood could and must be withheld in the interest of regional and international order. Yet even when faced with such discouraging signals, the Kosovo Albanians' determination to achieve independence has proved to be irrepressible. In the absence of a rights-respecting leadership in Serbia, moreover, persistent EU opposition to Kosovo independence has had the effect of facilitating Belgrade's violent assertion of control there – until March 1999, at least – while encouraging the Albanians to eschew passive resistance in favour of armed struggle.

The role that EC recognition played in the wars of Yugoslav dissolution has been poorly understood. Broadly speaking, the claims with respect to its negative impact on the violent conflict have been greatly overstated. The prospect of recognition played no significant role in Slovenia's and Croatia's determination to initiate and sustain their campaigns for independence and therefore bears little responsibility for the first phase of the war. In Croatia, recognition, together with the deployment of UN peacekeepers, may even have had a mitigating effect. Only in BiH is there any relationship between the granting of recognition and an intensification of hostilities. But in that case it is doubtful that non-recognition or delayed recognition would have prevented the eruption of generalised violence since Bosnian Serb aspirations for an ethnically homogeneous state entity could not be realised without resort to violence. Indeed delayed recognition and non-recognition did little to improve the strategic climate in Macedonia and Kosovo; to some degree it made the climate worse. This is not to suggest that recognition

---

[200] For a discussion of the last attempt at a diplomatic solution prior to the NATO air campaign, see Marc Weller, 'The Rambouillet Conference on Kosovo', 75 *International Affairs* (1999), 211–51.
[201] UN Security Council Res 1244, 10 June 1999.

– and the EC's distinctive approach in particular – offered a panacea. Yet, in a number of cases, EC recognition certainly created opportunities for conflict prevention, attenuation and resolution that the international community did not exploit.

The EC's strategic use of recognition in Yugoslavia provides only limited experience from which to draw conclusions about the possible value of political conditionality as an instrument of conflict management. Historical precedents may be of some relevance – the League of Nations system in particular – and they are therefore deserving of re-examination in the light of the EC's experiences. But the current context differs in important respects from the conditions that prevailed after the First World War. Among other things, the European integration process today offers distinct opportunities to reinforce the EC's goals in the Balkans – through the disbursal of aid and in the admission of states to the various antechambers of the European Union. The renewable character of these opportunities bears some resemblance to another use of political conditionality altogether: as part of the EC's and other states' development assistance programmes. It is these experiences that we will now consider for what they suggest about the possible utility of conditional recognition in support of strategic aims.

5   Political conditionality and conflict management

The EC's policy of conditional recognition, we have seen, represents a significant departure from legal thinking and historic state practice as well as a novel approach to conflict management. It is not, however, the first time that conditionality has been used in support of political aims. For more than two decades, states and multilateral organisations have been employing political conditionality in their relations with developing countries, often in pursuit of objectives akin to those of the EC in Yugoslavia, such as the promotion of human rights and, more recently, democratisation and 'good governance'. Indeed, since the 1970s the EC/EU itself has used and continues to use political conditionality as part of its trade and aid programmes, imposing on recipient states requirements relating to their domestic political structures that in many ways are not unlike the requirements it stipulated for the new state authorities in Yugoslavia.

This final chapter examines these parallel uses of political conditionality for what they suggest about the potential for, and the limitations of, conditional recognition as an instrument of conflict management. It charts the evolution of these policy initiatives and the thinking behind them – politically conditioned aid in particular – and explores the similarities they bear to the EC's use of conditional recognition. It also looks at how effective political conditionality has been and identifies factors that may account for its successes and shortcomings. Finally, it attempts to draw lessons from these experiences for the use of conditional recognition in support of conflict mitigation and prevention. Although aid and trade conditionality may not seem immediately germane to the subject at hand, these experiences, it will become apparent, provide a useful optic through which to analyse the possible utility of conditional recognition.

Prior uses of conditionality

Conditionality – the tying of aid, trade or other concessions to prescribed changes in a recipient's behaviour – has long been a part of international relations. Indeed, if one interprets concessions broadly enough to

146

include the cessation of violent attacks by one state against another, contingent upon the target state's compliance with the assailant's demands, then the earliest recorded histories of inter-'state' relations reveal conditionality at work.[1] Such extreme forms of pressure, however, are perhaps more accurately described as 'strategic coercion'.[2]

The conditions that donors may attach to concessions will vary depending in part on whether the considerations that underpin the conditions are political or economic. Yet even ostensibly economic conditionality may be motivated by political concerns. The economic conditions associated with US aid to Western Europe under the Marshall Plan, for instance, can be said to have had fundamentally political underpinnings. One of the requirements for delivery of Marshall aid was that the recipient countries agree to administer the funds jointly.[3] This coordinated approach arguably made more sense economically than would have a series of bilateral arrangements, since it allowed for better responsiveness to relative trade and payments deficits among the participating states, but it was also seen to offer important political advantages. For one thing, a coordinated approach meant a *European*-led recovery, which was critical to winning support from a US Congress wary of prolonged US entanglement on the continent after the war. Moreover, it was only in the context of an integrated Europe (and a continued US presence) that it was possible to allay European concerns about the resuscitation of the German economy.[4]

There have been other, more overtly political uses of conditionality in recent history. In the early 1960s, West Germany, concerned lest the partition of Germany become permanent, tied its aid to non-recognition of East Germany by recipient states. This policy – an inversion, in effect, of conditional recognition – did not work because other donor states were unwilling to follow suit.[5] Similarly political, and evidently no more

---

[1] Herodotus's 'Persian History' (*c.* 442 BC), one of the earliest surviving accounts of international relations, is filled with many such examples.

[2] The threatened use of force would seem to distinguish strategic coercion from other forms of conditionality. See Alexander George, *Forceful Persuasion: Coercive Diplomacy as an Alternative to War* (Washington, DC: United States Institute of Peace Press, 1991); and Lawrence Freedman, *Strategic Coercion: Concepts and Cases* (Oxford: Oxford University Press, 1998), ch. 1.

[3] Derek W. Urwin, *The Community of Europe: A History of European Integration Since 1945* (London: Longman, 1991), pp. 18–19.

[4] Melvyn P. Leffler, 'The United States and the Strategic Dimensions of the Marshall Plan', 12 *Diplomatic History* (1988), 290, 305.

[5] See Peter P. Waller, 'Aid and Conditionality: The Case of Germany, with Particular Reference to Kenya', in Olav Stokke (ed.), *Aid and Political Conditionality* (London: Frank Cass, 1995), p. 112. Taiwan has pursued a similar policy, with no greater success, to discourage recognition of the People's Republic of China.

successful, were US efforts to liberalise Soviet emigration policies in the mid-1970s. The Jackson–Vanik amendment to the Trade Act of 1974 withheld most-favoured-nation status and US credits from the Soviet Union as long as Moscow denied its citizens – Soviet Jews in particular – the right to emigrate.[6] The Soviet Union responded by reducing Jewish emigration – from 20,628 in 1974 to 13,221 in 1975 – rather than raising it. (Senator Henry Jackson, the sponsor of the legislation, had expected an increase to 60,000 Jewish emigrants a year.)[7] Trade with the United States, the presumed pressure point, was apparently not as important to Moscow as had been assumed, accounting as it did for less than 5 per cent of total Soviet hard currency trade. Moreover, Moscow was able to compensate for the loss of US technology and credits through increased trade with Western Europe and Japan.

Human rights, a fundamental concern behind the Jackson–Vanik initiative, have been the principal focus of politically conditioned aid measures since the end of the Second World War. Emblematic of this concern, more broadly, was the legislation passed by the US Congress in 1975 – the Harkin Amendment to the Foreign Assistance Act of 1961 – that requires the US government to condition economic aid on a recipient country's respect for human rights. Under this provision, no US assistance may be provided to the government of any country that engages in a consistent pattern of gross violations of human rights.[8] These same concerns were extended to US participation in multilateral aid organisations. Section 701 of the International Financial Assistance Act of 1977 mandates US representatives in multilateral banks 'to advance the cause of human rights, including by seeking to channel assistance towards countries other than those whose governments engage in gross violations of internationally recognized human rights'.[9] Neither of these measures, however, has been implemented in a consistent manner.[10]

The United States has not been alone in seeking to enhance the protection of human rights through conditioned aid. In 1984 Norway

---

[6] David P. Forsythe, 'Congress and Human Rights in U. S. Foreign Policy: The Fate of General Legislation', 9 *Human Rights Quarterly* (1987), 400–3.

[7] George Perkovich, 'Soviet Jewry and American Foreign Policy', 5 *World Policy Journal* (1988), 456.

[8] Joan M. Nelson with Stephanie J. Eglinton, *Encouraging Democracy: What Role for Conditioned Aid?* Policy Essay No. 4 (Washington, DC: Overseas Development Council, 1992), p. 27.

[9] Cited in *ibid*.

[10] See David Carleton and Michael Stohl, 'The Role of Human Rights in U. S. Foreign Assistance Policy: A Critique and Reappraisal', 31 *American Journal of Political Science* (1987), 1002–18.

indicated that it would cut off aid 'when the government of the recipient country takes part in, tolerates or directly executes [persistent or gross and systematic] violations of human rights'.[11] Canada, similarly, has denied aid to countries that contravene the Universal Declaration of Human Rights.[12] And British Prime Minister Margaret Thatcher sought to incorporate explicit human rights conditions into the criteria for the allocation of European aid to Third World countries that were party to the Lomé Convention when the treaty was being renegotiated in 1984. Her efforts, however, were unsuccessful. As Christopher Clapham observes, 'Regarded with horror by the African, Caribbean and Pacific states which adhered to the Convention, and receiving little support from most of her European Community partners, the attempt was watered down into a pious and unenforceable aspiration.'[13] West European states were more willing to adopt punitive trade and investment policies designed to pressure South Africa to abolish apartheid – policies that this time the Thatcher government opposed.

These latter uses of conditionality are examples of what is known as 'negative conditionality' because they entail a suspension or termination of benefits in reaction to non-compliance by a target state. 'Positive conditionality', by contrast, is characterised by the delivery of benefits as a reward for the performance of prescribed behaviour.[14] Conditional recognition – the promise of diplomatic recognition in exchange for fulfilling certain criteria – is a form of positive conditionality. On the whole the EC has tended to favour positive over negative conditionality and in 1992 even formalised this preference. The European Commission declared at the time: 'The Community approach is geared to the principle that international cooperation must focus especially on positive measures providing incentives for the promotion of democracy and human rights; the use of sanctions should be considered only if all other means have failed.'[15] One reason why the EC/EU has tended to prefer

[11] From a 1984 White Paper cited in Katarina Tomaševski, *Between Sanctions and Elections: Aid Donors and their Human Rights Performance* (London: Pinter, 1997), p. 24.

[12] Mark Robinson, 'Will Political Conditionality Work?' 24(1) *IDS Bulletin* (1993), 59.

[13] Christopher Clapham, 'Political Conditionality and Structures of the African State', 25(2) *Africa Insight* (1995), 93. By the late 1980s, however, the Community was united in pressing for the inclusion of references to human rights in the Lomé convention. See Karen E. Smith, 'The Use of Political Conditionality in the EU's Relations with Third Countries: How Effective?' 3 *European Foreign Affairs Review* (1998), 262.

[14] Waller, 'Aid and Conditionality', p. 126.

[15] European Commission, 'Report from the Commission to the Council and the European Parliament on the Implementation in 1993 of the Resolution of the Council and of the Member States Meeting in the Council on Human Rights, Democracy and

positive measures to negative sanctions is that these measures are considered to be less disruptive of donor–recipient relations. Another reason is that EC/EU member states have managed to achieve greater consistency in their application of positive as opposed to negative measures – precisely because they have been wary of disruption.[16] The EC's performance is discussed in greater detail below.

Despite its widespread use in the post-Second World War period, political conditionality has tended to be *ad hoc* and highly selective. This is largely because of the nature and the weight of geopolitical considerations that influenced aid giving and other concessions during the Cold War. Although ideological and strategic considerations have long influenced decisions about aid, and continue to do so, these priorities were especially pronounced in the Cold War years. The democratic complexion of a recipient state, however relevant it would later seem to economic development, social justice and regional stability, was subordinated to the imperative of building and maintaining alliances at the time of the US–Soviet contest. Thus Jimmy Carter, who more than any other Cold War-era US president sought to introduce a degree of consistency to US aid policies based on human rights considerations, was severely constrained in his efforts by geopolitics. Carter succeeded in cutting security assistance to several authoritarian regimes, especially in Latin America, but he was unable to reduce support, or only nominally, to others, notably the Philippines, South Korea, Iran and Zaire.[17] Jeane Kirkpatrick, later to become US ambassador to the United Nations under Ronald Reagan, legitimated US support for allied military dictatorships with her famous distinction between authoritarian and totalitarian (communist) regimes – the former alone, she argued, exhibiting a capacity for democratic transformation.[18]

On the other hand, most *systematic* conditionality – systematic because it has been applied in both a more methodical and more overt fashion –

Development, Adopted on 28 November 1991', COM(94) 42 final, 23 February 1994, p. 11.

[16] Demetrios James Marantis, 'Human Rights, Democracy, and Development: The European Community Model', 7 *Harvard Human Rights Journal* (1994), 12–16.

[17] Stephen B. Cohen, 'Conditioning U.S. Security Assistance on Human Rights Practices', 76 *American Journal of International Law* (1982), 256–61.

[18] See Jeane Kirkpatrick, *Dictatorships and Double Standards: Rationalism and Reason in Politics* (New York: American Enterprise Institute/Simon & Schuster, 1982), pp. 23–52. Henry Kissinger offered a similar analysis at the time: 'modern authoritarianism is a vestige of traditional personal rule. This is why some authoritarian governments have been able to evolve into democracies and why no totalitarian state has ever done so.' See his *Years of Upheaval* (London: Weidenfeld & Nicolson and Michael Joseph, 1982), p. 313.

has until fairly recently been economic in orientation. The first generation of systematic conditionality has its origins in the severe economic crisis in large parts of the Third World at the end of the 1970s. Declining official aid flows and increased indebtedness, together with deteriorating terms of trade, combined to produce a desperate economic situation for many Third World states, particularly in Latin America and sub-Saharan Africa.[19] Many poor countries, it was feared, might default on their debts to Northern countries. The crisis reached such proportions as to threaten the integrity of the international financial system. With commercial banks unwilling to extend additional credits, the World Bank and, to a lesser extent, the International Monetary Fund (IMF) were asked to step in to assist.

The multilateral financial institutions identified the roots of the crisis as structural in nature. As they saw it, excessive and unproductive spending by Third World governments was generating unmanageable budget deficits and fuelling inflation. Overvalued currencies were seen to be favouring 'wasteful' consumer imports rather than income-generating exports. And price controls that kept the price of food low for urban consumers were discouraging rural producers, farmers especially. The World Bank thus agreed to lend new monies to these troubled states but only on the condition that the recipient countries restructure their economies – through import and exchange liberalisation, currency devaluation, the elimination of price biases, the privatisation of government enterprises and deficit reduction.[20] Thus were established the first structural adjustment loans (SALs).[21] By the latter half of the 1980s, sixty-one countries had been recipients of World Bank loans conditioned on economic reforms, and roughly one-third of the Bank's total lending was made up of such loans.[22]

---

[19] On declining aid flows, see Joan Edelman Spero, *The Politics of International Economic Relations*, 4th edn (New York: St. Martin's Press, 1990), pp. 162–4; on increased Third World indebtedness, see Altaf Gauhar, 'Arab Petrodollars: Dashed Hope for a New Economic Order', 4 *World Policy Journal* (1997), 443–64; on the Third World economic crisis generally, see Bernard D. Nossiter, *The Global Struggle for More: Third World Conflicts with the Rich Nations* (New York: Harper & Row, 1987).

[20] The World Bank identified these reform priorities in its 1981 report *Accelerated Development in Sub-Saharan Africa: An Agenda for Action*. For an overview of this reform agenda, see Peter Gibbon, 'The World Bank and the New Politics of Aid', in Stokke, *Aid and Political Conditionality*, pp. 38–40.

[21] SALs, in fact, had an earlier incarnation in the IMF's stabilisation (or austerity) programmes of the early 1970s. See Cheryl Payer, *Lent and Lost: Foreign Credit and Third World Development* (London: Zed Books, 1991), ch. 12.

[22] Joan M. Nelson, 'Good Governance: Democracy and Conditional Economic Aid', in Paul Mosely (ed.), *Development Finance and Policy Reform* (London: Macmillan, 1992), p. 311.

To say that economic conditionality was more systematic than other uses of conditionality at the time is not to suggest that it was non-ideological. The prescribed reforms clearly reflected a market-oriented, neo-liberal perspective that, to the minds of some critics, served the West's interests (particularly those of the exposed commercial banks) better than they did the interests of Third World states or poor people in those states.[23] But decisions about whether to extend assistance were taken on the basis of considerations that were not as *overtly* political as were those of many bilateral aid programmes. Thus, for instance, because Chile's economic policies were essentially sound from the Bank's standpoint, the World Bank continued to lend to Chile throughout the Pinochet dictatorship despite objections from several European countries to Chile's poor human rights performance. At the same time the Bank refused to lend to Idi Amin's Uganda, which had an appalling human rights record, but for administrative rather than political reasons: the civil war in the country made it impossible for the Bank to carry out an effective programme. Meanwhile, communist Hungary joined the Bank in 1982 – at the height of the second Cold War – and by the mid-1980s was also a recipient of structural adjustment loans.[24] 'The political regime, whether it is democracy, whether it is authoritarian, whether it is a military dictatorship, is nothing the Bank does concern itself with', Michael Stevens, a senior World Bank official, would later explain. 'But the process by which power is exercised in a country to manage its economic and social resources and the capacity of governments to design effective government programmes and policies are areas that the Bank is concerned about.'[25] Stevens overstates the Bank's apolitical posture – leading states have sometimes succeeded in blocking loans for political reasons[26] – but, again, it is fair to say that political

---

[23] See, in this regard, David Felix, 'Latin America's Debt Crisis: Overselling the Market Solution', 7 *World Policy Journal* (1990), 733–71.

[24] For many years Soviet bloc countries were virtually excluded from World Bank lending because of Moscow's refusal to allow its allies to be members of the Bank. See Spero, *The Politics of International Economic Relations*, pp. 306–7.

[25] Michael Stevens, 'The World Bank and the New Political and Economic Order: The Political Conditionalities', paper presented at a conference on 'The New Political Conditionalities of Development Assistance: Human Rights, Democracy and Disarmament' organised by the Vienna Institute for Development and Cooperation (VIDC), 23–25 April 1992. Report Series 2/92, p. 58 (hereafter VIDC conference).

[26] From 1983, for instance, the United States blocked several World Bank loans to the revolutionary Sandinista government of Nicaragua. See Hazel Smith, *Nicaragua: Self-Determination and Survival* (London: Pluto Press, 1993), p. 253.

considerations have had less bearing on Bank policies than they have had on many national aid programmes.[27]

And yet, despite the Bank's apparent aversion to politics, its experiences with economic conditionality and the lessons it has drawn from those experiences have led it to become increasingly preoccupied with questions of governance, thus contributing to and reinforcing an emergent trend in favour of more systematic policies of political conditionality among donor states in the post-Cold War period – a trend, we will see, that extends to the EC's use of conditional recognition. What explains this shift on the part of the Bank was the gradual realisation, in the absence of a definitive success for structural adjustment, that 'getting the prices right' was a necessary but not a sufficient condition for economic development.[28] The persistence of corruption and inefficiency in the use of public sector resources in recipient states and the absence of an adequate legal infrastructure, among other governance problems, meant that economic reform needed to be accompanied by political reform ('capacity building') if it were to be effective, the Bank reasoned. National leaders had to be more accountable for receipts and expenditures, their transactions more transparent and donor funds better administered. 'None of [our] measures will go far, nor will much external aid be forthcoming, unless governance in Africa improves', the Bank declared in 1989.[29]

In emphasising the importance of good governance, the Bank was not necessarily advocating democratic rule. Its definition of governance ('the manner in which power is exercised in the management of a country's economic and social resources for development')[30] meant that the Bank could still be the broad church that Stevens describes. Indeed some in the development field have gone even further, at times suggesting that

---

[27] There is a statutory basis for this restriction. Article 4, Section 10 of the World Bank's Articles of Agreement limits the Bank to economic activities: 'The Bank and its officers shall not interfere in the political affairs of any member; nor shall they be influenced in their decisions by the political character of the member or members concerned. Only economic considerations shall be relevant to their decisions. . .'

[28] For a negative assessment of the results of structural adjustment lending, see Frances Stewart, 'The Many Faces of Adjustment', in Mosely, *Development Finance and Policy Reform*, pp. 176–231. World Bank officials, naturally, are less disparaging of the performance of SALs. See, for instance, Vittorio Corbo and Stanley Fischer, 'Adjustment Programmes and World Bank Support: Rationale and Main Results', in *ibid.*, pp. 157–75.

[29] World Bank, *Sub-Saharan Africa: From Crisis to Sustainable Growth* (Washington, DC: World Bank, 1989), p. 15. Also, see pp. 60–1, where the Bank attributes much of the blame for Africa's continued economic malaise to a 'crisis of governance'.

[30] World Bank, *Governance and Development* (Washington, DC: World Bank, 1992), p. 1.

authoritarian regimes might be more effective administrators of the bitter pill of structural adjustment. (Chile and the 'Asian Tigers' are often invoked as examples.)[31] With the end of the Cold War, however, many donor states and multilateral organisations began to take a different view, arguing that democracy was a requirement for development. '[T]here is a vital connection, now more widely appreciated, between open, democratic and accountable political systems, individual human rights and effective and equitable operation of economic systems', the Development Assistance Committee of the Organisation for Economic Co-operation and Development (OECD) asserted in 1989 in a manner representative of the new thinking.[32]

Echoes of this new thinking could be heard throughout Europe. Thus Jacques Pellier, the French minister of co-operation and development, in a speech in January 1990 declared that development was not feasible without democracy.[33] Six months later, President François Mitterrand put French African leaders on notice that henceforth France would 'link its financial efforts to the efforts made towards liberty in African countries', although he did not go so far as to say that France would tie aid to specific conditions regarding democratic practice.[34] That same month British Foreign Secretary Douglas Hurd, in an address to the Overseas Development Institute, emphasised 'the need to move away from inefficient, authoritarian models of the past'. 'Economic success', he said, 'depends to a very large extent on effective and honest government, political pluralism . . . observance of the rule of law [and] freer and more open economies . . . Economic and political liberalisation go together.'[35] And in September 1990, the Nordic Ministers of Development Co-operation, meeting at Molde in Norway, issued a communiqué in which they declared, 'The connection between democracy, human rights and sustainable development has become more and more evident . . . It has now been recognised that open democratic systems and respect for

---

[31] See, for instance, H. W. Singer, *Aid Conditionality* (Brighton: Institute of Development Studies, 1994), p. 13: '[I]n some ways authoritarian regimes may be in an even better position to enforce strict adjustment programmes and maintain them through the inevitable initial period of disruption and sacrifice; while fully democratic governments depending on the results of the next election might not be able to afford such a long-term outlook.'

[32] Cited in Olav Stokke, 'Aid and Political Conditionality: Core Issues and State of the Art', in Stokke, *Aid and Political Conditionality*, p. 23.

[33] *Ibid.*, p. 22, fn. 16.

[34] Peter Uvin, '"Do as I Say, Not as I Do": The Limits of Political Conditionality', in Georg Sørensen (ed.), *Political Conditionality* (London: Frank Cass, 1993), p. 66.

[35] 'Prospects for Africa in the 1990s', transcript of speech delivered at the Overseas Development Institute, London, 6 June 1990, pp. 3, 8.

human rights give impetus to efforts to achieve development, economic efficiency and equitable distribution.'[36]

What was surprising about these and the many comparable pronouncements made at the time is that they could not be said to reflect any new consensus among economists and political scientists as to the link between democracy and development – a scepticism that persists to this day. 'There is no systematic evidence that more "democratic" types of regime – in the sense of being popularly elected, politically competitive and having respect for civil and political rights – are more successful in achieving economic growth', John Healey and Mark Robinson observed in their study of democracy and development in sub-Saharan Africa. At the same time, the authors added, 'authoritarian regimes cannot be expected to perform better on these criteria'.[37] Adam Przeworski and Fernando Limongi, in their survey of 139 countries between 1950 and 1990, also found no obvious relationship between democracy, on the one hand, and economic success or failure, on the other.[38] In its own development report for 1991 the World Bank hedged its bets, observing that there was no specific link between the type of regime and rates of growth but conceding that 'dictatorships have proven disastrous for development in many economies'.[39]

---

[36] Cited in Gordon Crawford, 'Promoting Democracy, Human Rights and Good Governance through Development Aid: A Comparative Study of the Policies of Four Northern Donors', Working Paper on Democratization No. 1 (Leeds: Centre for Democratization Studies, University of Leeds, 1996), p. 16.

[37] John Healey and Mark Robinson, *Democracy, Governance and Economic Policy: Sub-Saharan Africa in Comparative Perspective* (London: Overseas Development Institute, 1992), p. 122. For an overview of the debate in the context of sub-Saharan Africa, see 'The Rulers, the Ruled and the African Reality', *The Economist*, 20 September 1997.

[38] Adam Przeworski and Fernando Limongi, 'Democracy and Development', in Axel Hadenius (ed.), *Democracy's Victory and Crisis* (Cambridge: Cambridge University Press, 1997), pp. 163–94. Surjit Bhalla, writing in the same volume, concluded to the contrary that political and civil liberties, together with economic freedom, helped to improve economic performance. See 'Freedom and Economic Growth: A Virtuous Cycle?', in *ibid.*, pp. 195–241.

[39] World Bank, *World Development Report 1991: The Challenge of Development* (Oxford: Oxford University Press, 1991), p. 133. The US Agency for International Development (USAID) exhibited even greater intellectual confusion. In a 1990 report the agency was unambiguous about the relationship between democracy and development: 'Democracy is complementary to and supportive of the transition to market-oriented economies and sustained, broadly based economic development.' USAID, *The Democracy Initiative* (Washington, DC: USAID, December 1990), p. 1. One year later the agency was decidedly more cautious: 'The debate about the relationship between democracy and sustained economic development is substantial, but thus far yields no firm conclusions concerning any direct, causal link between democracy and development.' USAID, *Democracy and Governance* (Washington, DC: USAID, November 1991), pp. 5–6.

Clearly, then, the new-found interest in democratisation – and aid conditionality linked to democratisation – had its basis in something other than undisputed economic analysis. (Of course, donor states were conflating various concerns; it was particular characteristics generally associated with democratic regimes – for instance, their accountability and transparency – rather than democracy itself that had mattered originally to the World Bank.)[40] Indeed, there were several other reasons why donor states were showing a heightened interest in democratisation and associated political goals worldwide.

One reason was that the end of the Cold War meant that Western states – the major aid donors – no longer felt constrained to put traditional security considerations above all others. Absent the Soviet threat, these states no longer found it necessary to support Third World authoritarian regimes simply because they were anti-communist. (Yugoslavia suffered a similar fate because of its declining strategic importance in a unipolar age.) Moreover, the spread of democratic openings throughout the developing world – in Latin America, Eastern Europe, Asia and sub-Saharan Africa – meant that there was an indigenous constituency demanding democratic reform that, as their voices grew louder, became harder to ignore.[41] This is not to suggest, however, that Western states ceased their support for repressive regimes altogether.

Another reason, related to the first, was that with the end of the Cold War many Western foreign assistance programmes seemed costly and unnecessary to the voting public, who, in some countries, especially the United States, tended to be critical of aid levels even in the best of times. Increased concerns about international competitiveness and pressures to reduce government deficits brought renewed calls for cuts in foreign aid.[42] At the same time, global interest groups – more numerous and sophisticated than ever in their campaign efforts – were bringing greater scrutiny to bear on foreign assistance programmes whose Cold War rationale could no longer be easily sustained.[43] Human rights groups such as Amnesty International and Human Rights Watch were particularly active in both mobilising members and lobbying donor

---

[40] The World Bank, too, began to blur these distinctions. In its 1991development report it defined as the aim of development 'to increase the economic, political and civil rights of all people across gender, ethnic groups, religions, races, regions, and countries'. See World Bank, *World Development Report 1991*, p. 31.

[41] Nelson, 'Good Governance', p. 309.

[42] Tomaševski, *Between Sanctions and Elections*, p. 3.

[43] Michael Clough, 'Grass-Roots Policymaking', 73(1) *Foreign Affairs* (1994), 2–7.

governments about recipient countries' human rights records. Western governments were therefore under pressure to provide new justification for aid programmes or to shift the priorities within them. Even the Pentagon established its own Office of Democracy Promotion (later renamed the Office for Foreign Civil-Military Affairs) in an apparent effort to deflect pressures for expenditure cuts.[44]

Finally, the triumph of the West and the perceived failure of the socialist model contributed to the notion, especially prevalent in the United States, of the universal validity of so-called Western values and to the belief, therefore, that worldwide economic and political liberalisation is a good thing in itself.[45] The use of conditionality by the multilateral aid agencies earlier lent legitimacy to what was perceived to be a powerful and potentially effective instrument for this larger purpose. Although states evinced some sensitivity to the dangers of seeking to impose 'alien' Western practices on non-Western cultures,[46] critics in the Third World nonetheless viewed the West's heightened interest in democratisation, human rights and good governance – along with the use of conditionality to promote those goals – as a form of 'neo-neo-colonialism'.[47]

The new political conditionalities

Many Western states fashioned new policies of political conditionality in the immediate aftermath of the Cold War, with Britain among the first EC member states to do so. Prior to 1990 Britain employed no formal political criteria in the allocation of its aid. In June of that year the

[44] Laurence Whitehead, 'Concerning International Support for Democracy in the South', in Robin Luckham and Gordon White (eds.), *Democratization in the South: The Jagged Wave* (Manchester: Manchester University Press, 1996), p. 248.

[45] Many Europeans made the same assumption with respect to their own continent. As Michael Steiner, the German diplomat who served as deputy high representative in Bosnia and Herzegovina until June 1997, describes post-Cold War thinking among his colleagues: 'Our mindset was determined by Francis Fukuyama's *The End of History*. We had a peaceful Europe, and we believed we were entering a new era of common values where everything would be different from the past.' Steiner quoted in 'Don't Fool Around with Principles', *Transitions*, August 1997, p. 38.

[46] In announcing the British government's decision to increase aid for 'good government' nearly two-fold, Lynda Chalker, minister for overseas development, denied that British policy was an attempt to promote Westminster-style democracy. 'Good Government and the Aid Programme', transcript of speech delivered at the Royal Institute of International Affairs, London, 25 June 1991, p. 1.

[47] See, for instance, Samir Amin, 'The Issue of Democracy in the Contemporary Third World', in Barry Gills, Joel Rocamora, and Richard Wilson (eds.), *Low Intensity Democracy: Political Power in the New World Order* (London: Pluto Press, 1993), pp. 59–79.

government announced that it was adopting new measures in support of 'pluralism, public accountability, respect for the rule of law, human rights and market principles' – measures that would rely, in part, on conditionality for their implementation.[48] 'The principle of conditionality has been clearly laid down by the British Government, by the European Community and by the USA', Hurd declared at the time.[49] A further articulation of what Britain termed its 'good government' policy was provided one year later by Lynda Chalker, the minister for overseas development. She identified three elements of the policy: the promotion of 'sound social and economic policies' that are market oriented and private-sector friendly; enhanced 'competence' of governments, including open and accountable practices, pluralism and democracy; and 'respect for human rights and the rule of law'.[50] In subsequent years Britain would reaffirm the promotion of good government as one of its chief objectives, and would maintain that it was taking the quality of government into account in its annual allocations of aid.[51]

Other states announced changes in their development assistance programmes along similar lines. Democracy and human rights were already priority aid concerns in Sweden but the Social Democratic government, in power until 1991, had been opposed to conditionality, preferring dialogue to 'democracy on demand', as Lena Hjelm-Wallén, the minister for international development cooperation, put it.[52] With the coming to power of a centre-right coalition that year, however, Sweden moved to adopt a policy of conditionality, the immediate effects of which were a reduction in aid to Vietnam and a termination of small-scale assistance to Cuba. Denmark, too, incorporated what it called 'negative incentives' in its aid strategy. 'Continued violations of human rights and lack of interest within the programme countries to enter into a dialogue on these issues will be reflected in the extent and character of Danish development assistance', the government announced in 1994.[53] Other countries proclaimed their support for the promotion of human rights, democracy

---

[48] Hurd, 'Prospects for Africa in the 1990s', p. 3.
[49] Cited in Salim Lone, 'Donors Demand Political Reforms', 4(2) *Africa Recovery* (1990), 28.
[50] Chalker, 'Good Government and the Aid Programme', pp. 2–3.
[51] Crawford, 'Promoting Democracy, Human Rights and Good Governance through Development Aid', p. 9.
[52] Cited in Gordon Crawford, 'Promoting Political Reform through Aid Sanctions: Instrumental and Normative Issues', Working Paper on Democratization (Leeds: Centre for Democratization Studies, University of Leeds, 1997), p. 7.
[53] Ministry of Foreign Affairs/Danida, 'A Developing World. Strategy for Danish Development Policy Towards the Year 2000', March 1994, pp. 8, 9–10 cited in Tomaševski, *Between Sanctions and Elections*, p. 27.

and good governance without necessarily embracing conditionality overtly. But it was widely understood, in many cases, that democratic and rights-respecting states would receive more favourable consideration from donors in the allocation of aid.

Much like the economic conditionality that preceded it, but in contrast with earlier uses of political conditionality, the new post–Cold War political conditionalities have tended to be more systematic and less *ad hoc*. Thus we see attempts by some Western states to *institutionalise* their relations with developing countries on the basis of respect for human rights and the promotion of democracy. The EC, for instance, on 28 November 1991 – less than a month before the adoption of its policy of conditional recognition – announced that, henceforth, considerations of human rights and democracy would have a major bearing on the Community's relations with all developing countries. The EC 'will give high priority to a positive approach that stimulates respect for human rights and encourages democracy', the EC's Development Council resolution stated. '[I]n the event of grave and persistent human rights violations or serious interruption of democratic processes', the Council warned, 'the Community and its Member States will consider appropriate responses in the light of the circumstances, guided by objective and equitable criteria.'[54]

It would not be until 1995, however, that the EU would effectively instrumentalise this commitment, with the May 1995 decision by the Development Council to include a suspension mechanism in all of its aid agreements with third countries. That decision resulted in the adoption of amendments to the Lomé Convention in November 1995 that allow for the partial or complete suspension of the convention for any party that fails to fulfil its essential obligations, including respect for human rights and democratic principles.[55] But already in 1991 the EC had begun to introduce changes of a similar nature in its relations with the states of Central and Eastern Europe and the former Soviet Union. The European Bank for Reconstruction and Development (EBRD), established in 1991 with strong EC participation, became the first multilateral lending institution with a statutory requirement to base its loan decisions on the democratic credentials of its recipient countries, among other

---

[54] 'Resolution of the Council and of the Member States Meeting in the Council on Human Rights, Democracy and Development', 28 November 1991, *Bulletin of the European Communities* 11–1991, § 2.3.1.

[55] Smith, 'The Use of Political Conditionality in the EU's Relations with Third Countries', p. 264.

criteria.[56] And in May 1992 the European Council decided that all future cooperation and association agreements between the EC and CSCE states should contain a clause allowing for their suspension in the event that the signatories failed to respect human rights, democratic rule and the principles of the market economy. The trade and cooperation agreements concluded with Albania (1992), the Baltic states (1993) and Slovenia (1993) all contain such a clause.[57]

Not only have the new political conditionalities tended to be more systematic but they have also often been broader in scope, aiming at fairly extensive political and administrative reforms in target countries. Under the revamped German aid programme in 1991, for instance, Bonn's new criteria for development assistance included respect for human rights, popular participation in the political process, observance of the rule of law, a 'market-friendly' approach to economic development and a clear commitment to development on the part of the recipient country.[58] Germany indicated further that it would also take environmental protection and military spending into account when allocating aid.[59] Britain's good government programme was similarly far-reaching, extending to corruption control, freedom of expression, the

---

[56] Stephen D. Krasner, 'Compromising Westphalia', 20(3) *International Security* (1995/96), 132. Article 1 of the 'charter' of the European Bank for Reconstruction and Development requires a commitment to 'the principles of multiparty democracy [and] pluralism' on the part of recipients of Bank funds. Article 38 allows for the suspension of any member who fails to fulfil its obligations to the Bank. See 'Agreement Establishing the European Bank for Reconstruction and Development' (29 May 1990), available at http://www.ebrd.co.uk/about/basics/index.htm.

[57] Smith, 'The Use of Political Conditionality in the EU's Relations with Third Countries', 261. The EC's first three association agreements – signed with Czechoslovakia, Hungary and Poland in December 1991 – did not contain suspension clauses but democratic criteria were an explicit basis for the EC's decision to conclude these agreements.

[58] Klemens Van de Sand, 'New Political Criteria: The German Concept', VIDC conference, p. 53. West Germany had already signalled its support for development aid associated with human rights and democratisation with the Bundestag's adoption of a resolution in 1982, which states:

In its development cooperation, the Federal Republic of Germany regards the implementation of human rights as an essential goal of the federal government . . . [T]hose countries should be especially supported which try to establish democratic structures . . . [I]n states where despotism, intimidation and physical threat characterise the relationship between the governing and the governed, only those projects can be supported which benefit directly the oppressed population.

Cited in Waller, 'Aid and Conditionality', p. 112.

[59] Nelson and Eglinton, *Encouraging Democracy*, p. 17.

strengthening of civil society and the mitigation of gender and racial inequalities, among other objectives.[60]

Not all the initiatives spawned by these policies have relied on conditionality. In many cases where recipient government practices have been inimical to the new policy objectives, donor states have made funds available to local and/or international non-governmental organisations working in the target countries to promote the realisation of these aims. For instance, independent media and human rights organisations in Serbia benefited significantly from funding under these schemes in the 1990s when much official assistance to Belgrade was suspended. These 'circumgovernmental' efforts have also been supported by a vast array of private foundations, such as the Ford Foundation, the Open Society Fund and the MacArthur Foundation in the United States.[61]

How effectively have governments implemented the new political conditionalities? In his analysis of the aid policies of four official donors – the European Union, the United Kingdom, Sweden and the United States – Gordon Crawford found that aid sanctions were applied in twenty-nine country cases in the period between January 1990 and January 1996.[62] The EU and the US used sanctions most often (twenty-two cases each), which Crawford attributes largely to the magnitude of their respective aid schemes. (The EU and the US have programmes in more countries than any other donors apart from the multilateral aid agencies.) Sanctions have involved a partial or total suspension of aid or a termination of assistance altogether. The most common reason offered for aid sanctions in this period, in at least seventeen cases, was the failure to respect democratic principles.[63]

The EU's experience merits closer examination because of its particular relevance to this study.[64] EU sanctions were applied to countries in every region of the developing world: Latin America/Caribbean, the Middle East, Asia and especially sub-Saharan Africa. In the majority of cases the EU chose to suspend development assistance either fully (Burundi, Liberia, Nigeria, Rwanda, Somalia, Sudan, Haiti and Turkey) or partially (Gambia, Malawi, Niger, Togo, Zaire, China, Guatemala,

---

[60] Crawford, 'Promoting Democracy, Human Rights and Good Governance through Development Aid', table 3 (pp. 45–50).

[61] Joel D. Barkan, 'Can Established Democracies Nurture Democracy Abroad? Lessons from Africa', in Axel Hadenius (ed.), *Democracy's Victory and Crisis* (Cambridge: Cambridge University Press, 1997), pp. 372–3.

[62] Crawford, 'Promoting Political Reform through Aid Sanctions', p. v.

[63] *Ibid.*

[64] For annual assessments of the performance of other donors, see Judith Randel and Tony German (eds.), *The Reality of Aid: An Independent Review of International Aid* (London: ActionAid, 1993 and subsequent years).

Peru and Syria). Full suspension entailed a withdrawal of all financial and technical assistance but not of humanitarian aid. (In two cases – Liberia and Somalia – civil war and the collapse of the government brought about a *de facto* total suspension.) Partial suspension generally entailed non-delivery of new project aid while ongoing projects continued to receive funding. In three other cases (Lesotho, Sierra Leone and El Salvador), the EU only threatened to implement aid sanctions if certain conditions were not met.[65]

The EU has therefore been fairly vigorous in its use of politically conditioned aid. However, it has not been consistent in its application. A number of countries have received EU and member-state assistance (or have been subject only to nominal sanctions) despite their failure to satisfy the EU's stated political requirements for aid. These countries include China, Nigeria, Turkey, Indonesia, Sri Lanka, Algeria, Egypt and Colombia – each of which either engaged in gross violations of human rights or failed to respect democratic principles in the period under review.[66] China, for instance, was subject to only mild and short-lived sanctions following the Tiananmen Square massacre in June 1989. The EU postponed its examination of new World Bank credits and suspended its own new project aid.[67] But despite Beijing's continued crackdown on democracy in subsequent years, even these weak restrictions were lifted gradually from October 1990.[68] Indonesia, on the other hand, suffered no diminution of EU aid in the period under review despite a pattern of serious human rights abuses on the part of the government and its continuing occupation of East Timor where, in November 1991, an estimated 200 unarmed civilians were killed by the Indonesian army in Dili. EU member states, moreover, failed to adopt a common response to the crisis. In contrast, Dutch efforts at punitive sanctions (the Netherlands suspended aid amounting to $91 million) were undermined by French and British aid increases (a 250 per cent rise in the case of Britain).[69]

It is not hard to understand why the EU was not more faithful to its policies of aid conditionality in both of these cases. In each instance it was impossible to achieve a consensus among the Twelve, as European Political Cooperation (EPC) required, because commercial and strategic

[65] Crawford, 'Promoting Political Reform through Aid Sanctions', p. 20.
[66] *Ibid.*, pp. 48–61.
[67] EPC 'Declaration on China', 26–27 June 1990, *Bulletin of the European Communities*, 6–1989, § 1.1.24.
[68] Clemens Stubbe Østergaard, 'Values for Money? Political Conditionality in Aid – The Case of China', in Sørensen, *Political Conditionality*, p. 117.
[69] Tomaševski, *Between Sanctions and Elections*, pp. 124–5.

considerations outweighed other concerns for many member states.[70] Access to China's large and expanding market was perceived as simply too important for these states to jeopardise with punitive sanctions.[71] And Britain and France, in particular, needed China's cooperation on the UN Security Council for a number of strategic initiatives. Indonesia, too, was a major trading and investment partner for EU member states in this period. Britain, in particular, became the world's largest supplier of arms to Indonesia in 1992.[72] Indeed in some cases there is often a strong correlation between aid and exports, with some aid actually being 'tied' to the purchase of goods or services from the donor. (Job creation in Canada has been one of the stated goals of the Canadian aid programme.)[73] The sale of arms, however, points to a further tension in the new aid conditionality since the weapons are sometimes used by the recipient government, as they have been by the Indonesian government, in the commission of human rights violations.[74] Moreover, weapons are purchased at the expense of other donor priorities – even donor conditions for aid – such as a demonstrable commitment to poverty-focused development. Indeed in 1992, according to the United Nations Development Programme, high military spenders attracted roughly twice as much aid per capita as low spenders.[75]

Lessons for conditional recognition

Despite uneven implementation of political conditionality, there has been sufficient experience with the policy to be able to make some broad observations about its effectiveness, and to draw some tentative lessons from these experiences for the use of conditional recognition. The emphasis here is on 'broad' and 'tentative', for we are talking about enormously complex social realities whose dynamics, while not opaque, are certainly not entirely transparent either. Although theirs was admittedly a more ambitious undertaking, it is worth bearing in mind the cautionary note with which Guillermo O'Donnell and Philippe Schmitter

---

[70] Title III of the Single European Act exhorts member states 'to inform and consult' one another about foreign policy and 'to endeavour' to harmonise positions, for which purpose European Political Cooperation (EPC) was established. For a discussion of EPC, see S. J. Nuttall, *European Political Cooperation* (Oxford: Clarendon Press, 1992).

[71] Østergaard, 'Values for Money?', p. 127.

[72] Crawford, 'Promoting Political Reform through Aid Sanctions', p. 53.

[73] Tomaševski, *Between Sanctions and Elections*, p. 26.

[74] See the annual *Human Rights Watch World Report* (New York: Human Rights Watch, 1991–).

[75] United Nations Development Programme, *Human Development Report 1992* (New York: Oxford University Press, 1992), p. 25 and table 3.13.

concluded their magisterial study (with Laurence Whitehead) into transitions from authoritarian rule:

> If we ever have the temerity to formulate a theory of such a process [of transition], it would have to be a chapter in a much larger inquiry into the problem of 'underdetermined' social change, of large-scale transformations which occur when there are insufficient structural or behavioral parameters to guide and predict the outcome. Such a theory would include elements of accident and unpredictability, of crucial decisions taken in a hurry with very inadequate information, of actors facing irreconcilable ethical dilemmas and ideological confusions, of dramatic turning points reached and passed without an understanding of their future significance. In it the unexpected and the possible are as important as the usual and the probable.[76]

Generally speaking, aid conditionality has had mixed results but overall it does not seem to have made more than a modest contribution to political reform. Sanctions failed to improve the political climate in nearly two-thirds (eighteen out of twenty-nine) of the country cases that Crawford considered in his study.[77] And in most of the other cases only a partial success could be claimed. (Poor results, it is worth noting, have also been observed for economic conditionality.)[78] These experiences, including additional cases outside the parameters of Crawford's study, are nonetheless instructive for what they reveal about the strengths and limitations of political conditionality and, by extension, the potential for conditional recognition as an instrument of conflict management.

In those instances where donor sanctions have been at all effective, the recipient country has been highly dependent on aid or at least vulnerable to significant shortfalls in aid. This would account, in part,

[76] Guillermo O'Donnell and Philippe C. Schmitter, 'Introducing Uncertainty', in Guillermo O'Donnell, Philippe C. Schmitter, and Laurence Whitehead (eds.), *Transitions from Authoritarian Rule: Prospects for Democracy* (Baltimore: The Johns Hopkins University Press, 1986), part IV, pp. 3–4.

[77] Crawford, 'Promoting Political Reform through Aid Sanctions', p. 38. Similar conclusions were reached by Peter Uvin in his 1999 study of the impact of aid conditionality on conflict situations. See Peter Uvin, 'The Influence of Aid in Situations of Violent Conflict', Development Assistance Committee, Informal Task Force on Conflict, Peace and Development Co-operation, Organisation for Economic Co-operation and Development, September 1999, para. 53.

[78] Paul Mosley *et al.* found high rates of non-compliance ('slippage') among recipient governments, whereas Frances Stewart found little evidence to suggest that 'adjusting' states performed better economically. See Paul Mosley, Jane Harrigan and John Toye, *Aid and Power: The World Bank and Policy-based Lending* (London: Routledge, 1991), vol. I, pp. 134–45, 299–302; and Stewart, 'The Many Faces of Adjustment', pp. 176–231. The World Bank disputed these conclusions. See Corbo and Fischer, 'Adjustment Programmes and World Bank Support: Rationale and Main Results', pp. 157–75.

for the responsiveness of Surinam to Dutch pressures in the 1980s – an oft-cited example in the literature. In 1983 the Netherlands suspended its development assistance to Surinam following the abduction and killing of fifteen opposition leaders. Dutch aid constituted 25 per cent of the government's budget at the time and the loss was palpable, notwithstanding some compensatory assistance from Libya and Brazil. Observers credit the Dutch policy for helping to foster Surinam's halting progress towards democratisation subsequently: a new constitution was drafted followed by multiparty elections and the installation of a civilian government. A further suspension of Dutch aid appears to have undermined the military regime that, having seized power unlawfully in 1990, subsequently yielded to a new civilian government.[79]

By contrast, Dutch aid to Indonesia was relatively small – amounting to less than 2 per cent of total foreign assistance to Jakarta – and Indonesia, therefore, was scarcely affected by Dutch punitive measures following the Dili massacre in 1991. Nor, as we saw earlier, was the Soviet Union especially vulnerable to US trade pressures to relax emigration restrictions in the 1970s, because Moscow was largely able to offset the losses. It is interesting to note that the peaks in Soviet emigration occurred in 1972–73 and again in 1979, when the strategic arms control agreements, SALT I and II, were being negotiated and signed. Emigration fell again in late 1979 when US ratification of SALT II seemed unlikely following the Soviet invasion of Afghanistan. These particular arms control accords, it would seem, mattered much more to the Soviet Union than did trade with the United States, and Moscow was therefore willing to make the right gestures to ensure their successful negotiation.[80]

The Dutch–Indonesian experience points to another factor that bears on the effectiveness of conditionality: the importance of donor coordination. Dutch actions could not be expected to have much impact on their own; the Netherlands, however, was unable to persuade most other donors to adopt a similar course of action. (Only Denmark joined the Netherlands in suspending aid, although Canada halted discussions on future aid.) Indonesia, in fact, turned the tables and succeeded in marginalising the Netherlands: at Jakarta's insistence, the next donors' meeting (in July 1992) was chaired by the World Bank in Paris, rather than by the Dutch government at The Hague, as had previously been the practice. In Paris, donors pledged some $5 billion, exceeding World

---

[79] Tomaševski, *Between Sanctions and Elections*, pp. 22–3; Robinson, 'Will Political Conditionality Work?' p. 65.
[80] Perkovich, 'Soviet Jewry and American Foreign Policy', 458.

Bank recommendations and their own volume of assistance the year before – a reflection, again, of the relative weight of trade and strategic considerations in donors' minds.[81]

Donors achieved far greater coordination in their efforts to pressure Kenya's President Daniel Arap Moi to partially reform his authoritarian regime in 1991, thus preventing the Kenyan government from playing one donor agency against the other. At the November 1991 meeting in Paris between the donors and the government of Kenya, the donors agreed to suspend all quick-disbursing aid until the government demonstrated progress towards greater political pluralism, re-established a multiparty system of government, reduced corruption and implemented economic reforms. Diplomats had appealed before to Moi to improve human rights, democracy and the rule of law in Kenya, but never had the donor agencies taken such strong, concerted measures (Norway and Denmark were alone in suspending aid the year before).[82] Kenya was highly dependent on aid, and Moi therefore responded promptly: he amended the constitution less than two weeks before the fateful Paris meeting, thus legalising opposition parties, and multiparty elections were held one year later, in December 1992.[83] What is noteworthy here is not just the importance of donor coordination but also the perceived weight of political conditionality. Although more than three-quarters of the suspended aid was tied to economic reforms, Kenya was accustomed to economic conditionality. Donors had imposed economic conditions on aid to Kenya – to no avail – for many years. When the donors actually suspended aid to Kenya in 1991 and the only new elements were the political demands, the Kenyan government understandably interpreted the motivation for sanctions as political. Thus Moi was especially responsive to the demands for political reforms because, as one senior Kenyan official later acknowledged, it was clear to the government that donors were serious about political change.[84]

The EC, by comparison, failed to achieve effective coordination in the implementation of its policy of conditional recognition. But whereas aid

---

[81] Tomaševski, *Between Sanctions and Elections*, p. 23; Stokke, 'Aid and Political Conditionality', p. 48.

[82] Hans H. Bass, 'The Human Rights Dimension of Germany's Development Aid: Two Examples', 6 *Berichte und Analysen Dritte Welt* (1994), 1–26.

[83] Stokke, 'Aid and Political Conditionality', pp. 48–50; Crawford, 'Promoting Political Reform through Aid Sanctions', appendix 1. Because the opposition was divided, Moi was able to remain in power with only 33.4 per cent of the vote.

[84] Samantha Gibson, 'Can Donors Impose Democracy? Political Conditionality in Kenya and Malawi 1990–1996', paper presented at the African Studies Seminar, University of Cambridge, 24 February 1997. Gibson conducted extensive interviews with Kenyan officials involved in aid negotiations at the time.

conditionality is often difficult to coordinate for political and bureau-
cratic reasons (for instance, budgetary reallocations may be subject to
approval by a national legislature), the EC faced only political obstacles
to the coordination of its recognition policy. In the case of Croatia, it was
clear by the end of December 1991 that Germany was prepared to
recognise the republic unilaterally. Furthermore, Germany was willing
to extend recognition without insisting on Zagreb's strict compliance
with EC requirements for minority protections. (It was a German
lawyer, after all, who with Bonn's blessing advised the Croatian government on the statutory reforms it needed to adopt to be in compliance.)[85]
The EC's determination to act in unison thus meant that unity would
be achieved on the basis of the lowest common denominator – on the
basis of Germany's own assessment of Croatia's eligibility, in other
words. The absence of any defectors among the Twelve with regard to
policy towards Macedonia, on the other hand, meant that Skopje
faced unmitigated pressure to bow to EC demands, notwithstanding
the impatience of some member states with Greek intransigence. Macedonia accepted the provisions from Chapter II of the Carrington draft
Convention regarding minority rights and renounced all territorial
claims against neighbouring states (i.e., Greece), thus satisfying the
Badinter Commission that it had fully met the EC's requirements for
recognition.[86]

Macedonia was willing to make these changes precisely because of
the importance it attached to recognition. What Dutch aid had been to
Surinam, EC recognition was to Macedonia – only more so. Recognition
is bound up with the question of identity,[87] and for Macedonia, whose
legitimacy as a nation-state dates largely from the establishment of the
Yugoslav Socialist Republic of Macedonia, recognition has been critical
to consolidating a fragile sense of national identity.[88] As we saw in
Chapter 4, Serbs, Bulgarians and Greeks have all been sceptical about
the authenticity of Macedonian nationhood at various times in the recent
past. Many Serbs recall that Macedonia was once southern Serbia, while
Bulgarians view their neighbours as western Bulgarians, and Greeks
refuse to accept that there is any Macedonia outside of northern

---

[85] See Chapter 1 of this study.
[86] Opinion No. 6 of the (Badinter) Arbitration Committee, 11 January 1992, 31 *International Legal Materials* (1992), 1507–12.
[87] For a discussion of identity and recognition, see Charles Taylor, *Multiculturalism and
"The Politics of Recognition"* (Princeton: Princeton University Press, 1992).
[88] Duncan M. Perry, 'Macedonia: A Balkan Problem and a European Dilemma', *RFE/RL
Research Report*, 19 June 1992, p. 36.

Greece.[89] In the circumstances, international recognition has helped to dispel many doubts about Macedonia's distinctive identity; indeed, recognition has arguably been constitutive of Macedonia's identity.

Important though recognition has been to the Macedonians, there has been a limit to the concessions that Skopje has been willing to make to secure it. In particular, Skopje has steadfastly refused to abandon use of the name 'Macedonia', as Greece (but not the EU) insisted.[90] In view of the weak foundations of Macedonia's identity, the Slav Macedonians fear that to yield on the name would be tantamount to national suicide. As Denko Maleski, Macedonia's foreign minister, explained in 1992:

We have used that name for centuries [*sic*] to try to draw a line of distinction between us as a people and the surrounding people, the Bulgarians, the Serbs, the Greeks, the Albanians. The word 'Macedonia' for us is not just a word, a name or a state. The word 'Macedonia' is part of our history, it is part of our literature, it is part of our children's tales, it is part of our songs. It is very important to our identity. So if we eliminate the word 'Macedonia' from our name we would in fact create a crisis of identity . . . and we would open again a century-long debate on who these people who live here are.[91]

What this suggests is that political conditionality will not work if the demands for reform are so radical as to threaten the very foundations of a state or a regime. Western demands for the Soviet Union to abandon communism, similarly, would have fallen on deaf ears. Even a country that is highly dependent on aid or international commerce may be able to resist such demands if its government is in control of key state resources, as Iraq under Saddam Hussein showed.

There is a corollary to this observation: political conditionality has a greater likelihood of success when there is internal support for the reforms being sought. If we read 'political conditionality' for 'intervention', this is essentially John Stuart Mill's argument in his essay, 'A Few Words on Non-intervention', published in 1859. '[T]he evil is', Mill wrote, 'that if [a people] have not sufficient love of liberty to be able to wrest it from merely domestic oppressors, the liberty which is bestowed on them by

[89] John B. Allcock, 'The Dilemmas of an Independent Macedonia', *ISIS Briefing* No. 42 (London: International Security Information Service, June 1994), p. 3.
[90] Macedonia, however, would agree several years later to forsake the sixteen-pointed Star of Vergina as a national symbol, which Greece claimed as part of its unique historic patrimony. The concession was part of an agreement reached in 1995 to end the Greek trade embargo against Macedonia. See Anthony Borden and Richard Caplan, 'The Former Yugoslavia: The War and the Peace Process', in *SIPRI Yearbook 1996* (Oxford: SIPRI/Oxford University Press, 1996), p. 226.
[91] Cited in Duncan M. Perry, 'The Republic of Macedonia and the Odds for Survival', *RFE/RL Research Report*, 20 November 1992, p. 14.

other hands than their own, will have nothing real, nothing permanent.'[92] And so it has frequently been with human rights and democratic reform. In the absence of sufficient support from either within the government or from key sections of the population, target states have often made a nod in the direction of donors' conditions (if they have responded at all) but then have failed to meet those conditions in a meaningful or lasting way. 'Outsiders' pressures can often make a difference', Joan Nelson observes, 'but there is no substitute for genuine conviction by the government and/ or coherent demands from domestic groups.'[93]

The Croatian experience provides evidence for this observation. There was clearly no support within the Tudjman government for the establishment of the 'special status' that the EC was seeking for Croatia's Serbs. Nor was there very much enthusiasm for the idea among the Croatian population, with most Croats tending to view Serbs as a 'fifth column' and many Serbs preferring secession. Only moderate Serbs in Croatia supported some form of autonomy but, as we saw in Chapter 5, they were too marginalised to be able to exert any real influence on policy.[94] In Kenya, on the other hand, political reform had been a priority objective of indigenous opposition groups. The Forum for the Restoration of Democracy (FORD) had campaigned actively for political reform since its formation in mid-1990 and enjoyed broad public support for its aims.[95] Aid sanctions echoed the demands of these opposition groups and thus amplified their importance, providing 'the extra push necessary to induce a systemic political transition'.[96]

Political conditionality also tipped the balance in favour of forces within Hungary and Romania who, at the end of the Cold War, were

[92] John Stuart Mill, 'A Few Words on Non-intervention', in *Essays on Politics and Culture*, edited by Gertrude Himmelfarb (Gloucester, MA: Peter Smith, 1973), p. 381. For a discussion of the enduring relevance of Mill's insights to contemporary humanitarian dilemmas, see Edward Mortimer, 'Under What Circumstances Should the UN Intervene Militarily in a "Domestic" Crisis?' in Olara A. Otunnu and Michael W. Doyle (eds.), *Peacemaking and Peacekeeping for the New Century* (Lanham, MD: Rowman & Littlefield, 1998), pp. 111–44.

[93] Nelson, 'Good Governance: Democracy and Conditional Economic Aid', p. 314. Similarly, it has been found, most countries that have implemented structural adjustment reforms successfully have had governments already committed to the policies. Uvin, '"Do as I Say, Not as I Do"', p. 74.

[94] See also Milorad Pupovac, 'A Settlement for the Serbs', in Anthony Borden *et al.* (eds.), *Breakdown: War & Reconstruction in Yugoslavia* (London: Institute for War and Peace Reporting, 1992), pp. 17–18. Pupovac was co-founder of the Serbian Democratic Forum in Croatia.

[95] Mark Robinson, 'Aid, Democracy and Political Conditionality in sub-Saharan Africa', in Sørensen, *Political Conditionality*, p. 95.

[96] Crawford, 'Promoting Political Reform through Aid Sanctions', p. 39.

prepared to sign a treaty to resolve long-standing border and minority questions between the two countries. For years Hungary and Romania had been unable to negotiate a treaty but when NATO made resolution of these issues a condition for membership in the organisation, negotiations were successfully concluded and a basic treaty was signed on 16 September 1996.[97] 'We have to face the fact that without the resolution of problems in a European manner neither Hungary nor her neighbours can enter the European Union and NATO', László Kovács, the Hungarian foreign minister, had declared the year before.[98] Although conditional membership would seem to offer diplomatic 'donors' a distinct advantage over conditional recognition, since membership in an organisation is in principle revocable, it is difficult to imagine a member state being forced out of NATO for reasons of border disputes, as tolerance for occasional flare-ups between Turkey and Greece would suggest. Indeed there are no provisions in the North Atlantic Treaty for the suspension or termination of member participation in NATO, only for a party's own denunciation of its membership.[99]

While political conditionality is likely to be more effective if there are elements within the government and/or an organised internal opposition supportive of political reform, there may be value to using conditionality even in the absence of these factors. Conditional recognition, or membership, may help to initiate or further a process of political liberalisation, much as the 'recognition' conferred by the Helsinki Final Act did within the Soviet bloc. The Final Act, signed by the United States, the Soviet Union and most other European countries in 1975, in effect recognised the territorial status quo of post-Second World War Europe in exchange for the acceptance of common human rights standards.[100] The accord spurred the emergence of human rights groups in the Soviet bloc (the various 'Helsinki committees') that were able to point to the failure of their political leaders to honour their commitments, thus helping to erode the legitimacy of the communist regimes.[101] In a similar

---

[97] Joel Blocker, 'Romania/Hungary: Historic Basic Treaty Signed Today', *RFE/RL Weekday Magazine*, 16 September 1996, available at http://www.rferl.org.

[98] Kovács cited in Zsuzsanna Dákai, 'NATO as an Issue in Hungarian Domestic Politics from 1994 to 1997', M.Phil. thesis, University of Oxford, Faculty of Social Studies, 1999, p. 21.

[99] The North Atlantic Treaty, Article 13.

[100] Conference on Security and Co-operation in Europe, Final Act, Helsinki 1975.

[101] John Feffer, *Shock Waves: Eastern Europe after the Revolutions* (Boston: South End Press, 1992), pp. 61, 176. See also Daniel C. Thomas, 'The Helsinki Accords and Political Change in Eastern Europe', in Thomas Risse, Stephen C. Ropp and Kathryn Sikkink (eds.), *The Power of Human Rights: International Norms and Domestic Change* (Cambridge: Cambridge University Press, 1999), pp. 205–33.

fashion, the formal requirements that the Yugoslav republic authorities were required to adopt as a condition for EC recognition established an agreed-upon standard that local interest groups could – and did – invoke in support of political reform.

The danger, however, is that standards may be debased if recognition or membership is extended to states that seem to fall short of satisfying the requirements. Such was the concern raised with the admission of Russia and Croatia to the Council of Europe in 1996. Critics argued that the two states did not genuinely meet the democratic criteria for membership whereas defenders maintained that membership would help to strengthen democracy in what they admitted were weak candidates.[102] At least the Council of Europe, unlike NATO, has provisions for the suspension or termination of membership in the event of a serious violation of its principles.[103] And while the exercise of provisions of this kind is rare for any multilateral organisation, it is not unheard of. The Council itself suspended the participation of Greece from 1969 to 1974 in response to the seizure of power by the military junta in April 1967 and its subsequent curtailment of Greek democratic freedoms.[104] Similarly, the CSCE, at a meeting of its Committee of Senior Officials in July 1992, suspended the participation of the Federal Republic of Yugoslavia (Serbia and Montenegro) in the organisation because of Belgrade's failure to comply with the 'principles, commitments and provisions of the CSCE' as evidenced by its continuing military support for the Bosnian Serbs.[105]

The importance of internal support for what could be considered outsiders' agendas has led some donors to eschew punitive measures in favour of dialogue. The UNDP, for instance, although it has strongly supported a broadening of the development agenda to include democracy and human rights, has opposed the use of negative conditionality and other external pressures for this purpose. 'Democracy is a native plant – it may wilt under foreign pressure', the agency observed in its 1992 *Human Development Report*. '[I]nformal dialogue', it suggests, 'may be more effective than formal conditionality.'[106] Dialogue is certainly less heavy-handed than conditionality and is therefore less likely to breed

---

[102] For membership requirements, see the Statute of the Council of Europe (1949), Article 3.

[103] Statute of the Council of Europe, Article 8.

[104] Committee of Ministers, Resolutions (69) 51 (12 December 1969) and (74) 34 (28 November 1974).

[105] 'Decisions of the Committee of Senior Officials', Thirteenth Meeting of the Committee of Senior Officials (Helsinki), *Journal* No. 7, 7 July 1992, Annex.

[106] UNDP, *Human Development Report 1992*, p. 25.

resentment on the part of target governments. Moreover, it makes target governments 'stakeholders' in reform processes. But dialogue itself would seem to require a pre-existing disposition towards reform if it is to be anything more than a dialogue of the deaf. It is difficult to see how dialogue alone would have yielded the results that the EC sought in Croatia.

Where for principled and other reasons donors have been opposed to punitive measures, or where target governments resistant to reform would appear to be impervious to such measures, donors have sometimes chosen to support whatever positive initiatives a government might be willing to undertake or to direct their resources to relevant civil society initiatives instead. Thus China and Israel have been largely exempt from sanctions while indigenous human rights organisations in both countries have received donor funding.[107] This approach is generally viewed as an alternative to negative conditionality, but it could in fact serve as a complementary measure – especially to conditional recognition, given the non-renewable nature of recognition. Of course there is nothing to prevent the further use of negative conditionality in the case of states that have been accorded recognition and have subsequently failed to respect the conditions of recognition. For instance, negative conditionality might have been used to greater effect against Croatia to ensure better treatment of its Serb minority,[108] just as it has been used on occasion to leverage political reform in Republika Srpska, the Bosnian Serb sub-state entity that gained recognition with the 1995 Dayton peace agreement.[109]

But the Bosnian experience also points to an inherent difficulty in the use of negative conditionality. In 1996 the international community withheld reconstruction aid from Republika Srpska, in part because

---

[107] The British government-sponsored Westminster Foundation, for example, has funded NGOs working to support the promotion of human rights in China and Palestine. See Westminster Foundation for Democracy, *Annual Report 1995–96* (London: Westminster Foundation, 1996), pp. 45–6.

[108] Negative conditionality was employed against Croatia on a limited basis. According to the UN, for instance, leading Western states persuaded the World Bank not to lend to Croatia without taking into account the government's compliance with its obligations to the UN peace-support operation in Eastern Slavonia (UNTAES). See United Nations, Department of Peacekeeping Operations, *The United Nations Transitional Administration in Eastern Slavonia, Baranja and Western Sirmium (UNTAES) January 1996 – January 1998: Lessons Learned* (New York: UN Department of Peacekeeping Operations, 1998), p. 7. For a discussion of Croatian government-sanctioned violations of Serbian civil and political rights, see Human Rights Watch, *Civil and Political Rights in Croatia* (New York: Human Rights Watch, 1995).

[109] General Framework Agreement for Peace in Bosnia and Herzegovina, Annex 4, Article I.3.

the Pale authorities refused to implement key provisions of the Dayton accords.[110] The withholding of aid arguably facilitated the ascent of reformists within the Bosnian Serb leadership who were able to promise the electorate an improvement in living standards in exchange for co-operation with the international community. However, strong international support for reformist candidates in BiH's September 1998 elections – including pledges of additional financial assistance in support of their policies – failed to secure their victory and may even have contributed to their defeat, as voters resented the intervention of the major powers.[111]

Critics of conditionality will invoke examples of backlash of this kind in support of a less heavy-handed approach to political reform but this is not a uniform reaction, as some of the other experiences above (e.g., Surinam, Kenya, Macedonia) make clear.[112] What these experiences tell us, instead, is that no single strategy is appropriate for all circumstances. For that matter, there may be times when no strategy will work at all. But clearly there is some scope for the effective use of political conditionality, including conditional recognition, especially where it acts in tandem with indigenous dynamics of reform. The possible utility of conditionality, however, can only be determined on a case-by-case basis.

Normative considerations

We have been discussing political conditionality entirely in utilitarian terms. However, the use of so powerful and invasive an instrument also raises a number of important normative issues, in the ethical sense of the term, which are often overlooked by policy planners. The irony is that political conditionality itself is underpinned by normative concerns, although it is sometimes difficult to distinguish these concerns from other more parochial interests, as has been the case with *missions*

---

[110] Republika Srpska received only 2 per cent of all reconstruction aid to BiH in 1996. See Ibrahim Polimac and Tihomir Loza, 'Uneasy Money', *War Report* No. 53 (August 1997), pp. 7–9.

[111] International Crisis Group, 'State of the Balkans', *ICG Balkans Report No. 47* (Brussels: International Crisis Group, 4 November 1998), p. 13.

[112] Indeed, in October 1999 even Milorad Dodik, prime minister of Republika Srpska, would urge that Karadžić and other indicted war criminals be brought to the Hague tribunal so as not to prevent Republika Srpska from receiving international aid and investments. See 'Bosnian Serb Prime Minister Says "Send Karadzic and Milosevic to The Hague"', *RFE/RL Balkan Report*, 15 October 1999, available at http://www.rferl.org/balkan-report.

civilisatrices historically.[113] Of course, national interests may be served by the establishment and reinforcement of particular norms, as we saw in Chapter 3, and the distinction between interests and norms, therefore, is not always a sharp one. The promotion of human rights worldwide, for instance, may help to prevent mass migrations and the spillover of conflict closer to home. Normative issues thus deserve some consideration not only, but especially, because they, too, may bear on the effectiveness of political conditionality – and conditional recognition in particular.

The two principal normative issues that relate to the use of political conditionality are legitimacy and consistency. The challenge of legitimacy manifests itself in different ways. To begin with, the legitimacy of a reform agenda may be compromised by virtue of its foreign parentage, as we saw above in the case of Republika Srpska. A political programme that owes its origin and design to external powers may be seen as alien, unresponsive to local needs and threatening to a state's (or regime's) interests. This is a problem that any state, developed or developing, may experience: witness the hostile reaction that certain judgements of the European Court of Human Rights have elicited from Britain's political leaders, notwithstanding Britain's voluntary acceptance of the Court's jurisdiction.[114] This difficulty is compounded by the uneasy relationship that many developing countries (the targets of most conditionality) have had with the major Western powers (the architects of conditionality). Historic patterns of exploitation contribute to the view that Western policy today has little to do with a genuine interest in democracy and human rights and more to do with a determination to establish new forms of domination. As John-Jean Barya, a Ugandan legal scholar, expresses this view:

There is no doubt . . . that the project of the new political conditionalities is none other than an attempt by the big western capitalist powers to create a new legitimacy in a new post–Cold War world order whereby discredited dictatorial/authoritarian regimes in Africa or elsewhere in the Third World are replaced by new leaders under the ideology of pluralism, democracy and free enterprise (the market system) while maintaining hegemony over countries which are economically and politically useful to those western powers.[115]

---

[113] See, for example, Anthony Pagden, *Lords of All the World: Ideologies of Empire in Spain, Britain and France c.1500–c.1800* (New Haven: Yale University Press, 1995), ch. 2.

[114] See, for instance, 'Major Weighs Case for Leaving Euro-court', *Daily Telegraph*, 25 September 1995.

[115] John-Jean B. Barya, 'The New Political Conditionalities of Aid: An Independent View from Africa', VIDC conference, p. 34.

Whether or not one subscribes to this view of Western interests, there are two factors that mitigate the charges of illegitimacy, partially at least. The first is that donors are pursuing a political agenda that, without gainsaying its indigenous critics, often enjoys the support of significant elements within the target-state populations. Kenya's Forum for the Restoration of Democracy is just one of thousands of indigenous organisations around the globe working to advance the same goals of liberal democracy and human rights that international donors are seeking to advance. Local actors and the international community may differ as to the specific content of these goals. Not all democratic reformers in the former Soviet bloc, for instance, favoured the wholesale dismantling of their socialist systems – the price of much Western assistance.[116] But it is fair to say that most reformers have generally welcomed the role of political conditionality in helping to sustain the impetus for democratic reform.

The challenge to the legitimacy of political conditionality is further mitigated by the fact that many of the values it represents and the goals it pursues are enshrined in international treaties that most, if not all, of the target states have ratified, including the Universal Declaration of Human Rights and the International Covenant on Civil and Political Rights. And despite the appeal that arguments for cultural relativism may have, states have largely rejected the view – as they did at the June 1993 World Conference on Human Rights in Vienna – that some human rights are optional or subordinate to cultural traditions and practices.[117] However objectionable, therefore, are the pressures from donors for the protection of rights enumerated in these treaties, the legitimacy of the rights themselves can hardly be disputed. And whereas minority rights – a central concern of the EC in former Yugoslavia – do not enjoy the same degree of legal recognition as human rights more generally, they are nonetheless acknowledged in a number of international and regional conventions to which Yugoslavia was a party.[118] Moreover, there are precedents in

---

[116] For East German calls for a 'third way', see Michael Lucas and Adrienne Edgar, 'Germany after the Wall: Interviews with Bärbel Bohley, Harald Lange, Karsten Voigt, and Yuri Davidov', 7 *World Policy Journal* (1989–90), 189–214.

[117] The Vienna Declaration and Programme of Action, adopted unanimously by the Conference, reaffirms the universality of all human rights: 'While the significance of national and regional particularities and various historical, cultural and religious backgrounds must be borne in mind, it is the duty of States, regardless of their political, economic and cultural systems, to promote and protect all human rights and fundamental freedoms.' UN Doc. A/Conf.157/23, 12 July 1993, I.5.

[118] See Patrick Thornberry, 'International and European Standards on Minority Rights', in Hugh Miall (ed.), *Minority Rights in Europe: The Scope for a Transnational Regime* (London: RIIA/Pinter, 1994), pp. 14–21; and Jennifer Jackson Preece, 'Minority

Yugoslavia's own constitutional history, including autonomous arrangements for its nationalities, that affirm the legitimacy of minority rights locally.[119] It cannot be said, then, that the notion of minority rights is an alien concept that the EC imposed on the new state authorities in former Yugoslavia. And the idea of a 'special status' for minorities in particular, it is worth recalling, originated with Milošević – however disingenuously.[120]

The second normative challenge for political conditionality is the issue of consistency. The inconsistent implementation of a sanctions policy may make its use seem arbitrary and lead states to believe that they are being singled out unfairly for punishment. Inconsistency can thus undermine a policy's legitimacy. The British Foreign and Commonwealth Office (FCO) has recognised this challenge for its human rights policies generally. In a 1991 policy document, the FCO wrote: 'It is important that the FCO should take and be seen to be taking a positive and consistent interest in the promotion of human rights world-wide. The charge of inconsistency is damaging to the potential success of our representations abroad.'[121]

As we have seen, the donor states and the EU in particular have not been consistent in their use of aid conditionality. And it can hardly be said that the EU has applied its policy of conditional recognition consistently. That policy, after all, was designed exclusively for new states in Eastern Europe and the Soviet Union, with the republics of Yugoslavia having to accept additional requirements. But the problem may not actually be one of consistency so much as one of coherence. As Thomas Franck explains: '[A] rule's inconsistent application does not necessarily undermine its legitimacy as long as the inconsistencies can be explained to the satisfaction of the community by a justifiable (i.e., principled) distinction.'[122] A credible justification for differential treatment thus imparts coherence to inconsistencies and helps to assure its legitimacy. Progressive tax rates have legitimacy because equity suggests that individuals of modest means should not bear the same tax burden as wealthy individuals. But should new candidates for state recognition be expected to satisfy requirements that already existing states have not had to meet?

Rights in Europe: From Westphalia to Helsinki', 23(1) *Review of International Studies* (1997), 75–92.
[119] Zoran Pajic, 'The Former Yugoslavia', in Miall, *Minority Rights in Europe*, p. 63.
[120] See Chapter 1 of this study.
[121] Foreign and Commonwealth Office, *Human Rights in Foreign Policy*, Foreign Policy Document No. 215 (London: January 1991), para 29.
[122] Thomas M. Franck, *The Power of Legitimacy Among Nations* (New York: Oxford University Press, 1990), p. 163.

Should Croatia be subject to more strenuous requirements for recognition than, say, Bangladesh was? And should European candidates for recognition face greater hurdles than their non-European contemporaries? Should Macedonia be required to offer guarantees that it will not engage in hostile propaganda activities against its neighbours while no such demands were placed on Eritrea, for instance?[123]

What lends coherence to this double standard from an *historical* perspective is, quite simply, the evolution of norms – or what in a less relativistic age one would call 'progress'. To paraphrase James Crawford, references to democracy, human rights and peaceful relations are entering into the justification of legal and political decision-making in new ways.[124] There is now not only greater scope for the consideration of these principles in law and diplomacy – a consequence, in part, of the gradual erosion of state sovereignty – but to some minds even an imperative to take them into account.[125]

What lends coherence to this double standard from a *regional* perspective, on the other hand, is the principle of self-help.[126] States, or in the case of the EU, groups of states, can be expected to take measures to enhance their security if and when they can. (The range of measures states may take is, of course, circumscribed by a number of factors – capabilities, the balance of power, legal and other norms, etc. – but these constraints need not concern us here.) It is only natural for the EU, moreover, to perceive a greater threat to its security arising from a war of state dissolution on its own doorstep as opposed to a conflict of this nature occurring elsewhere in the world – other things, of course, being equal. It does not matter that these developments may pose no direct threat to the EU or its member states. 'It is bad for the neighbourhood', as the Paris-based *New York Times* correspondent, Flora Lewis, later wrote in a related context.[127] It is therefore not surprising that the EU

---

[123] Since it gained independence in 1993, Eritrea has warred with Ethiopia over disputed borderlands and has threatened to overthrow the Sudanese government. See 'Why Are They Fighting?' *The Economist*, 13 June 1998.

[124] See Chapter 3 of this study.

[125] This point is illustrated especially well by the British House of Lords decision in November 1998 to allow General Augusto Pinochet Ugarte to be extradited to Spain to be tried for crimes under international law that he allegedly committed while Chilean head of state. See Michael Byers, 'A Safer Place for All', *The World Today*, January 1999, pp. 4–6.

[126] For a discussion of the concept of self-help in international relations, see Kenneth N. Waltz, *Theory of International Politics* (Reading, MA: Addison-Wesley, 1979), ch. 5.

[127] Flora Lewis, 'A New Consensus that Limits Must Be Imposed', *International Herald Tribune*, 26 March 1999. Lewis was writing specifically about Belgrade's treatment of Kosovo Albanians.

should seek the enhancement of national and regional security that more stringent criteria for the recognition of neighbouring states might offer.

But the EU is also a civilizational project – a community of states engaged in a self-conscious attempt to create 'an ever closer union' on the basis of, *inter alia*, 'liberty, democracy and respect for human rights and fundamental freedoms and of the rule of law', in the words of its charter.[128] The EU's backyard is its future. This is as much the view from Brussels as it is from Prague, Warsaw, Ljubljana and in time, one can imagine, even Belgrade.[129] If the EU thus imposes on its neighbours unique requirements, including exceptional standards for the treatment of minorities, it is because it seeks to lay the foundation for that future, however uncertain it may be.[130]

Can there, then, be any utility to the use of conditional recognition as an instrument of conflict management? The answer is a qualified 'yes'. The critical importance of recognition to a nascent state means that it will generally be prepared to go to great lengths to satisfy the requirements of the international community, or leading members within that community, provided that those requirements are not so onerous as to threaten the very foundations of the state or regime in question. Zagreb's acceptance of the Vance Plan, which helped to keep the peace in Croatia, and Skopje's adoption of confidence-building measures with respect to Greece were both conflict-mitigating developments whose achievement can be attributed largely to the allure of recognition. Other factors – the coordination of recognition policies among the relevant powers and support for reform within the target state or government – may also be necessary to ensure positive results. At the very least the presence of these factors increases the likelihood of conditional recognition's success in achieving its objectives.

Conditional recognition, however, is no magic bullet. It is a one-time measure: a state, once recognised, need not – indeed cannot – seek recognition again. The potency of conditional recognition, therefore,

---

[128] Preamble, Treaty on European Union.

[129] 'We remain committed to Yugoslavia's integration into Europe', Milo Đukanović, the president of Montenegro, and Zoran Đinđić, the head of the Democratic Party in Serbia, declared in May 1999. See their 'Toward a New Start for Yugoslavia, With Outside Help', *International Herald Tribune*, 10 May 1999.

[130] For an eloquent statement of Europe representing 'the idea of the free citizen as the source of all power' and a vision of a Europe of 'human beings [freed] from the bondage of ethnic collectivism', see Václav Havel, 'The Hope for Europe', *New York Review of Books*, 20 June 1996, pp. 38–41.

although considerable, is not enduring, while the reforms it seeks to effect need to be. Moreover, conditional recognition, an exogenous stimulus of social and political change, lacks the legitimacy of indigenous initiatives. For that reason it may be resented, even resisted, by the leadership and people of the target state. Of course these inherent limitations may not always prove fatal. Complementary follow-on measures – including conditional aid giving and conditional membership in regional and international organisations – can extend the power of conditional recognition. And national leaders will sometimes find advantage in foreign pressures that tip the balance of forces in favour of reforms that they are powerless to achieve otherwise. Limited a measure though it is, conditional recognition provides diplomats with valuable political capital.

Conclusion

Writing in 1861, John Stuart Mill expressed a general pessimism about the capacity of pluralistic societies for representative government: 'Free institutions are next to impossible in a country made up of different nationalities', Mill argued. 'Among a people without fellow-feeling, especially if they read and speak different languages, the united public opinion, necessary to the working of representative government, cannot exist.'[1]

In its response to the collapse of communist Europe and the emergence of new states in its wake, the European Community took a very different view of pluralistic societies in relation to 'free institutions'. Not only was it possible for such societies to function democratically, the EC maintained, but a democratic Europe at the end of the twentieth century required pluralism. For where multinational societies might predominate – as they do in much of East-Central Europe – states wishing to achieve the relative homogeneity that Mill's logic seemed to recommend could only do so through the elimination of ethnic differences.[2] The use of violent means for such a purpose, including the forcible redrawing of boundaries, was, however, anathema to the EC.[3] Even non-coercive instruments, such as assimilation, could be problematic in an era when it was accepted that minority communities were

---

[1] John Stuart Mill, 'Representative Government', in *Utilitarianism, Liberty, and Representative Government* (London: J. M. Dent & Sons, 1940), p. 361.

[2] For the attraction of the notion of a homogeneous state to militant nationalists in Croatia and Serbia, see Zarko Puhovski, 'The Real Democracy Deficit', *War Report* No. 58 (February/March 1998), pp. 44–5; and Sonja Biserko and Seška Stanojlović (eds.), *Radicalisation of the Serbian Society: Collection of Documents* (Belgrade: Helsinki Committee for Human Rights in Serbia, 1997).

[3] A *voluntary* redrawing of borders, however, was proposed by the Netherlands in July 1991 but the proposal was rejected by the other EC countries. See David Owen, *Balkan Odyssey* (New York: Harcourt Brace & Company, 1995), pp. 31–4, and Norbert Both, *From Indifference to Entrapment: The Netherlands and the Yugoslav Crisis 1990–1995* (Amsterdam: Amsterdam University Press, 2000), pp. 107–9.

entitled to preserve their distinctiveness consistent with the right to self-determination.

The EC's conditional recognition of new states in Yugoslavia reflected this belief in both the possibility and the imperative for the maintenance of pluralistic societies in Europe. As this book has shown, the architects of the EC's policy were motivated in part by the view that peace in the region would not be assured as long as minority populations adversely affected by the disintegration of Yugoslavia remained vulnerable. The EC thus sought to strengthen the position of these groups within the newly created states in the hope that such measures would undercut the dynamic of violent conflict. The prospect of recognition, the EC reasoned, would induce the emerging states to adopt policies towards its national minorities that might mitigate and perhaps even eliminate some of the presumed sources of the conflict. This was not the only reason why the EC adopted its particular requirements for recognition – other, more parochial interests, we have seen, bore on policymaking as well – but it was certainly one important reason.

The EC's leaders set great store – too great, it is now evident – by the Community's ability to influence the course of events in its own back-yard. It was 'the hour of Europe', Jacques F. Poos, Luxembourg's foreign minister, declared famously in June 1991 as the EC attempted single-handedly to resolve the Yugoslav crisis.[4] Yet although EC member states overestimated the influence they could wield, there was reason to believe at the time that the skilful use of non-military inducements could be effective in moulding the regional strategic environment, as the EC's prior experience with political conditionality in East-Central Europe seemed to suggest. In April 1989, well before the collapse of the Soviet bloc, the EC adopted a 'carrot and stick' approach towards reform in Eastern Europe: it offered economic rewards to reform-minded Poland and Hungary and meted out economic punishment (the suspension of trade and economic cooperation talks) to Romania and Bulgaria because of their human rights violations.[5] Satisfied with the results of this ap-proach, the EC, at its Paris Summit in November 1989, decided to offer aid and trade concessions – known as association agreements – to other Central and East European countries on the basis of four political conditions: rule of law, respect for human rights, political pluralism

---

[4] Cited in 'Ceasefire in Slovenia', *The Independent*, 29 June 1991.

[5] John Pinder, 'Community against Conflict: The European Community's Contribution to Ethno-National Peace in Europe', in Abram Chayes and Antonia Handler Chayes (eds.), *Preventing Conflict in the Post-Communist World* (Washington, DC: The Brookings Institution, 1996), p. 182.

(defined as a multiparty system) and free and fair elections in 1990, in addition to a fifth, economic condition: liberalisation in support of a market economy.[6]

Conditionality also seemed to make good sense because the most salient structural factors recommended such an approach. For the East European, and later the former Soviet republics, the benefits of closer association with the EC were perceived to be very great, even vital. As the Georgian geographer and political scientist Alex Rondeli would later put it: 'Europe means almost too much to us. It is magic. It is everything. Everything that can join us to Europe is wanted and everything which separates us exists to be overcome.'[7] It was assumed, therefore, that these countries would be willing to comply with what were essentially modified 'Helsinki' requirements – the catalogue of rights enumerated in the CSCE's Helsinki Final Act of 1975 – in exchange for stronger links with the European Community. Not only were the former communist countries attracted to the benefits of closer association with the Community but they were also highly exposed economically – a condition that the EC thought it could exploit in the interest of enhancing security as well as reshaping the region's economic and political structures. Among other things, the EC was by far the most important trading partner for Eastern Europe, accounting for nearly 30 per cent of imports from and exports to the region.[8]

Yugoslavia was especially vulnerable in this regard. More than half of the country's trade in mid-1991 was with the EC.[9] Additionally, Yugoslavia was in desperate need of international financial assistance: its foreign debt, totalling $18 billion in early 1991, could not be sustained without fresh loans and debt rescheduling from the EC and the World Bank.[10] In addition to the relative weakness and dependency of Yugoslavia on the West, years of EC experience in supporting Yugoslavia (in tacit exchange for Belgrade's continued non-aligned orientation) contributed to the view, as the crisis in that country unfolded, that it could be brought into line using economic and political levers.

---

[6] *Agence Europe* (Brussels), No. 5194 (15 February 1990), p. 7.

[7] Cited in Martin Woollacott, 'Craving the European Club', *War Report* No. 44 (August 1996), p. 16.

[8] Peter Ludlow, 'The Foreign Policy of the Union', in Peter Ludlow (ed.), *Setting European Community Priorities 1991–92* (London: CEPS/Brassey's, 1991), p. 108, Table 1. Eastern Europe here comprises Bulgaria, Czechoslovakia, Hungary, Poland, Romania and Yugoslavia.

[9] 'Yugoslavian Government Seeks $4bn Boost', *Financial Times*, 3 June 1991.

[10] Mario Zucconi, 'The European Union in the Former Yugoslavia', in Chayes and Chayes, *Preventing Conflict in the Post-Communist World*, p. 239.

Two economic cooperation agreements had already been signed with Yugoslavia and a third was being negotiated on the eve of the crisis. As with the rest of Eastern Europe, Yugoslavia's clear interest in building stronger ties to the EC reinforced the belief among West European officials that Belgrade would be susceptible to pressure by Brussels. By February 1990 Yugoslavia had applied for associate status in the European Community, as well as membership in the Council of Europe and the Organisation for Economic Cooperation and Development (OECD)[11] – a significant policy shift for a country that valued its autonomous position in the world community.

Conditional recognition was just one of several policy instruments, then, that the EC employed on the assumption that its security environment could be managed with a judicious mixture of carrots and sticks – more specifically, that the former communist countries could be induced to meet the EC's demands for economic, political and security reforms in exchange for closer association with the Community. Conditional recognition can thus be seen to have been not merely an *ad hoc* measure in response to the crisis arising from assertions of independence in former communist Europe but part of a general approach that reflected the EC's confidence in the influence at its disposal.

Did the EC's policy, however, make any actual contribution to peace in the former Yugoslavia? It might seem cynical to pose such a question in light of the failure of EC diplomacy to prevent the eruption of further violence in the region and given the brutal atrocities that have been visited upon various minority populations since the EC implemented its policy. Yet, it has been noted here, positive trends in respect of minority rights can in fact be attributed to the pressure exerted by the Community. The legislation of minority rights guarantees throughout the region, most notably, owes itself in part to the EC's recognition policy, and that legislation has contributed, in some cases at least, to the maintenance of peaceful interethnic relations. Of course, some of these states would likely have adopted such legislation anyway in their attempts to conform to European standards but this does not detract from the value of EC policy in helping to reinforce a tendency.

In those cases where the impact of the recognition criteria was slight, in Croatia in particular, the EC's failure to take its own conditions of recognition more seriously is partly to blame for the lack of progress. Yet even in those cases, it is important not to allow short-term negative

[11] As reported by Budimir Lončar, Yugoslavia's foreign minister. Foreign Broadcast Information Service, *Daily Report: Eastern Europe*, FBIS-EEU-90-034, 20 February 1990, pp. 72–3.

trends to obscure the gains that may still be reaped from the EU's approach in the future. For many years the Helsinki process, too, was derided for its inability to ameliorate the human rights situation in Eastern Europe to any significant degree. In retrospect, however, it seems fair to say that the CSCE's affirmation of the importance of human rights helped to legitimise these rights as a matter of international concern and, moreover, helped to foster a shared political sensibility across the continent that has made it easier to safeguard human rights in the post-communist successor regimes.[12] Indeed, with the collapse of the Tudjman regime in Croatia in 2000 and the establishment of a successor government more interested in international and regional cooperation, EU pressures on behalf of the Croatian Serb minority would find greater reception.

Recognition also created opportunities for conflict prevention and attenuation that third parties, however, did not exploit. Recognition conferred international personality on the republics, thus entitling them to a greater degree of protection from the use of force. Several European governments – Germany, Denmark and Austria, in particular – argued in favour of the prompt recognition of Slovenia and Croatia on these very grounds. But, for a variety of reasons, EC member states – individually and collectively – were either unable or unwilling to deploy their military forces to the region. An early show of resolve, which recognition now made easier, might have deterred some of Serbia/Yugoslavia's aggression.[13]

The rules and norms of EC recognition have played a more fundamental role beyond their conflict regulation function. They have also had an important constitutive effect. By insisting on respect for minority rights as a condition for diplomatic recognition, the EC has given new definition to what it means to be a state today – in Europe, at least. (Respect for minority rights would soon also become a key requirement for accession to the EU with the European Council's adoption of the 'Copenhagen criteria' for membership in 1993.)[14] Of course, how effective such an approach will be in the end will depend in part on whether this and any other requirements are satisfied in a meaningful way. But there can be no doubt that EC policy has contributed to the further entrenchment of democratic norms in international society.

---

[12] Vojtech Mastny, *The Helsinki Process and the Reintegration of Europe, 1986–1991: Analysis and Documentation* (London: Pinter Publishers, 1992), pp. 1–49.

[13] Former US ambassador to Yugoslavia, Warren Zimmermann, argued this point in his book, *Origins of a Catastrophe* (New York: Times Books/Random House, 1996), p. 158.

[14] 'Conclusions of the Presidency', European Council, Copenhagen, 21–22 June 1993.

For all that may have recommended the EC's approach, it has also been argued here that the architects of the EC's recognition policy overestimated the security dividends that their policy could yield – and not just because of overconfidence on the EC's part. Even if the EC had been able to secure credible guarantees for the Serb populations in Croatia and Bosnia and Herzegovina at an early stage of the crisis, these guarantees alone might not have succeeded in mitigating the conflict because they did not address the external sources of the conflict (i.e., support from Belgrade), which had little to do with objective threats to security. At the same time, it has been argued here that the responsibility that recognition is thought to bear for the violent conflict in the former Yugoslavia is generally overstated. While EC recognition clearly had an impact on the conflict dynamics, the forces of violence in the region were to a large degree operating independently of the factor of recognition.

The limitations of its recognition policy notwithstanding, the EU enjoys a distinct and continuing advantage in its efforts to achieve greater regional stability through the strengthening of minority rights. This advantage derives from the process of integration at work in Europe. The prospect of closer association with the EU means that East-Central European states are willing to go to considerable lengths to satisfy West European demands – for restructuring their economies, for reforming their administrations and, it is increasingly apparent, for treating their minority populations fairly.[15] The advantage that the EU possesses in this regard is amplified by the prevailing asymmetries of power: Croatia, before its accession to the EU in 2004, could not, after all, prescribe the terms of its relations with the EU the way that China could. These asymmetries of power translate into greater influence for the EU but not into double human rights standards, broadly speaking. For unlike during the inter-war period, when the victorious powers adopted a two-tier system of minority rights guarantees, the human rights norms that the EU has been seeking to promote in post-Cold War Europe do not apply solely to the smaller and weaker states of the region. Rather, these are *common* European norms applicable to all European states, as the many judgements of the European Court of Human Rights against the major West European states make clear.

---

[15] The European Commission, in a November 1998 report, noted progress in the protection of minority rights in Latvia and Romania as part of these states' efforts to gain accession to the EU. See European Commission, 'Reports on Progress Towards Accession by each of the Candidate countries', 4 November 1998, available at http://europa. eu.int/comm/enlargement/report_11_98/pdf/en/composite_en.pdf.

The growing importance of Brussels also means increased opportunities for the protection of minority rights throughout the European Union itself, thus sparing national leaders the sometimes punishing political embarrassment they may suffer when they are perceived at home to be capitulating to minorities' demands. If cultural or political autonomy is the price one has to pay for adhesion to the Union, then it may no longer be seen only or even principally as a concession granted to one's minorities. Of course, however influential the EU may be, in the end it cannot simply impose its human rights norms on a state. Such norms, if they are to find meaningful expression in a state's institutions and practices, must have sufficient indigenous support. As Jack Donnelly has observed: 'Stable regimes that protect internationally recognized human rights over the long run almost always have arisen, and must arise, from sustained national political struggle and vigilance.'[16]

Whatever the verdict on the EC's particular efforts, conditional recognition continues to inspire responses to the challenge posed by secessionist violence.[17] Indeed, seven years after the EC's experiment, a group of leading lawyers was once again calling for the recognition of a Yugoslav entity – this time Kosovo – on the condition, in part, that the entity safeguard the rights of all minority populations within its territory.[18] Similarly, the Independent International Commission on Kosovo recommended 'conditional independence' for Kosovo following NATO's 'humanitarian war' against Belgrade in 1999.[19] Given the renewed force of self-determination in international politics after the Cold War, and the prospect of further state fragmentation as a consequence, the appeal of conditional recognition as an instrument of conflict management is unlikely to disappear any time soon.

---

[16] Jack Donnelly, 'The Past, the Present and the Future Prospects', in Milton J. Esman and Shibley Telhami (eds.), *International Organizations and Ethnic Conflict* (Ithaca, NY: Cornell University Press, 1995), p. 70.

[17] See, for instance, Adam Roberts, 'Communal Conflict as a Challenge to International Organization: The Case of the Former Yugoslavia', in Olara A. Otunnu and Michael W. Doyle (eds.), *Peacemaking and Peacekeeping for the New Century* (Lanham, MD: Rowman & Littlefield Publishers, 1998), p. 48.

[18] Public International Law & Policy Group, 'Intermediate Sovereignty as a Basis for Resolving the Kosovo Crisis', *ICG Balkans Report No. 46* (Brussels: International Crisis Group, 9 November 1998), p. 2.

[19] Independent International Commission on Kosovo, *The Kosovo Report: Conflict, International Response, Lessons Learned* (Oxford: Oxford University Press, 2000), ch. 9.

Appendix 1: EPC Declaration on the Recognition of New States in Eastern Europe and the Soviet Union (16 December 1991)

In compliance with the European Council's request, Ministers have assessed developments in Eastern Europe and in the Soviet Union with a view to elaborating an approach regarding relations with new States.

In this connection they have adopted the following guidelines on the formal recognition of new states in Eastern Europe and in the Soviet Union:

"The Community and its member States confirm their attachment to the principles of the Helsinki Final Act and the Charter of Paris, in particular the principle of self-determination. They affirm their readiness to recognise, subject to the normal standards of international practice and the political realities in each case, those new States which, following the historic changes in the region, have constituted themselves on a democratic basis, have accepted the appropriate international obligations and have committed themselves in good faith to a peaceful process and to negotiations.

Therefore, they adopt a common position on the process of recognition of these new States, which requires:

- respect for the provisions of the Charter of the United Nations and the commitments subscribed to in the Final Act of Helsinki and in the Charter of Paris, especially with regard to the rule of law, democracy and human rights
- guarantees for the rights of ethnic and national groups and minorities in accordance with the commitments subscribed to in the framework of the CSCE
- respect for the inviolability of all frontiers which can only be changed by peaceful means and by common agreement
- acceptance of all relevant commitments with regard to disarmament and nuclear non-proliferation as well as to security and regional stability

     — commitment to settle by agreement, including where appropriate by recourse to arbitration, all questions concerning State succession and regional disputes.

The Community and its member States will not recognise entities which are the result of aggression. They would take account of the effects of recognition on neighbouring States.

The commitment to these principles opens the way to recognition by the Community and its member States and to the establishment of diplomatic relations. It could be laid down in agreements."

Appendix 2: EPC Declaration on Yugoslavia (16 December 1991)

The European Community and its member States discussed the situation in Yugoslavia in the light of their guidelines on the recognition of new states in Eastern Europe and in the Soviet Union. They adopted a common position with regard to the recognition of Yugoslav Republics. In this connection they concluded the following:

The Community and its member States agree to recognise the independence of all the Yugoslav Republics fulfilling all the conditions set out below. The implementation of this decision will take place on January 15, 1992.

They are therefore inviting all Yugoslav Republics to state by 23 December whether:

— they wish to be recognized as independent States
— they accept the commitments contained in the above-mentioned guidelines
— they accept the provisions laid down in the draft Convention
— especially those in Chapter II on human rights and rights of national or ethnic groups – under consideration by the Conference on Yugoslavia
— they continue to support
  — the efforts of the Secretary General and the Security Council of the United Nations, and
  — the continuation of the Conference on Yugoslavia.

The application of those Republics which reply positively will be submitted through the Chair of the Conference to the Arbitration Commission for advice before the implementation date.

In the meantime, the Community and its member States request the UN Secretary General and the UN Security Council to continue their efforts to establish an effective cease-fire and promote a peaceful and negotiated outcome to the conflict. They continue to attach the greatest importance to the early deployment of a UN peace-keeping force referred to in UN Security Council Resolution 724.

The Community and its member States also require a Yugoslav Republic to commit itself, prior to recognition, to adopt constitutional and political guarantees ensuring that it has no territorial claims towards a neighbouring Community State and that it will conduct no hostile propaganda activities versus a neighbouring Community State, including the use of a denomination which implies territorial claims.

Appendix 3: Treaty Provisions for the Convention (at 4 November 1991)

Chapter II Human rights and rights of national or ethnic groups

Article 2

(a)   *Human rights*

1. The Republics shall guarantee the following human rights:
   (a) the right to life
   (b) the right not to be subjected to torture or to inhuman or degrading treatment
   (c) the right not to be subjected to slavery or compulsory labour
   (d) the right to liberty
   (e) the right to a fair and public hearing by an impartial tribunal and not to be subject to retrospective criminal proceedings
   (f) the right to respect for private and family life, the home and correspondence
   (g) the right to freedom of thought, conscience and religion
   (h) the right to freedom of expression
   (i) the right of freedom of peaceful assembly and freedom of association
   (j) the right to marry and form a family
   (k) the right to an effective remedy determined by law and available to all persons whose human rights have been violated, and
   (l) all the other rights envisaged in the instruments listed below, subject only to the exceptions and restrictions set out in those instruments, and without discrimination on any ground such as sex, race, colour, language, religion, political or other opinion, national or social origin, association with a national minority, property, birth or other status.

The instruments referred to above are:

— the Universal Declaration of Human Rights, the International Covenant on Civil and Political Rights, the International Covenant on Economic, Social and Cultural Rights of the United Nations;
— the Final Act of the Conference on Security and Co-operation in Europe, the Charter of Paris for the New Europe and the other CSCE documents relating to the human dimension, in particular the Document of the Copenhagen Meeting of the Conference on the Human Dimension of the CSCE and the document of the Moscow meeting of the Conference on the Human Dimension of the CSCE;
— The Council of Europe Convention for the Protection of Human Rights and Fundamental Freedoms and the Protocols to that Convention.

(b)   Rights of members of national or ethnic groups

2. The Republics shall guarantee human rights as applied to national or ethnic groups, in particular, and embodied in:
— the instruments of the United Nations, CSCE and the Council of Europe referred to in paragraph 1 of this Article;
— the Convention on the Elimination of Racial Discrimination, the Convention on the Prevention and Punishment of the Crime of Genocide and the Convention on the Rights of the Child of the United Nations;
— the report of the CSCE meeting of experts on national minorities held in Geneva.

In giving effect to this Convention, they shall also take appropriate account of

— proposals for a United Nations Declaration on the Rights of Persons belonging to National or Ethnic, Religious and Linguistic Minorities;
— the proposals for a Convention for the Protection of Minorities of the European Commission for Democracy and Law in the framework of the Council of Europe.

3. The Republic shall guarantee to persons belonging to a national or ethnic group the following rights:
— the principle of non-discrimination as set out in the legal instruments mentioned in paragraph 2 of this Article;

- the right to be protected against any activity capable of threatening their existence;
- all cultural rights as set out in the instruments mentioned in paragraph 2 of this Article, in particular the right to identity, culture, religion, use of language and alphabet, both in public and in private, and education;
- protection of equal participation in public affairs, such as the exercise of political and economic freedoms, in the social sphere, in access to the media and in the field of education and cultural affairs generally;
- the right to decide to which national or ethnic group he or she wishes to belong, and to exercise any rights pertaining to this choice as an individual or in association with others. No disadvantage shall arise from a person's choice to belong or not to belong to a national or ethnic group. This right shall particularly apply in the case of marriage between persons of different national or ethnic groups.

Those persons of the same national or ethnic group living distant from others of the same origin, for example, in isolated villages, shall be granted self-administration, to the extent that it is practicable.

The above principles shall also apply in areas where members of the main national or ethnic group of a Republic are numerically inferior to one or more other national or ethnic groups in that area.

4. The Republics shall guarantee to persons belonging to a national or ethnic group forming a substantial percentage of the population in the Republic where they live but not forming a majority, in addition to the rights set out in paragraph 3 of this Article, a general right of participation of members of this group in public affairs, including participation in the government of the Republics concerning their affairs.

(c)   Special status

5. In addition, areas in which persons belonging to a national or ethnic group form a majority, shall enjoy a special status of autonomy. Such a status will provide for:

   a. the right to have and show the national emblems of that area;
   b. (deleted)
   c. an educational system which respects the values and needs of that group;
   d. i. a legislative body,

    ii. an administrative structure, including a regional police force, and

    iii. a judiciary,

responsible for matters concerning the area, which reflects the composition of the population of the area;

    e. provisions for appropriate international monitoring.

These areas are listed in Annex A.

5A. Such areas, unless they are defined in part by an international frontier with a State not party to this Convention, shall be permanently demilitarised and no military forces, exercises or activities on land or in the air shall be permitted in those areas.

5B.

    (a) The Republics shall provide for international monitoring of the implementation of the special status of autonomy. To this end, they shall conclude agreements which would provide for a permanent international body to monitor implementation of this paragraph.

    (b) The monitoring missions thus established shall
      — report to the Republics in question as well as to the other parties to the agreement, and
      — as appropriate formulate recommendations on the implementation of the special status.

    (c) The Republics shall give effect to such recommendations through legislation or otherwise. In case of dispute, the Court of Human Rights shall be requested to give its decision.

6. (deleted)

(d)   *General provisions*

7. Persons belonging to a national or ethnic group, in exercising their rights, respect the rights of the majority and of persons belonging to other groups.

8. The Republics should jointly, or individually as the case may be, become parties to international instruments in the field of human rights, including all related complaint procedures.

9. The Republics shall provide, by legislation and through national institutions, in respect of the rights referred to in this Article,

full implementation of the rights and an effective remedy for breaches of any of those rights.

10. As none of the Republics will have an ethnically homogeneous population, they shall cooperate and consult one another directly or through a mixed commission in respect of matters dealt with in paragraph 3 to 5 of this Article.

Bibliography

PRIMARY MATERIALS

TREATIES

Agreement Establishing the European Bank for Reconstruction and Development (1990)
Convention on Rights and Duties of States (1933)
Covenant of the League of Nations (1919)
General Framework Agreement for Peace in Bosnia and Herzegovina (1995)
International Bank for Reconstruction and Development Articles of Agreement (as amended in 1989)
North Atlantic Treaty (1949)
Polish Minorities Treaty (1919)
Single European Act (1986)
Statute of the Council of Europe (1949)
Statute of the International Court of Justice (1945)
Treaty of Berlin (1878)
Treaty on European Union (1992)
United Nations Charter (1945)
Vienna Convention on the Law of Treaties (1969)

DOCUMENTS

Conference on Security and Co-operation in Europe (CSCE)
Conference on Security and Co-operation in Europe, Final Act (1 August 1975)
'The Situation in Yugoslavia', Third Additional Meeting of the Committee of Senior Officials, Prague, 10 October 1991
'Decisions of the Committee of Senior Officials', Thirteenth Meeting of the Committee of Senior Officials, Helsinki, 7 July 1992

Council of Europe
Committee of Ministers Resolution (69) 51 (12 December 1969)
Committee of Ministers Resolution (74) 34 (28 November 1974)

European Community
EPC 'Declaration on China', 26–27 June 1990
European Parliament, 'Resolution on the Situation in Yugoslavia', 15 March
    1991
'Common Declaration on the Peaceful Resolution of the Yugoslav Crisis' (Brioni
    Agreement), 7 July 1991
EPC 'Declaration on Yugoslavia', 27 August 1991
'Joint Statement', 28 August 1991
'Declaration on Yugoslavia', Informal Meeting of Ministers of Foreign Affairs
    (Haarzuilens), 6 October 1991
'Declaration on Yugoslavia', Extraordinary EPC Ministerial Meeting (Rome),
    8 November 1991
'Resolution of the Council and of the Member States Meeting in the Council on
    Human Rights, Democracy and Development', 28 November 1991
'Declaration on the "Guidelines on the Recognition of New States in Eastern
    Europe and in the Soviet Union"', Extraordinary EPC Ministerial Meeting
    (Brussels), 16 December 1991
'Declaration on Yugoslavia', Extraordinary EPC Ministerial Meeting (Brussels),
    16 December 1991
'Conclusions of the Presidency', European Council, Copenhagen, 21–22 June
    1993
European Commission, 'Report from the Commission to the Council and the
    European Parliament on the Implementation in 1993 of the Resolution of
    the Council and of the Member States Meeting in the Council on Human
    Rights, Democracy and Development, Adopted on 28 November 1991',
    COM(94) 42 final, 23 February 1994
'Declaration by the Presidency on Behalf of the European Union Concerning
    Chechnya', Council of the European Union, 17 January 1995
'Presidency Statement on Behalf of the European Union Concerning the
    Member States' Recognition of the Federal Republic of Yugoslavia',
    9–10 April 1996 (Rome and Brussels)
European Commission, Composite Paper, 'Reports on Progress Towards Acces-
    sion by Each of the Candidate Countries', 4 November 1998, available at
    http://europa.eu.int/comm/enlargement/report_11_98/intro/index.htm

EC Arbitration Commission (Badinter Commission)
Opinion No. 1 (29 November 1991)
Letter from Dr Franjo Tudjman, President of Croatia, to Mr Robert Badinter,
    Chairman of the Arbitration Commission (11 January 1992)
Opinion No. 2 (11 January 1992)
Opinion No. 3 (11 January 1992)
Opinion No. 4 (11 January 1992)
Opinion No. 5 (11 January 1992)
Opinion No. 6 (11 January 1992)
Opinion No. 7 (11 January 1992)
Interlocutory Decision (4 July 1992)
Opinion No. 8 (4 July 1992)

Opinion No. 9 (4 July 1992)
Opinion No. 10 (4 July 1992)
Comments on the Republic of Croatia's Constitutional Law of 4 December 1991, as last amended on 8 May 1992 (4 July 1992)

EC Conference on Yugoslavia
Background briefing by Ambassador Geert Ahrens (6 October 1991)
Arrangements for a General Settlement (18 October 1991)
Treaty Provisions for the Convention (23 October 1991)
Treaty Provisions for the Convention (4 November 1991)
Statement of Principles for New Constitutional Arrangements for Bosnia and Herzegovina (18 March 1992)
Working Group on Ethnic and National Communities and Minorities, Sub-Group on Macedonia, 'Present State of the Talks with Representatives of the Macedonian Government and of the Albanians from Macedonia' (*c.* July 1993)
Biannual Report of the Co-Chairmen of the Steering Committee on the Activities of the International Conference on the Former Yugoslavia, UN Doc. S/1994/1454, 29 December 1994, Annex

United Nations
General Assembly and Security Council Resolutions
UN General Assembly Res 1497 (XV), 31 October 1960
UN General Assembly Res 2625 (XXV), 24 October 1970
UN General Assembly Res 31/4, 21 October 1976
UN Security Council Res 169 (1961), 15 November 1961
UN Security Council Res 217 (1965), 12 November 1965
UN Security Council Res 678 (1990), 29 November 1990
UN Security Council Res 713 (1991), 25 September 1991
UN Security Council Res 1244 (1999), 10 June 1999

Reports
Report of the Secretary-General Pursuant to Paragraph 3 of Security Council Resolution 713 (1991), UN Doc. S/23169 (25 October 1991)
Report of the Secretary-General Pursuant to Security Council Resolution 721 (1991), UN Doc. S/23280, 11 December 1991
Further Report of the Secretary-General Pursuant to Security Council Resolution 721 (1991), UN Doc. S/23363, 5 January 1992
Further Report of the Secretary-General Pursuant to Security Council Resolution 721 (1991), UN Doc. S/23513, 4 February 1992
Report of the Secretary-General Pursuant to Security Council Resolution 749 (1992), UN Doc. S/23836, 24 April 1992
Further Report of the Secretary-General Pursuant to Security Council Resolution 749 (1992), UN Doc. S/23844, 24 April 1992
'The Situation in Bosnia and Herzegovina', Report of the Secretary-General, UN Doc. A/47/747, 3 December 1992
Report of the Secretary-General Pursuant to Resolution 871 (1993), UN Doc. S/1994/300, 16 March 1994

Final Report of the United Nations Commission of Experts Established Pursuant to Security Council Resolution 780 (1992), UN Doc. S/1994/674, 27 May 1994

Other UN documents
UN Security Council, *Official Records*, 383rd meeting (2 December 1948)
'The Status of the German-speaking Element of Bolzano (Bozen)', UN General Assembly, 16th Session, Special Political Committee, 289th Meeting, UN Doc. A/SPC/SR.289 (15 November 1961)
UN Security Council, Provisional Verbatim Record of the 1606th meeting, UN Doc. S/PV. 1606 (4 December 1971)
An Agenda for Peace: Preventive Diplomacy, Peacemaking and Peacekeeping, UN Doc. A/47/277 (1992)
Vienna Declaration and Programme of Action, UN Doc. A/Conf.157/23 (12 July 1993)
Letter dated 30 October 1991 from the Permanent Representatives of Belgium, France and the United Kingdom of Great Britain and Northern Ireland to the United Nations Addressed to the President of the Security Council, UN Doc. S/23181 (30 October 1991), Annex
Letter dated 26 November 1991 from the Permanent Representative of Yugoslavia to the United Nations Addressed to the President of the Security Council, UN Doc. S/23240 (26 November 1991)
Letter of the SFRY Presidency to the President of the UN Security Council of 19 December 1991, Embassy of the Socialist Federal Republic of Yugoslavia (London)
Letter dated 25 January 1993 from the Permanent Representative of Greece to the United Nations Addressed to the Secretary-General, UN Doc. S/25158 (25 January 1993), Appendix
United Nations, Department of Peacekeeping Operations, *The United Nations Transitional Administration in Eastern Slavonia, Baranja and Western Sirmium (UNTAES) January 1996 – January 1998: Lessons Learned* (New York: UN Department of Peacekeeping Operations, 1998)

Other documents
'The Aaland Islands Question', report submitted to the Council of the League of Nations by the Commission of Rapporteurs, Doc. B.7.21/68/106 (1921)
Address of 19 March 1992 by Dr Borisav Jović in the Assembly of the Socialist Federal Republic of Yugoslavia
Constitution of Bosnia and Herzegovina (1995)
Constitution of the Republic of Croatia (1990)
Constitution of the Republic of Macedonia (1991)
Constitution of the Republic of Slovenia (1991)
Constitution of the Socialist Federal Republic of Yugoslavia (1974)
Constitutional Act on Human Rights and Freedoms and the Rights of Ethnic and National Communities and Minorities (Croatia), 4 December 1991
Democracy and Human Rights in Eastern Europe, Advisory Report No. 11 (The Hague: Advisory Committee on Human Rights and Foreign Policy, 12 November 1990)

Digest of United States Practice in International Law 1976 (Washington, DC: US Government Printing Office, 1977)

Foreign and Commonwealth Office, *Human Rights in Foreign Policy*, Foreign Policy Document No. 215 (London: January 1991)

Foreign Office (Bonn), 'Recognition of the Yugoslav Successor States', mimeo, 10 March 1993

House of Commons, Foreign Affairs Committee, First Report, *Central and Eastern Europe: Problems of the Post-Communist Era* (HC 21-II), vol. II, Minutes of Evidence, HC Session 1991–92

'Instructions for the Organisation and Activity of Organs of the Serbian People in Bosnia and Herzegovina in Extraordinary Circumstances', 19 December 1991, unpublished English translation of Bosnian Serb document (Copy No. 096) submitted as evidence at the International Criminal Tribunal for the Former Yugoslavia in Case No. IT-95-18-R61, *Prosecutor of the Tribunal v Radovan Karadžić and Ratko Mladić*

Letter dated 21 December 1991 by the Government of the Republic of Kosovo to the extraordinary EPC ministerial meeting in Brussels

Memo dated 20 March 1992 from General Milutin Kukanjac, the JNA commander of Sarajevo, to the General Staff of the Armed Forces SFRY

'Naputak za izradu ustava Republike Hrvatske', notes for a Croatian constitution by Slaven Letica, advisor to President Franjo Tudjman, with marginalia of President Tudjman, 14 July 1990

'Naredba SDS Sarajevo' [Orders of SDS Sarajevo], 29 October 1991

Il nuovo Statuto di Autonomia (Trentino–Alto Adige) (1972)

Parliamentary Debates (Hansard), 1980–95

'Polazišta za rješenje Srpskog pitanja u Hrvatskoj', memorandum of Milorad Pupovac, co-founder of the Serbian Democratic Forum, discussing resolution of the Serbian question in Croatia in relation to the Conference on Yugoslavia, October 1991

La politique étrangère de la France: textes et documents (Paris: Ministère des Affaires Étrangères, 1989–91)

'The Position of the SFRY Presidency on the Legal Aspect of the Yugoslav Crisis', statement of the Embassy of the Socialist Federal Republic of Yugoslavia (London), 11 December 1991

'Post Report for September and October 1992', US Government memorandum, Skopje, 26 October 1992

'Primjedbe na nacrt ustava Republike Hrvtske', memorandum from Jovan Rašković, co-founder of the Serbian Democratic Forum, to Slaven Letica, 11 December 1990

'Promemorija o položaju Srpskog naroda u Republici Hrvatskoj', memorandum of the Serbian Democratic Forum to the Conference on Yugoslavia, 25 September 1991

Statement of 30 April 1993 by the government of the Federal Republic of Yugoslavia

Statistisches Jahrbuch für die Bundesrepublik Deutschland (Wiesbaden: Statistisches Bundesamt, 1995)

US Agency for International Development, *The Democracy Initiative* (Washington, DC: USAID, December 1990)

Democracy and Governance (Washington, DC: USAID, November 1991)

US Commission on Security and Cooperation in Europe, *Minority Rights: Problems, Parameters, and Patterns in the CSCE Context* (Washington, DC: Congressional Information Service, 1991)

Verhandlungen des deutschen Bundestages, 12.Wahlperiode. Drucksache 12/1591 (14.11.91)

Westminster Foundation for Democracy, *Annual Report 1995–96* (London, Westminster Foundation for Democracy: 1996)

WEU Ministerial Statement (Document 1280), Vianden, Luxembourg, 27 June 1991

CASES

The City of Berne Bank v Bank of England (1804)

Deutsche Continental Gas Gesellschaft v Polish State (1929)

Frontier Dispute Case (Burkina Faso v Republic of Mali) (1985)

Nicaragua v USA (1986)

Republic of Somalia v Woodhouse Drake & Carey (Suisse) SA (1992)

Application of the Convention on the Prevention and Punishment of the Crime of Genocide (Bosnia-Herzegovina v Yugoslavia) (1993)

Prosecutor of the Tribunal v Dusko Tadić (Case No. IT-94-1-T) (1994)

INTERVIEWS

Bavčar, Igor: independent Slovenia's first minister of the interior. Ljubljana, 4 June 1997

Bavcon, Ljubo: former president of Slovenia's Council of Human Rights and Fundamental Freedom. Ljubljana, 5 June 1997

Begić, Kasim: professor of international law, University of Sarajevo. Sarajevo, 20 June 1997

Biserko, Sonja: former head of the Department for Analysis and Strategy, Yugoslav Ministry of Foreign Affairs. London, 12 December 1996

Brejc, Miha: independent Slovenia's first director of intelligence. Ljubljana, 4 June 1997

Bučar, France: former speaker of the Slovene Assembly. Ljubljana, 3 June 1997

Budiša, Dražen: member of Croatian Parliament, minister without portfolio from August 1992 to February 1992, former president of the Croatian Social Liberal Party. Zagreb, 11 July 1997

Čamu, Mensur: Bosnian journalist with *Slobodna Bosna*. London, 17 October 1996

Chrobog, Jürgen: former German political director, 3 June 1999 (telephone)

Dejammet, Alain: former French political director. New York, 21 November 1996

Divjak, Jovan: former Bosnian Serb commander of the Bosnian territorial defence and deputy commander of independent Bosnia and Herzegovina's army. Sarajevo, 19 June 1997

Dizdarević, Zlatko: editor of the Sarajevo daily *Oslobodjenje*. Sarajevo, 16 June 1997

Filipović, Muhamed: vice-president of the Bosnian Liberal Party. Sarajevo, 18 June 1997

Hopkinson, William: former British assistant under-secretary of state (policy). London, 10 September 1996

Kacin, Jelko: independent Slovenia's first minister of information. Ljubljana, 5 June 1997

Kosin, Marko: former Yugoslav and then Slovene ambassador to Italy. Ljubljana, 4 June 1997

Ladjević, Peter: co-founder of the Serbian Democratic Forum. Zagreb, 12 June 1997

Letica, Slaven: former advisor to Croatian President Franjo Tudjman. Zagreb, 12 and 13 June 1997

Lever, Paul: former head of the Security Policy Department of the Foreign and Commonwealth Office. London, 14 November 1996

Mesić, Stipe: Croatia's representative on the Federal Presidency and former advisor to President Tudjman. Zagreb, 12 June 1997

Neville-Jones, Pauline: former British political director. London, 30 October 1996

Pajić, Zoran: former professor of law, University of Sarajevo. London, 28 April 1997

Peterle, Lojze: independent Slovenia's first prime minister. Ljubljana, 3 June 1997

Pupovac, Milorad: co-founder of the Serbian Democratic Forum. Zagreb, 10 July 1997

Šeparović, Zvonimir: former Croatian minister of foreign affairs. Zagreb, 14 July 1997

Silajdzić, Haris: former foreign minister of Bosnia and Herzegovina. Sarajevo, 16 June 1997

Šinkovec, Matjaž: member of the Slovene delegation to the Conference on Yugoslavia. London, 21 May 1997

Škare-Ožbolt, Vesna: deputy chief of the Office of the President. Zagreb, 11 July 1997

Tharoor, Shashi: special assistant to the UN head of peacekeeping operations. New York, 28 April 1994

Tus, Antun: former head of Croatian armed forces. Zagreb, 11 July 1997

Van den Broek, Hans: former Dutch foreign minister. 19 February 1998 (telephone)

Van Walsum, Peter: former Dutch political director. 24 March 1998 (telephone)

Williams, Paul: former legal adviser in the US State Department. London, 15 March 1996

Wynaendts, Henry: deputy to Lord Carrington at the Conference on Yugoslavia. 5 December 1997 (telephone)

Zimmermann, Warren: former US ambassador to Yugoslavia. New York, 20 November 1996

Zorc, Milovan: former JNA commander and later adviser to the Slovene president. Ljubljana, 6 June 1997

INTERVIEWS FOR `THE DEATH OF YUGOSLAVIA´ TELEVISION SERIES

Babić, Milan: leader of the Krajina Serb rebellion in Croatia. Liddell Hart Centre for Military Archives, King's College London (hereafter LHCMA), undated, Box 18, File 1

Bulatović, Momir: political ally of Milošević and former president of Montenegro. LHCMA, 7 October 1994, Box 18, File 1

Carrington, Lord Peter: chairman of the EC Conference on Yugoslavia. LHCMA, 4 April 1995, Box 18, File 1

Ganić, Ejup: former vice-president of independent Bosnia and Herzegovina. LHCMA, undated, Box 18, File 1

Genscher, Hans-Dietrich: former German foreign minister. LHCMA, undated, Box 18, File 1

Izetbegović, Alija: president of Bosnia and Herzegovina. LHCMA, undated, Box 18, File 2

Jović, Borisav: Serbia's representative on the Yugoslav Federal Presidency. LHCMA, undated, Box 18, File 2

Karadžić, Radovan: Bosnian Serb leader from 1990. LHCMA, undated, Box 18, File 2

Koljević, Nikola: Bosnian Serb vice-president. LHCMA, undated, Box 18, File 2

Kostić, Branko: former acting president of rump Yugoslavia. LHCMA, 8 August 1994, Box 18, File 2

Rupel, Dimitrij: first foreign minister of independent Slovenia. LHCMA, undated, Box 18, File 4

Šešelj, Vojislav: Serb ultranationalist who commanded a paramilitary unit during the war. LHCMA, undated, Box 18, File 4

Tudjman, Franjo: president of Croatia. LHCMA, undated, Box 18, File 4

SPEECHES

Chalker, Lynda: 'Good Government and the Aid Programme', Royal Institute of International Affairs, London, 25 June 1991

Hurd, Douglas: 'Prospects for Africa in the 1990s', Overseas Development Institute, London, 6 June 1990

Janša, Janez: Remarks delivered at the Department of War Studies, King's College London, 1 November 1995

Thant, U: Remarks delivered in Accra, Ghana on 9 January 1970 and published as 'Secretary-General's Press Conferences', *UN Monthly Chronicle* (7)(2) (February 1970), 36–44

CORRESPONDENCE

Letter to the author from Geert-Hinrich Ahrens, head of the working group on human and minority rights; drafted Chapter II of the Treaty Provisions for the Convention, 27 November 1997

Letter from US Congressman Lee H. Hamilton to Acting US Secretary of State Lawrence Eagleburger, 22 October 1992

Letter to the author from Stjepan Kljuić, Croat member of the Bosnian Presidency, 31 July 1998
Letter to the author from Paul Sizeland, Carrington's private secretary, 3 November 1997
Letter from A. P. van Walsum, Dutch ambassador to Germany, to Michael Libal, Head of OSCE Mission to Georgia, 13 March 1998

NEWSPAPERS AND BROADCASTING SERVICES

Agence Europe (Brussels)
Daily Telegraph
Das Parlament (Bonn)
Die Presse (Vienna)
The Economist
European Parliament, The Week (Strasbourg)
Financial Times
Foreign Broadcast Information Service, *Daily Report: East Europe*
Frankfurter Allgemeine Zeitung
The Guardian
The Independent
International Herald Tribune
Keesing's Record of World Events
Le Monde
New York Times
The Observer
RFE/RL Balkan Report
RFE/RL Research Report ('Weekly Review')
RFE/RL Weekday Magazine
The Times
Washington Post

SECONDARY MATERIAL

BOOKS, PERIODICALS AND REPORTS

Abbott, Kenneth W., 'International Law and International Relations Theory: Building Bridges – Elements of a Joint Discipline', 86 *Proceedings of the American Society of International Law* (1992), 167–72.
'Modern International Relations Theory: A Prospectus for International Lawyers', 14 *Yale Journal of International Law* (1989), 335–411.
Academy of Sciences of the Republic of Albania, Institute of History (ed.), *The Truth on Kosova* (Tirana: Encyclopaedia Publishing House, 1993).
Acheson, Dean, 'Remarks', 57 *Proceedings of the American Society of International Law* (1963), 13–15.
Akehurst, Michael, 'Custom as a Source of International Law', 47 *British Year Book of International Law* (1974–75), 1–53.
Alcock, Antony E., *The History of the South Tyrol Question* (London: Michael Joseph, 1970).

Alker, Jr., Hayward R., 'A Methodology for Design Research on Interdependence Alternatives', 31 *International Organization* (1977), 29–63.

Allcock, John B., 'The Dilemmas of an Independent Macedonia', *ISIS Briefing*, No. 42 (London: International Security Information Service, June 1994).

Allcock, John B., *et al.* (eds.), *Border and Territorial Disputes*, 3rd edn (Harlow: Longman, 1992).

Amin, Samir, 'The Issue of Democracy in the Contemporary Third World', in Barry Gills, Joel Rocamora and Richard Wilson (eds.), *Low Intensity Democracy* (London: Pluto Press, 1993), pp. 59–79.

Anderson, Jeffrey J. and Goodman, John B., 'Mars or Minerva? A United Germany in a Post-Cold War Europe', in Robert O. Keohane, Joseph S. Nye and Stanley Hoffmann (eds.), *After the Cold War: International Institutions and State Strategies in Europe, 1989–1991* (Cambridge, MA: Harvard University Press, 1993), pp. 23–62.

Andrejevich, Milan, 'Bosnia and Herzegovina: A Precarious Peace', *RFE/RL Research Report*, 28 February 1992, pp. 6–14.

Annual Digest of Public International Law Cases (London: Longmans, Green & Co., 1935), vol. V (1929–30).

Attali, Jacques, *Verbatim* (Paris: Fayard, 1995), vol. III.

Austin, John, *The Province of Jurisprudence Determined*, 5th edn (London: John Murray, 1885).

Bagwell, Ben, 'Yugoslavian Constitutional Questions: Self-Determination and Secession of Member Republics', 21 *Georgia Journal of International and Comparative Law* (1991), 489–523.

Barkan, Joel D., 'Can Established Democracies Nurture Democracy Abroad? Lessons from Africa', in Axel Hadenius (ed.), *Democracy's Victory and Crisis* (Cambridge: Cambridge University Press, 1997), pp. 371–403.

Bass, Hans H., 'The Human Rights Dimension of Germany's Development Aid: Two Examples', 6 *Berichte und Analysen Dritte Welt* (1994), 1–26.

Baylies, Carolyn, '"Political Conditionality" and Democratisation', 65 *Review of African Political Economy* (1995), 321–37.

Beck, Robert J., Arend, Anthony Clark and Vander Lugt, Robert D. (eds.), *International Rules: Approaches from International Law and International Relations* (New York: Oxford University Press, 1996).

Bennett, Christopher, *Yugoslavia's Bloody Collapse: Causes, Course and Consequences* (London: C. Hurst & Co., 1995).

Bhalla, Surjit, 'Freedom and Economic Growth: A Virtuous Cycle?' in Axel Hadenius (ed.), *Democracy's Victory and Crisis* (Cambridge: Cambridge University Press, 1977), pp. 195–241.

Bieber, Roland, 'European Community Recognition of Eastern European States: A Perspective for International Law', 86 *Proceedings of the American Society of International Law* (1992), 374–8.

Bildt, Carl, *Peace Journey: The Struggle for Peace in Bosnia* (London: Weidenfeld & Nicolson, 1998).

Biserko, Sonja and Stanojlović, Seška (eds.), *Radicalisation of the Serbian Society: Collection of Documents* (Belgrade: Helsinki Committee for Human Rights in Serbia, 1997).

Blay, S. K. N., 'Self-determination in Cyprus: The New Dimensions of an Old Conflict', 10 *Australian Yearbook of International Law* (1987), 67–100.

Borden, Anthony and Caplan, Richard, 'The Former Yugoslavia: The War and the Peace Process', in *SIPRI Yearbook 1996* (Oxford: SIPRI/Oxford University Press, 1996), pp. 203–31.

Borden, Anthony and Hedl, Drago, 'How the Bosnians Were Broken: 21 Days at Dayton', *War Report* No. 39 (February/March 1996), pp. 26–42.

Bosnia and Herzegovina: Essential Texts, revised and updated edition (Brussels: Office of the High Representative, May 1997).

Both, Norbert, *From Indifference to Entrapment: The Netherlands and the Yugoslav Crisis 1990–1995* (Amsterdam: Amsterdam University Press, 2000).

Boyle, Francis Anthony, *World Politics and International Law* (Durham, NC: Duke University Press, 1985).

Brierly, J. R., *The Outlook for International Law* (Oxford: Clarendon Press, 1944).

Brilmayer, Lea, 'Secession and Self-Determination: A Territorial Interpretation', 16 *Yale Journal of International Law* (1991), 177–202.

Brown, Michael E. (ed.), *The International Dimensions of Internal Conflict* (Cambridge, MA: CSIA/MIT Press, 1996).

Brownlie, Ian, *Principles of Public International Law*, 2nd edn (Oxford: Oxford University Press, 1973).

'Recognition in Theory and Practice', in R. St. J. Macdonald and Douglas M. Johnston (eds.), *The Structure and Process of International Law: Modern Essays in Legal Philosophy, Doctrine and Theory* (The Hague: Martinus Nijhoff, 1983), pp. 627–41.

Brubaker, Rogers, *Nationalism Reframed: Nationhood and the National Question in the New Europe* (Cambridge: Cambridge University Press, 1996).

Bull, Hedley, *The Anarchical Society: A Study of Order in World Politics* (London: Macmillan, 1977).

'Recapturing the Just War for Political Theory', 31 *World Politics* (1979), 588–99.

Byers, Michael, 'A Safer Place for All', *The World Today*, January 1999, pp. 4–6.

Caplan, Richard, 'Conditional Recognition as an Instrument of Ethnic Conflict Regulation: The European Community and Yugoslavia', 8 *Nations and Nationalism* (2002), 157–77.

'The European Community's Recognition of New States in Former Yugoslavia: The Strategic Implications', 21(3) *The Journal of Strategic Studies* (1998), 24–45.

'International Diplomacy and the Crisis in Kosovo', 74 *International Affairs* (1998), 745–61.

International Governance of War-Torn Territories: Rule and Reconstruction (Oxford: Oxford University Press, 2005).

Caplan, Richard and Feffer, John (eds.), *Europe's New Nationalism: States and Minorities in Conflict* (New York: Oxford University Press, 1996).

Carleton, David and Stohl, Michael, 'The Role of Human Rights in U.S. Foreign Assistance Policy: A Critique and Reappraisal', 31 *American Journal of Political Science* (1987), 1002–18.

Carrington, The Rt Hon. Lord, 'Turmoil in the Balkans: Developments and Prospects', *RUSI Journal* (October 1992), 1–4.

Cassese, Antonio, *International Law in a Divided World* (Oxford: Clarendon Press, 1991).

Self-Determination of Peoples: A Legal Reappraisal (Cambridge: Cambridge University Press, 1995).

Čekić, Smail, *Agresija na Bosnu i Genocid nad Bošnjacima 1991–1993* (Sarajevo: Ljiljan, 1994).

Charpentier, Jean, 'Les déclarations des Douze sur la reconnaissance des nouveaux états', 96 *Revue générale de droit international public* (1992), 343–55.

Chayes, Abram and Chayes, Antonia Handler (eds.), *Preventing Conflict in the Post-Communist World* (Washington, DC: The Brookings Institution, 1996).

Chen, T. C., *The International Law of Recognition* (London: Stevens & Sons, 1951).

Cigar, Norman, *Genocide in Bosnia: The Policy of "Ethnic Cleansing"* (College Station, TX: Texas A & M University Press, 1995).

'The Serbo-Croatian War, 1991: Political and Military Dimensions', 16(3) *Journal of Strategic Studies* (1993), 297–338.

Clapham, Christopher, 'Political Conditionality and Structures of the African State', 25(2) *Africa Insight* (1995), 91–7.

Clark, Grenville and Sohn, Louis B., *World Peace Through World Law* (Cambridge, MA: Harvard University Press, 1958).

Clément, Sophia, *Conflict Prevention in the Balkans: Case Studies of Kosovo and the FYR of Macedonia*, Chaillot Paper No. 30 (Paris: Institute for Security Studies of the Western European Union, 1997).

Clough, Michael, 'Grass-Roots Policymaking', 73(1) *Foreign Affairs* (1994), 2–7.

Cohen, Lenard J., *Broken Bonds: Yugoslavia's Disintegration and Balkan Politics in Transition*, 2nd edn (Boulder, CO: Westview Press, 1995).

Cohen, Stephen B., 'Conditioning U.S. Security Assistance on Human Rights Practices', 76 *American Journal of International Law* (1982), 246–79.

Conversi, Daniele, *German-Bashing and the Breakup of Yugoslavia*, Donald W. Treadgold Paper No. 16 (Seattle, WA: The Henry M. Jackson School of International Studies/University of Washington, 1998).

Cooper, Robert and Berdal, Mats, 'Outside Intervention in Ethnic Conflicts', 35(1) *Survival* (1993), 118–42.

Corbo, Vittorio and Fischer, Stanley, 'Adjustment Programmes and World Bank Support: Rationale and Main Results', in Paul Mosely (ed.), *Development Finance and Policy Reform* (London: Macmillan, 1992), pp. 157–75.

Cossiga, Francesco, 'Perché contiamo poco', 3 *Limes* (1995), 13–21.

Craven, Matthew C. R., 'The European Community Arbitration Commission on Yugoslavia', 66 *British Year Book of International Law* (1995), 333–413.

Crawford, Beverly, 'Explaining Defection from International Cooperation: Germany's Unilateral Recognition of Croatia', 48 *World Politics* (1996), 482–521.

'German Foreign Policy and European Political Cooperation: The Diplomatic Recognition of Croatia in 1991', 13(2) *German Politics and Society* (1995), 1–34.

Crawford, Gordon, 'Promoting Democracy, Human Rights and Good Governance through Development Aid: A Comparative Study of the Policies of Four Northern Donors', Working Paper on Democratization No. 1 (Leeds: Centre for Democratization Studies, University of Leeds, 1996).

'Promoting Political Reform through Aid Sanctions: Instrumental and Normative Issues', Working Paper on Democratization (Leeds: Centre for Democratization Studies, University of Leeds, 1997).

Crawford, James, *The Creation of States in International Law* (Oxford: Clarendon Press, 1979).

'*Democracy in International Law*', inaugural lecture, University of Cambridge, 5 March 1993 (Cambridge: Cambridge University Press, 1994).

'Negotiating Global Security Threats in a World of Nation States', 38 *American Behavioral Scientist* (1995), 867–88.

'State Practice and International Law in Relation to Secession', 69 *British Year Book of International Law* (1998), 85–117.

Crnobrnja, Mihailo, *The Yugoslav Drama*, 2nd edn (London: I. B. Tauris, 1996).

Dalton, Richard, 'The Role of the CSCE', in Hugh Miall (ed.), *Minority Rights in Europe: The Scope for a Transnational Regime* (London: Pinter/RIIA, 1994), pp. 99–111.

D'Amato, Anthony, *International Law: Process and Prospect* (Dobbs Ferry, NY: Transactional Publishers, 1987).

Jurisprudence: A Descriptive and Normative Analysis of Law (Dordrecht: Martinus Nijhoff Publishers, 1984).

De Michelis, Gianni, 'Così cercammo di impedire la guerra', 1 *Limes* (1994), 229–36.

De Visscher, Charles, *Theory and Reality in Public International Law* (Princeton: Princeton University Press, 1957).

Diamond, Larry, 'Promoting Democracy', 87 *Foreign Policy* (1992), 25–46.

'Promoting Democracy in the 1990s: Actors, Instruments and Issues', in Axel Hadenius (ed.), *Democracy's Victory and Crisis* (Cambridge: Cambridge University Press, 1997), pp. 311–70.

Dixon, Martin and McCorquodale, Robert (eds.), *Cases and Materials on International Law* (London: Blackstone, 1991).

Djilas, Aleksa, *The Contested Country: Yugoslav Unity and Communist Revolution, 1919–1953* (Cambridge, MA: Harvard University Press, 1991).

Donnelly, Jack, 'International Human Rights: A Regime Analysis', 40 *International Organization* (1986), 599–642.

'The Past, the Present and the Future Prospects', in Milton J. Esman and Shibley Telhami (eds.), *International Organizations and Ethnic Conflict* (Ithaca, NY: Cornell University Press, 1995), pp. 48–71.

Dugard, John, *Recognition and the United Nations* (Cambridge: Grotius Publications, 1987).

Edwards, Geoffrey, 'European Responses to the Yugoslav Crisis: An Interim Assessment', in Reinhardt Rummel (ed.), *Toward Political Union: Planning a Common Foreign and Security Policy in the European Community* (Boulder, CO: Westview Press, 1992), pp. 161–86.

Esman, Milton J., *Ethnic Politics* (Ithaca, NY: Cornell University Press, 1994).

Falk, Richard A., 'The Relevance of Political Context to the Nature and Func-
tioning of International Law: An Intermediate View', in Karl W. Deutsch
and Stanley Hoffmann (eds.), *The Relevance of International Law* (Cam-
bridge, MA: Schenkman, 1968), pp. 133–52.
  The Status of Law in International Society (Princeton: Princeton University
Press, 1970).
Farer, Tom, 'A Paradigm of Legitimate Intervention', in Lori Fisler Damrosch
(ed.), *Enforcing Restraint: Collective Intervention in Internal Conflicts* (New
York: Council on Foreign Relations, 1993), pp. 316–47.
Feffer, John, *Shock Waves: Eastern Europe after the Revolutions* (Boston: South
End Press, 1992).
Felix, David, 'Latin America's Debt Crisis: Overselling the Market Solution',
7 *World Policy Journal* (1990), 733–71.
Forsythe, David P., 'Congress and Human Rights in U.S. Foreign Policy: The
Fate of General Legislation', 9 *Human Rights Quarterly* (1987), 382–404.
Foundation on Inter-Ethnic Relations, *The Role of the High Commissioner on
National Minorities in OSCE Conflict Prevention: An Introduction* (The
Hague: Foundation on Inter-Ethnic Relations, 1997).
Franck, Thomas M., 'The Emerging Right to Democratic Governance', 86
American Journal of International Law (1992), 46–91.
  The Power of Legitimacy Among Nations (New York: Oxford University Press,
1990).
Franck, Thomas and Rodley, Nigel, 'After Bangladesh: The Law of Humanitar-
ian Intervention by Military Force', 67 *American Journal of International Law*
(1973), 275–305.
Freedman, Lawrence (ed.), *Strategic Coercion: Concepts and Cases* (Oxford:
Oxford University Press, 1998).
Friedmann, Wolfgang, 'National Sovereignty, International Cooperation, and
the Reality of International Law', 10 *University of California Los Angeles
Law Review* (1962–3), 739–53.
Fuller, Lon L., 'Law as an Instrument of Social Control and Law as a Facilitation
of Human Interaction', 8 *Archiv für Rechts- und Sozialphilosophie* (1974),
99–105.
Gagnon, Jr, V. P., 'Ethnic Conflict as an Intra-Group Phenomenon: A Prelimi-
nary Framework', 26(1–2) *Revija za sociologiju* (Zagreb) (1995), 81–90.
  'Ethnic Nationalism and International Conflict: The Case of Serbia', 19(3)
International Security (1994/95), 130–66.
Galtung, Johan, 'The Problems of Recognition', *YugoFax* No. 9 (28 December
1991), 1.
Garrity, Patrick J., *Why the Gulf War Still Matters: Foreign Perspectives on the War
and the Future of International Security*, Report No. 13 (Los Alamos, NM:
Center for National Security Studies, July 1993).
Garton Ash, Timothy, *History of the Present* (London: Allen Lane/Penguin Press,
1999).
  In Europe's Name: Germany and the Divided Continent (London: Vintage,
1994).
Gauhar, Altaf, 'Arab Petrodollars: Dashed Hope for a New Economic Order', 4
World Policy Journal (1997), 443–64.

Genscher, Hans-Dietrich, *Erinnerungen* (Berlin: Siedler, 1995).
'Für Recht auf Selbstbestimmung', *Das Parlament* Nr. 47–48 (15/22 November 1991), 7.
George, Alexander L., *Forceful Persuasion: Coercive Diplomacy as an Alternative to War* (Washington, DC: United States Institute of Peace Press, 1991).
Gibbon, Peter, 'The World Bank and the New Politics of Aid', in Georg Sørensen (ed.), *Political Conditionality* (London: Frank Cass, 1993), pp. 35–62.
Glenny, Misha, 'Bosnia Means More Bad News for Balkans', *New Statesman & Society*, 17 April 1992, pp. 26–7.
The Fall of Yugoslavia: The Third Balkan War (London: Penguin, 1992).
Gnesotto, Nicole and Roper, John (eds.), *Western Europe and the Gulf* (Paris: Institute for Security Studies of Western European Union, 1992).
Gong, Gerrit W., *The Standard of 'Civilization' in International Society* (Oxford: Clarendon Press, 1984).
Gow, James, 'Coercive Cadences: The Yugoslav War of Dissolution', in Lawrence Freedman (ed.), *Strategic Coercion: Concepts and Cases* (Oxford: Oxford University Press, 1998), pp. 276–96.
'Deconstructing Yugoslavia', 33(4) *Survival* (1991), 291–311.
'The First Test Case for Integration', *War Report* No. 30 (December 1994/ January 1995), 25–6.
'One Year of War in Bosnia and Herzegovina', *RFE/RL Research Report*, 4 June 1993, pp. 1–13.
'The Role of the Military in the Yugoslav War of Dissolution', 9(1) *Storia delle Relazioni Internazionali* (1993), 111–27.
Triumph of the Lack of Will: International Diplomacy and the Yugoslav War (London: C. Hurst & Co., 1997).
Gow, James and Smith, James D. D., *Peace-making, Peace-keeping: European Security and the Yugoslav Wars*, London Defence Study No. 11 (London: Centre for Defence Studies/Brassey's, 1992).
Guicherd, Catherine, *L'Heure de L'Europe: premières leçons du conflit Yugoslav*, Les Cahiers du CREST No. 10 (Paris: CREST, 1993).
'International Law and the War in Kosovo', 41(2) *Survival* (1999), 19–34.
Gurr, Ted Robert, 'The Internationalization of Protracted Communal Conflicts since 1945: Which Groups, Where, and How', in Manus I. Midlarsky (ed.), *The Internationalization of Communal Strife* (London: Routledge, 1992), pp. 3–26.
Minorities at Risk: A Global View of Ethnopolitical Conflicts (Washington, DC: United States Institute of Peace Press, 1993).
Gurr, Ted Robert and Harff, Barbara, *Ethnic Conflict in World Politics* (Boulder, CO: Westview Press, 1994).
Hadenius, Axel (ed.), *Democracy's Victory and Crisis* (Cambridge: Cambridge University Press, 1977).
Halliday, Fred, *Rethinking International Relations* (Basingstoke: Macmillan, 1994).
Halperin, Morton H. and Scheffer, David J., *Self-Determination in the New World Order* (Washington, DC: Carnegie Endowment for International Peace, 1992).

Hannum, Hurst, *Autonomy, Sovereignty, and Self-Determination: The Accommodation of Conflicting Rights* (Philadelphia: University of Pennsylvania Press, 1990).

'Self-Determination, Yugoslavia, and Europe: Old Wine in New Bottles?' 3(1) *Transnational Law and Contemporary Problems* (1993), 58–69.

'The Specter of Secession: Responding to Claims for Ethnic Self-Determination', 77(2) *Foreign Affairs* (1998), 13–18.

Harris, D. J., *Cases and Materials on International Law*, 5th edn (London: Sweet & Maxwell, 1998).

Hart, H. L. A., *The Concept of Law*, 2nd edn (Oxford: Clarendon Press, 1994).

Havel, Václav, 'The Hope for Europe', *New York Review of Books*, 20 June 1996, pp. 38–41.

Healey, John and Robinson, Mark, *Democracy, Governance and Economic Policy: Sub-Saharan Africa in Comparative Perspective* (London: Overseas Development Institute, 1992).

Helsinki Watch, *Human Rights Abuses in Kosovo, 1990–1992* (New York: Human Rights Watch, 1992).

'Human Rights in the Former Yugoslav Republic of Macedonia', 6(1) *Helsinki Watch* (1994).

Henkin, Louis, 'The Connally Reservation Revisited and, Hopefully, Contained', 65 *American Journal of International Law* (1971), 374–77.

How Nations Behave: Law and Foreign Policy, 2nd edn (New York: Council on Foreign Relations/Columbia University Press, 1979).

Heraclides, Alexis, 'Secessionist Minorities and External Involvement', 44 *International Organization* (1990), 341–78.

Herodotus: the Histories, trans. by Aubrey de Sélincourt (Harmondsworth: Penguin Books, 1954).

Higgins, Rosalyn, *Problems & Process: International Law and How We Use It* (Oxford: Clarendon Press, 1994).

Hillgruber, Christian, 'The Admission of New States to the International Community', 9 *European Journal of International Law* (1998), 491–509.

Hoffmann, Stanley, 'The Study of International Law and the Theory of International Relations', 57 *Proceedings of the American Society of International Law* (1963), 26–35.

Holbrooke, Richard, *To End a War* (New York: Random House, 1998).

'The Road to Sarajevo', *The New Yorker*, 21 & 28 October 1996, pp. 88–104.

Hondius, Frits W., *The Yugoslav Community of Nations* (The Hague: Mouton, 1968).

Horowitz, Donald L., 'The Cracked Foundations of the Right to Secede', 14(2) *Journal of Democracy* (2003), 5–17.

'Ethnic Conflict Management for Policymakers', in Joseph V. Montville (ed.), *Conflict and Peacemaking in Multiethnic Societies* (Lexington, MA: Lexington Books, 1990), pp. 115–30.

Ethnic Groups in Conflict (Berkeley: University of California Press, 1985).

Human Rights Watch, *Civil and Political Rights in Croatia* (New York: Human Rights Watch, 1995).

Human Rights Watch World Report (New York: Human Rights Watch, 1991–).

Hurrell, Andrew, 'International Society and the Study of Regimes: A Reflective Approach', in Robert J. Beck, Anthony Clark Arend, and Robert D. Vander Lugt (eds.), *International Rules: Approaches from International Law and International Relations* (New York: Oxford University Press, 1996), pp. 206–26.

Independent International Commission on Kosovo, *The Kosovo Report: Conflict, International Response, Lessons Learned* (Oxford: Oxford University Press, 2000).

International Commission of Jurists, *The Events in East Pakistan, 1971* (Geneva: International Commission of Jurists, 1972).

International Commission on the Balkans, *Unfinished Peace: Report of the International Commission on the Balkans* (Washington, DC: Carnegie Endowment for International Peace, 1996).

International Crisis Group, 'Kosovo Spring', *ICG Balkans Report*, 20 March 1998 (ICG reports available at http://www.crisisweb.org).
    'Macedonia: No Time for Complacency', *Europe Report No. 149*, 23 October 2003.
    'State of the Balkans', *ICG Balkans Report No. 47*, 4 November 1998.

Jackson, Robert H., *Quasi-states: Sovereignty, International Relations and the Third World* (Cambridge: Cambridge University Press, 1990).

Jackson Preece, Jennifer, 'Minority Rights in Europe: From Westphalia to Helsinki', 23 *Review of International Studies* (1997), 75–92.
    National Minorities and the European Nation-States System (Oxford: Clarendon Press, 1998).

Jakobsen, Peter Viggo, 'Myth-making and Germany's Unilateral Recognition of Croatia and Slovenia', 4 *European Security* (1995), 339–415.

Janša, Janez, *The Making of the Slovenian State, 1988–1992* (Ljubljana: Založba Mladinska knjiga, 1994).

Jennings, Sir Robert and Watts, Sir Arthur (eds.), *Oppenheim's International Law*, 9th edn (Harlow: Longmans, 1992).

Jepperson, Ronald L., Wendt, Alexander and Katzenstein, Peter J., 'Norms, Identity, and Culture in National Security', in Peter J. Katzenstein (ed.), *The Culture of National Security: Norms and Identity in World Politics* (New York: Columbia University Press, 1996), pp. 3–75.

Johnson, A. Ross, *Impressions of Post-Tito Yugoslavia: A Trip Report*, Rand Note N-1813 (Santa Monica, CA: Rand Corporation, January 1982).

Jović, Borisav, *Poslednji dani SFRJ: izvodi iz dnevnika* (Belgrade: Politika, 1995).

Judt, Tony, 'Why the Cold War Worked', *New York Review of Books*, 9 October 1997, pp. 39–44.

Kadijević, General Veljko, *Moje Vidjenje Raspada: Vojska Bez Države* (Belgrade: Politika, 1993).

Kaplan, Robert D., 'History's Cauldron', *The Atlantic Monthly*, June 1991, pp. 92–104.

Katzenstein, Peter J. (ed.), *The Culture of National Security: Norms and Identity in World Politics* (New York: Columbia University Press, 1996).

Kelsen, Hans, *Law and Peace in International Relations* (Cambridge, MA: Harvard University Press, 1942).
    Pure Theory of Law (Berkeley: University of California Press, 1967).

Kennan, George F., *American Diplomacy*, expanded edn (Chicago: University of Chicago Press, 1984).

Kenney, George, 'Derecognition: Exiting Bosnia', *IGCC Policy Brief No. 5* (La Jolla, CA: Institute on Global Conflict and Cooperation, June 1995).

Keohane, Robert O., 'The Analysis of International Regimes: Towards a European-American Research Programme', in Volker Rittberger (ed.), *Regime Theory and International Relations* (Oxford: Clarendon Press, 1995), pp. 23–45.

'Compliance with International Commitments: Politics within a Framework of Law', 86 *Proceedings of the American Society of International Law* (1992), 176–80.

'The Demand for International Regimes', 36 *International Organization* (1982), 325–55.

International Institutions and State Power: Essays in International Relations Theory (Boulder, CO: Westview, 1989).

'The Theory of Hegemonic Stability and Changes in International Economic Regimes, 1967–1977', in Ole R. Holsti, Randolph M. Silverson, and Alexander L. George (eds.), *Change in the International System* (Boulder, CO: Westview, 1980), pp. 131–62.

Keohane, Robert O. and Nye, Joseph S., *Power and Interdependence: World Politics in Transition* (Boston: Little, Brown, 1977).

Keukeleire, Stephan, 'The European Community and Conflict Management', in Werner Bauwens and Lus Reychler (eds.), *The Art of Conflict Prevention* (London: Brassey's, 1994), pp. 137–79.

Kingsbury, Benedict, 'Claims by Non-State Groups in International Law', 25 *Cornell International Law Journal* (1992), 481–513.

Kirgis, Jr, Frederic L., 'The Degrees of Self-Determination in the United Nations Era', 88 *American Journal of International Law* (1994), 304–10.

Kirkpatrick, Jeane J., *Dictatorships and Double Standards: Rationalism and Reason in Politics* (New York: American Enterprise Institute/Simon & Schuster, 1982).

Kissinger, Henry A., *American Foreign Policy* (New York: W. W. Norton & Co., 1969).

Years of Upheaval (London: Weidenfeld & Nicolson and Michael Joseph, 1982).

Klotz, Audie, *Norms in International Relations: The Struggle Against Apartheid* (Ithaca, NY: Cornell University Press, 1995).

Koh, Harold Hongju, 'Review Essay: Why Do Nations Obey International Law?' 106 *Yale Law Journal* (1997), 2599–659.

Kondis, Basil, *et al.* (eds.), *Resurgent Irredentism: Documents on Skopje 'Macedonian' Nationalist Aspirations (1934–1992)* (Thessaloniki: Institute for Balkan Studies, 1993).

Krasner, Stephen D., 'Compromising Westphalia', 20(3) *International Security* (1995/96), 115–51.

'Structural Causes and Regime Consequences: Regimes as Intervening Variables', 36 *International Organization* (1982), 185–205.

Kratochwil, Friedrich V., *Rules, Norms, and Decisions: On the Conditions of Practical and Legal Reasoning in International Relations and Domestic Affairs* (Cambridge: Cambridge University Press, 1989).

Krieger, Wolfgang, 'Toward a Gaullist Germany? Some Lessons from the Yugoslav Crisis', 11(1) *World Policy Journal* (1994), 26–38.

Landell-Mills, Pierre and Serageldin, Ismaïl, 'Governance and the External Factor', *Proceedings of the World Bank Annual Conference on Development Economics 1991* (Washington, DC: World Bank, 1992), pp. 303–20.

Lauterpacht, Hersch, *Recognition in International Law* (Cambridge: Cambridge University Press, 1947).

Leffler, Melvyn P., 'The United States and the Strategic Dimensions of the Marshall Plan', 12 *Diplomatic History* (1988), 277–306.

Levine, Alicia, 'Political Accommodation and the Prevention of Secessionist Violence', in Michael E. Brown (ed.), *The International Dimensions of Internal Conflict* (Cambridge, MA: CSIA/MIT Press, 1996), pp. 311–40.

Libal, Michael, *Limits of Persuasion: Germany and the Yugoslav Crisis, 1991–1992* (Westport, CT: Praeger, 1997).

Lijphart, Arend, *Democracy in Plural Societies: A Comparative Exploration* (New Haven: Yale University Press, 1977).

Lone, Salim, 'Donors Demand Political Reforms', 4(2) *Africa Recovery* (1990), 3, 28–9.

Lowe, A. V. and Warbrick, Colin, 'Recognition of States', 41 *International and Comparative Law Quarterly* (1992), 473–82.

Loza, Tihomir, 'Kosovo Albanians: Closing the Ranks', *Transitions*, May 1998, pp. 16–37.

Lucarelli, Sonia, *Europe and the Breakup of Yugoslavia: A Political Failure in Search of a Scholarly Explanation* (The Hague: Kluwer Law International, 2000).

Lucas, Michael and Edgar, Adrienne, 'Germany after the Wall: Interviews with Bärbel Bohley, Harald Lange, Karsten Voigt and Yuri Davidov', 7 *World Policy Journal* (1989–90), 189–214.

Ludlow, Peter (ed.), *Setting European Community Priorities 1991–92* (London: CEPS/Brassey's, 1991).

Lukic, Reneo and Lynch, Allen, *Europe from the Balkans to the Urals: The Disintegration of Yugoslavia and the Soviet Union* (Oxford: SIPRI/Oxford University Press, 1996).

Macartney, C. A., *National States and National Minorities* (London: Oxford University Press, 1934).

Malcolm, Noel, *Kosovo: A Short History* (London: Macmillan, 1998).

Marantis, Demetrios James, 'Human Rights, Democracy, and Development: the European Community Model', 7 *Harvard Human Rights Journal* (1994), 1–32.

Mastnak, Tomaž, 'Fascists, Liberals, and Anti-Nationalism', in Richard Caplan and John Feffer (eds.), *Europe's New Nationalism: States and Minorities in Conflict* (New York: Oxford University Press, 1996), pp. 59–74.

Mastny, Vojtech, *The Helsinki Process and the Reintegration of Europe, 1986–1991: Analysis and Documentation* (London: Pinter Publishers, 1992).

Maull, Hans W., 'Germany in the Yugoslav Crisis', 37(4) *Survival* (1995–96), 99–130.

Mayall, James, *Nationalism and International Society* (Cambridge: Cambridge University Press, 1990).

McDougal, Myres S. and Lasswell, Harold D., 'The Identification and Appraisal of Diverse Systems of Public Order', in Richard A. Falk and Saul H. Mendlovitz (eds.), *The Strategy of World Order* (New York: World Law Fund, 1966), vol. II, pp. 45–74.

McGarry, John and O'Leary, Brendan (eds.), *The Politics of Ethnic Conflict Regulation: Case Studies of Protracted Ethnic Conflicts* (London: Routledge, 1993).

Medlicott, W. N., *The Congress of Berlin and After: A Diplomatic History of the Near Eastern Settlement 1878–1880* (London: Methuen & Co., 1938).

Meier, Viktor, *Yugoslavia: A History of its Demise* (London: Routledge, 1999).

Meiers, Franz-Josef, 'Germany: The Reluctant Power', 37(3) *Survival* (1995), 82–103.

Mendelson, M. H., 'Diminutive States in the United Nations', 21 *International and Comparative Law Quarterly* (1972), 609–30.

Miall, Hugh (ed.), *Minority Rights in Europe: The Scope for a Transnational Regime* (London: RIIA/Pinter Publishers, 1994).

Midlarsky, Manus I. (ed.), *The Internationalization of Communal Strife* (London: Routledge, 1992).

Mill, John Stuart, 'A Few Words on Non-intervention', in Gertrude Himmelfarb (ed.), *Essays on Politics and Culture* (Gloucester, MA: Peter Smith, 1973), pp. 368–84.

 'Representative Government', in *Utilitarianism, Liberty, and Representative Government* (London: J. M. Dent & Sons, 1940), pp. 171–393.

Minority Rights Group, 'Kosovo: Oppression of Ethnic Albanians' (London: Minority Rights Group, November 1992).

 'Minorities in Croatia' (London: Minority Rights Group, September 2003).

 (Hugh Poulton), 'Minorities in Southeast Europe: Inclusion and Exclusion' (London: Minority Rights Group, 1998).

Mitchell, C. R., 'External Peace-Making Initiatives and Intra-National Conflict', in Manus I. Midlarsky (ed.), *The Internationalization of Communal Strife* (London: Routledge, 1992), pp. 274–96.

Moore, Patrick, 'The "Albanian Question" in the Former Yugoslavia', *RFE/RL Research Report*, 3 April 1992, pp. 7–15.

 'Diplomatic Recognition of Croatia and Slovenia', *RFE/RL Research Report*, 24 January 1992, pp. 9–14.

 'The International Relations of the Yugoslav Area', *RFE/RL Research Report*, 1 May 1992, pp. 33–8.

Morgenthau, Hans J., 'Diplomacy', 55 *Yale Law Journal* (1946), 1067–80.

 'Positivism, Functionalism, and International Law', 34 *American Journal of International Law* (1940), 260–84.

 Politics Among Nations, revised by Kenneth W. Thompson (New York: McGraw-Hill, 1993).

Mortimer, Edward, 'Under What Circumstances Should the UN Intervene Militarily in a "Domestic" Crisis?' in Olara A. Otunnu and Michael W. Doyle (eds.), *Peacemaking and Peacekeeping for the New Century* (Lanham, MD: Rowman & Littlefield, 1998), pp. 111–44.

Mosely, Paul (ed.), *Development Finance and Policy Reform* (London: Macmillan, 1992).

Mosely, Paul, Harrigan, Jane and Toye, John, *Aid and Power: The World Bank and Policy-based Lending* (London: Routledge, 1991), vol. I.

Müller, Harald, 'German Foreign Policy after Unification', in Paul B. Stares (ed.), *The New Germany in the New Europe* (Washington, DC: The Brookings Institution, 1992), pp. 126–73.

Müllerson, Rein, *International Law, Rights and Politics* (London: LSE/Routledge, 1994).

Nedeva, Ivanka, 'Kosovo/a: Different Perspectives', in Thanos Veremis and Evangelos Kofos (eds.), *Kosovo: Avoiding Another Balkan War* (Athens: Hellenic Foundation for European and Foreign Policy, 1998), pp. 99–144.

Nelson, Joan M., 'Good Governance: Democracy and Conditional Economic Aid', in Paul Mosely (ed.), *Development Finance and Policy Reform* (London: Macmillan, 1992), pp. 309–16.

Nelson, Joan M., with Eglinton, Stephanie J., *Encouraging Democracy: What Role for Conditioned Aid?* Policy Essay No. 4 (Washington, DC: Overseas Development Council, 1992).

Neville-Jones, Pauline, 'Dayton, IFOR and Alliance Relations in Bosnia', 38(4) *Survival* (1996–7), 45–65.

Newhouse, John, 'Dodging the Problem', *The New Yorker*, 24 August 1992, pp. 60–71.

Nossiter, Bernard D., *The Global Struggle for More: Third World Conflicts with the Rich Nations* (New York: Harper & Row, 1987).

Nuttall, S. J., *European Political Cooperation* (Oxford: Clarendon Press, 1992).

Nuttall, Simon, 'The EC and Yugoslavia – *Deus ex Machina* or *Machina sine Deo?*' 32 *Journal of Common Market Studies* (Annual Review 1994), 11–25.

Nye, Jr, Joseph S., *Soft Power: The Means to Success in World Politics* (New York: PublicAffairs, 2004).

O'Connell, D. P., *International Law*, 2nd edn (London: Stevens & Sons, 1970), vol. I.

O'Donnell, Guillermo, Schmitter, Philippe C. and Whitehead, Laurence (eds.), *Transitions from Authoritarian Rule: Prospects for Democracy* (Baltimore: The Johns Hopkins University Press, 1986), part IV.

Osiander, Andreas, *The States System of Europe 1640–1990: Peacemaking and the Conditions of International Stability* (Oxford: Clarendon Press, 1994).

Østergaard, Clemens Stubbe, 'Values for Money? Political Conditionality in Aid – The Case of China', in Georg Sørensen (ed.), *Political Conditionality* (London: Frank Cass, 1993), pp. 112–34.

Otunnu, Olara A. and Doyle, Michael W. (eds.), *Peacemaking and Peacekeeping for the New Century* (Lanham, MD: Rowman & Littlefield, 1998).

Owen, David, *Balkan Odyssey* (New York: Harcourt Brace & Company, 1995).

Balkan Odyssey, CD-ROM, academic edition, version 1.1 (London: Apple/Electric company, 1995).

Pagden, Anthony, *Lords of All the World: Ideologies of Empire in Spain, Britain and France c.1500–c.1800* (New Haven: Yale University Press, 1995).

Pajic, Zoran, 'The Former Yugoslavia', in Hugh Miall (ed.), *Minority Rights in Europe: The Scope for a Transnational Regime* (London: RIIA/Pinter Publishers, 1994), pp. 56–65.

Parks, Tim, 'Tyrol: Retreat to Reality', *New York Review of Books*, 27 May 2004, pp. 50–2.

Payer, Cheryl, *Lent and Lost: Foreign Credit and Third World Development* (London: Zed Books, 1991).

Pellet, Alain, 'Note sur la Commission d'arbitrage de la Conférence européenne pour la paix en Yugoslavie', 37 *Annuaire français de droit international* (1991), 329–48.

'The Opinions of the Badinter Arbitration Committee: A Second Breath for the Self-Determination of Peoples', 3 *European Journal of International Law* (1992), 178–85.

Perkovich, George, 'Soviet Jewry and American Foreign Policy', 5 *World Policy Journal* (1988), 435–67.

Perry, Duncan M., 'Macedonia: A Balkan Problem and a European Dilemma', *RFE/RL Research Report*, 19 June 1992, pp. 35–45.

'The Republic of Macedonia and the Odds for Survival', *RFE/RL Research Report*, 20 November 1992, pp. 12–19.

Pettifer, James, 'The New Macedonian Question', 68 *International Affairs* (1992), 475–86.

Pinder, John, 'Community against Conflict: The European Community's Contribution to Ethno-National Peace in Europe', in Abram Chayes and Antonia Handler Chayes (eds.), *Preventing Conflict in the Post-Communist World* (Washington, DC: The Brookings Institution, 1996), pp. 147–96.

Polimac, Ibrahim and Loza, Tihomir, 'Uneasy Money', *War Report* No. 53 (August 1997), pp. 7–9.

Pollis, Adamantia, 'Strangers in a Strange Land', *War Report* No. 25 (March/April 1994), p. 12.

Poulton, Hugh, 'The Albanians of Macedonia', in *The Southern Balkans* (London: Minority Rights Group, 1994), pp. 25–31.

Przeworski, Adam and Limongi, Fernando, 'Democracy and Development', in Axel Hadenius (ed.), *Democracy's Victory and Crisis* (Cambridge: Cambridge University Press, 1997), pp. 163–94.

Public International Law & Policy Group, 'Intermediate Sovereignty as a Basis for Resolving the Kosovo Crisis', *ICG Balkans Report No. 46* (Brussels: International Crisis Group, 9 November 1998).

Puchala, Donald J. and Hopkins, Raymond F., 'International Regimes: Lessons from Inductive Analysis', 36 *International Organization* (1982), 245–75.

Puhovski, Zarko, 'The Real Democracy Deficit', *War Report* No. 58 (February/March 1998), pp. 44–5.

Pupovac, Milorad, 'A Settlement for the Serbs', in Anthony Borden *et al.* (eds.), *Breakdown: War & Reconstruction in Yugoslavia* (London: Institute for War and Peace Reporting, 1992), pp. 17–18.

Ramcharan, B. G. (ed.), *The International Conference on the Former Yugoslavia: Official Papers* (The Hague: Kluwer Law International, 1997), vol. II.

Ramet, Sabrina Petra, *Balkan Babel: The Disintegration of Yugoslavia from the Death of Tito to the War for Kosovo*, 3rd edn (Boulder, CO: Westview Press, 1999).

'The Macedonian Enigma', in Sabrina Petra Ramet and Ljubiša S. Adamovich (eds.), *Beyond Yugoslavia: Politics, Economics, and Culture in a Shattered Community* (Boulder, CO: Westview Press, 1995), pp. 211–36.

Ramet, Sabrina Petra, and Coffin, Letty, 'German Foreign Policy toward the Yugoslav Successor States, 1991–1999', 48(1) *Problems of Post-Communism* (2001), 48–64.

Randel, Judith and German, Tony (eds.), *The Reality of Aid: An Independent Review of International Aid* (London: ActionAid, 1993 & 1994).

Reychler, Luc, 'The Art of Conflict Prevention: Theory and Practice', in Werner Bauwens and Luc Reychler (eds.), *The Art of Conflict Prevention* (London: Brassey's, 1994), pp. 1–21.

Rich, Roland, 'Recognition of States: The Collapse of Yugoslavia and the Soviet Union', 4 *European Journal of International Law* (1993), 36–65.

Roberts, Adam, 'Communal Conflict as a Challenge to International Organization: The Case of the Former Yugoslavia', in Olara A. Otunnu and Michael W. Doyle (eds.), *Peacemaking and Peacekeeping for the New Century* (Lanham, MD: Rowman & Littlefield Publishers, 1998), pp. 27–58.

'NATO's "Humanitarian War" over Kosovo', 41(3) *Survival* (1999), 102–23.

Robinson, Mark, 'Aid, Democracy and Political Conditionality in Sub-Saharan Africa', in Georg Sørensen (ed.), *Political Conditionality* (London: Frank Cass, 1993), pp. 85–99.

'Will Political Conditionality Work?' 24(1) *IDS Bulletin* (1993), 58–66.

Roth, Brad R., *Governmental Illegitimacy in International Law* (Oxford: Clarendon Press, 1999).

Ruggie, John G., 'International Regimes, Transactions and Change: Embedded Liberalism in the Postwar Economic Order', 36 *International Organization* (1982), 379–415.

Rummel, Reinhardt, 'The European Union's Politico-Diplomatic Contribution to the Prevention of Ethno-National Conflict', in Abram Chayes and Antonia Handler Chayes (eds.), *Preventing Conflict in the Post-Communist World* (Washington, DC: The Brookings Institution, 1996), pp. 197–235.

Rupel, Dimitrij, 'Slovenia's Shift from the Balkans to Central Europe', in Jill Benderly and Evan Kraft (eds.), *Independent Slovenia: Origins, Movements, Prospects* (London: Macmillan, 1994), pp. 183–200.

Šahović, Milan, 'International Humanitarian Law in the "Yugoslav War"', in Sonja Biserko (ed.), *Yugoslavia: Collapse, War, Crimes* (Belgrade: Centre for Anti-War Action, 1993), pp. 141–59.

Salmon, Trevor C., 'Testing Times for European Political Cooperation: the Gulf and Yugoslavia, 1990–1992', 68 *International Affairs* (1992), 233–53.

Saussure, F. de, *Course in General Linguistics* (London: Duckworth, 1983).

Schmidt, Fabian, 'Teaching the Wrong Lesson in Kosovo', *Transition*, 12 July 1996, pp. 37–9.

Schöpflin, George, 'The Rise and Fall of Yugoslavia', in John McGarry and Brendan O'Leary (eds.), *The Politics of Ethnic Conflict Regulation: Case Studies of Protracted Ethnic Conflicts* (London: Routledge, 1993), pp. 172–203.

Shaw, M. N., *International Law*, 3rd edn (Cambridge: Cambridge University Press, 1994).

Shelley, Toby, *Endgame in the Western Sahara: What Future for Africa's Last Colony?* (London: Zed Books, 2004).

Shoup, Paul, 'The Bosnian Crisis in 1992', in Sabrina Petra Ramet and Ljubiša S. Adamovich (eds.), *Beyond Yugoslavia: Politics, Economics, and Culture in a Shattered Community* (Boulder, CO: Westview Press, 1995), pp. 155–87.

Silber, Laura and Little, Allan, *The Death of Yugoslavia* (London: Penguin, 1995).

Singer, H. W., *Aid Conditionality* (Brighton: Institute of Development Studies, 1994).

Skinner, Quentin, *The Foundations of Modern Political Thought* (Cambridge: Cambridge University Press, 1978), vol. I.

Slaughter Burley, Anne-Marie, 'International Law and International Relations Theory: A Dual Agenda', 87 *American Journal of International Law* (1993), 205–39.

Slaughter, Anne-Marie, Tulumello, Andrew S. and Wood, Stepan, 'International Law and International Relations Theory: A New Generation of Interdisciplinary Scholarship', 92 *American Journal of International Law* (1998), 367–97.

Smerdel, Branko, 'The Republic of Croatia: Three Fundamental Constitutional Choices', 1(1) *Croatian Political Science Review* (1992), 60–77.

Smith, Hazel, *Nicaragua: Self-Determination and Survival* (London: Pluto Press, 1993).

Smith, Karen E., 'The Use of Political Conditionality in the EU's Relations with Third Countries: How Effective?' 3 *European Foreign Affairs Review* (1998), 253–74.

Sørensen, Georg, 'Conditionality, Democracy and Development', in Olav Stokke (ed.), *Aid and Political Conditionality* (London: Frank Cass, 1995), pp. 392–409.

Sørensen, Georg (ed.), *Political Conditionality* (London: Frank Cass, 1993).

Spero, Joan Edelman, *The Politics of International Economic Relations*, 4th edn (New York: St. Martin's Press, 1990).

Stein, Arthur A., 'Coordination and Collaboration: Regimes in an Anarchic World', 36 *International Organization* (1982), 299–324.

Steiner, Michael, 'Don't Fool Around with Principles', *Transitions*, August 1997, pp. 34–40.

Stern, Brigitte (ed.), *Le statut des états issus de l'ex-Yougoslavie à l'ONU* (Paris: Montchrestien, 1996).

Stewart, Frances, 'The Many Faces of Adjustment' in Paul Mosely (ed.), *Development Finance and Policy Reform* (London: Macmillan, 1992), pp. 176–231.

Stokke, Olav, 'Aid and Political Conditionality: Core Issues and State of the Art', in Olav Stokke (ed.), *Aid and Political Conditionality* (London: Frank Cass, 1995), pp. 1–87.

Stokke, Olav (ed.), *Aid and Political Conditionality* (London: Frank Cass, 1995).

Strang, David, 'Contested Sovereignty: The Social Construction of Colonial Imperialism', in Thomas J. Biersteker and Cynthia Weber (eds.), *State Sovereignty as Social Construct* (Cambridge: Cambridge University Press, 1996), pp. 22–49.

Suny, Ronald Grigor, *The Revenge of the Past: Nationalism, Revolution and the Collapse of the Soviet Union* (Stanford, CA: Stanford University Press, 1993).

Surroi, Veton, 'The Albanian National Question: The Post-Dayton Pay-off', *War Report* No. 41 (May 1996), pp. 25–6.

Tanner, Marcus, *Croatia: A Nation Forged in War* (New Haven, CT: Yale University Press, 1997).

Taylor, Charles, *Multiculturalism and "The Politics of Recognition"* (Princeton: Princeton University Press, 1992).

Terrett, Steve, *The Dissolution of Yugoslavia and the Badinter Arbitration Commission* (Aldershot: Ashgate, 2000).

Thatcher, Margaret, *The Downing Street Years* (London: HarperCollins, 1993).

Thomas, Daniel C., 'The Helsinki Accords and Political Change in Eastern Europe', in Thomas Risse, Stephen C. Ropp, and Kathryn Sikkink (eds.), *The Power of Human Rights: International Norms and Domestic Change* (Cambridge: Cambridge University Press, 1999), pp. 205–33.

Thompson, Mark, *Forging War: The Media in Serbia, Croatia and Bosnia-Hercegovina* (London: Article XIX, 1994).

Thornberry, Patrick, 'International and European Standards on Minority Rights', in Hugh Miall (ed.), *Minority Rights in Europe: The Scope for a Transnational Regime* (London: RIIA/Pinter, 1994), pp. 14–21.

Tomaševski, Katarina, *Between Sanctions and Elections: Aid Donors and their Human Rights Performance* (London: Pinter, 1997).

Torres Bernádez, Santiago, 'The "Uti Possidetis Juris Principle" in Historical Perspective', in Konrad Ginther *et al.* (eds.), *Völkerrecht zwischen normativen Anspruch und politischer Realität* (Berlin: Duncker & Humblot, 1994), pp. 417–37.

Toscano, Mario, *Alto Adige – South Tyrol* (Baltimore: The Johns Hopkins University Press, 1975).

Trifunovska, Snezana (ed.), *Yugoslavia through Documents from its Creation to its Dissolution* (Dordrecht: Martinus Nijhoff, 1994).

Troebst, Stefan, *Conflict in Kosovo: Failure of Prevention?* ECMI Working Paper No. 1 (Flensburg, Germany: European Centre for Minority Issues, 1998).

Türk, Danilo, 'Remarks Concerning the Breakup of the Former Yugoslavia', 3 *Transnational Law and Contemporary Problems* (1993), 50–6.

United Nations Development Programme, *Human Development Report 1992* (New York: Oxford University Press, 1992).

Urwin, Derek W., *The Community of Europe: A History of European Integration Since 1945* (London: Longman, 1991).

Uvin, Peter, '"Do as I Say, Not as I Do": The Limits of Political Conditionality', in Georg Sørensen (ed.), *Political Conditionality* (London: Frank Cass, 1993), pp. 63–84.

'The Influence of Aid in Situations of Violent Conflict', Development Assistance Committee, Informal Task Force on Conflict, Peace and Development Co-operation, Organisation for Economic Co-operation and Development (September 1999).

Van Eekelen, Willem, *Debating European Security, 1948–1998* (The Hague and Brussels: Sdu Publishers/Centre for European Policy Studies, 1998).

Väyrynen, Raimo (ed.), *New Directions in Conflict Theory: Conflict Resolution and Conflict Transformation* (London: ISSC/SAGE Publications, 1991).

Védrine, Hubert, *Les mondes de François Mitterrand* (Paris: Fayard, 1996).

Verdross, Alfred, '*Jus Dispositivum* and *Jus Cogens* in International Law', 60 *American Journal of International Law* (1966), 55–63.

Verhoeven, Joe, 'La reconnaissance internationale: declin ou renouveau?', 39 *Annuaire français de droit international* (1993), 7–40.

Waller, Peter P., 'Aid and Conditionality: The Case of Germany, with Particular Reference to Kenya', in Olav Stokke (ed.), *Aid and Political Conditionality* (London: Frank Cass, 1995), pp. 110–28.

Waltz, Kenneth, 'The Stability of a Bipolar World', 93 *Daedalus* (1964), 881–909.

Theory of International Politics (New York: McGraw-Hill, 1979).

Warbrick, Colin, 'Current Developments: Public International Law: Recognition of States', 41 *International and Comparative Law Quarterly* (1992), 473–82.

'Current Developments: Public International Law: Recognition of States', 42 *International and Comparative Law Quarterly* (1993), 433–42.

Webster, C. K., *Britain and the Independence of Latin America, 1812–1830* (Oxford: Oxford University Press, 1938), vol. II.

Weller, Marc, 'The International Response to the Dissolution of the Socialist Federal Republic of Yugoslavia', 86 *American Journal of International Law* (1992), 569–607.

'Peace-Keeping and Peace-Enforcement in the Republic of Bosnia and Herzegovina', 56(1–2) *Zeitschrift für ausländisches öffentliches Recht und Völkerrecht* (1996), 70–177.

'The Rambouillet Conference on Kosovo', 75 *International Affairs* (1999), 211–51.

Whitehead, Laurence, 'Concerning International Support for Democracy in the South', in Robin Luckham and Gordon White (eds.), *Democratization in the South: The Jagged Wave* (Manchester: Manchester University Press, 1996), pp. 243–73.

Wilkinson, H. R., *Maps and Politics: A Review of the Ethnographic Cartography of Macedonia* (Liverpool: Liverpool University Press, 1951).

Williams, Paul R., 'The Treaty Obligations of the Successor States of the Former Soviet Union, Yugoslavia, and Czechoslovakia: Do They Continue in Force?' 23 *Denver Journal of International Law and Policy* (1994), 1–42.

Williams, Paul R. and Cigar, Norman, *A Prima Facie Case for the Indictment of Slobodan Milosevic* (London: Alliance to Defend Bosnia-Herzegovina, 1996).

Wilson, Duncan, *Tito's Yugoslavia* (Cambridge: Cambridge University Press, 1979).

Wolff, Stefan, 'Settling an Ethnic Conflict through Power-sharing: South Tyrol', in Ulrich Schneckener and Stefan Wolff (eds.), *Managing and Settling Ethnic Conflicts* (London: Hurst & Co., 2004), pp. 57–76.

Woodward, Susan L., *Balkan Tragedy: Chaos and Dissolution After the Cold War* (Washington, DC: Brookings Institution, 1995).

Woollacott, Martin, 'Craving the European Club', *War Report* No. 44 (August 1996), pp. 15–16.

World Bank, *Governance and Development* (Washington, DC: World Bank, 1992).

Sub-Saharan Africa: From Crisis to Sustainable Growth (Washington, DC: World Bank, 1989).

World Development Report 1991: The Challenge of Development (Oxford: Oxford University Press, 1991).

Wrede, Hans-Heinrich, 'Die deutsche Balkanpolitik im Einklang mit den Partnern', *Das Parlament*, Nr. 40 (1 October 1993), 14.

'"Friendly Concern" – Europe's Decision-making on the Recognition of Croatia and Slovenia', 4(3) *The Oxford International Review* (1993), 30–2.

Wynaendts, Henry, *L'engrenage: Chroniques yougoslaves, juillet 1991–août 1992* (Paris: Denoël, 1993).

Young, Oran R., *International Cooperation: Building Regimes for Natural Resources and the Environment* (Ithaca, NY: Cornell University Press, 1989).

Zametica, John, *The Yugoslav Conflict*, Adelphi Paper 270 (IISS/Brassey's, 1992).

Zimmermann, Warren, 'The Last Ambassador', 74(2) *Foreign Affairs* (1995), 2–20.

'A Pavane for Bosnia', 37 *The National Interest* (1994), 75–9.

Origins of a Catastrophe (New York: Times Books/Random House, 1996).

Zucconi, Mario, 'The European Union in the Former Yugoslavia', in Abram Chayes and Antonia Handler Chayes (eds.), *Preventing Conflict in the Post-Communist World* (Washington, DC: The Brookings Institution, 1996), pp. 237–78.

CONFERENCE REPORTS AND SEMINAR PAPERS

Barya, John-Jean B., 'The New Political Conditionalities of Aid: An Independent View from Africa', paper presented at a conference on 'The New Political Conditionalities of Development Assistance: Human Rights, Democracy and Disarmament', organised by the Vienna Institute for Development and Cooperation (VIDC), 23–25 April 1992. Report Series 2/92.

Gibson, Samantha, 'Can Donors Impose Democracy? Political Conditionality in Kenya and Malawi 1990–1996', paper presented at the African Studies Seminar, Faculty of Social and Political Studies, University of Cambridge, 24 February 1997.

Stevens, Michael, 'The World Bank and the New Political and Economic Order: The Political Conditionalities', paper presented at a conference on 'The New Political Conditionalities of Development Assistance: Human Rights, Democracy and Disarmament', organised by the Vienna Institute for Development and Cooperation (VIDC), 23–25 April 1992. Report Series 2/92.

Van de Sand, Klemens, 'New Political Criteria: The German Concept', paper presented at a conference on 'The New Political Conditionalities of Development Assistance: Human Rights, Democracy and Disarmament', organised by the Vienna Institute for Development and Cooperation (VIDC), 23–25 April 1992. Report Series 2/92.

UNPUBLISHED MANUSCRIPTS

Dákai, Zsuzsanna, 'NATO as an Issue in Hungarian Domestic Politics from 1994 to 1997', M.Phil. thesis, University of Oxford, Faculty of Social Studies, 1999.

Divjak, Jovan, 'Nastanak, Razvoj i Perspektive Armije RBiH – Vojske Federacije', unpublished manuscript, 1997.

Hassner, Pierre, 'The European Union and the Balkans', background paper submitted to the International Commission on the Balkans, 1996.

Loza, Tihomir, 'Getting to Dayton', contribution to unpublished edited volume, *Implementing Dayton*, 1997.

Miller, Hugo, 'German Foreign Policy Since Reunification: The Case Study of German Recognition of Croatia and Slovenia in 1991', M.Phil. thesis, University of Cambridge, Centre for International Studies, 1996.

Warnes, Kevin Robert, 'West European Foreign and Security Policy-Making: National Interests and Regional Cooperation (1990–1994)', Ph.D. dissertation, University of Bradford, Department of Peace Studies, 1995.

Index

Conference on Yugoslavia 4, 22, 33, 34, 66, 109–110, 113, 132, 139
and recognition of new states in Yugoslavia 48, 96, 108, 110, 120
Carrington Plan 16, 22, 24, 29–30, 34–35, 40, 110, 113, 117, 139, 167
Carter, Jimmy 150
Centre for Applied Policy Research 32
Chalker, Lynda 157, 158
Charter of Paris 2, 23, 35, 192
Chechnya 50, 70, 95, 128
China
aid conditionality and 162, 163, 165, 172
and Croatia/Slovenia 104
EU relations with 185
Chrobog, Jürgen 23, 35
Clapham, Christopher 149
Cold War 78, 79
aid policies 150, 156
and recognition of states 9, 50–51, 85
conditionality
economic conditionality 147, 151–153, 159, 164, 166
political conditionality 7, 8, 145, 147–150, 153–155, 157–163, 164
see also recognition of states
Conference of London (1913) 64
Conference on Security and Co-operation in Europe (CSCE)
and crisis in Yugoslavia 18, 20, 100, 171, 187, 192
and European Community 160
Germany and 27, 44
and human rights 182, 184
Conference on Yugoslavia 16, 19, 22, 24, 33, 34, 36, 40, 108, 140, 189
see also Carrington Plan
conflict management 4–5
Congo 53, 85, 114
Connally reservation 92
Copenhagen Declaration (1993) 93
Council of Europe 85, 93, 171, 183, 192
Craven, Matthew 37, 56, 68
Crawford, Beverly 47
Crawford, Gordon 161, 164
Crawford, James 51, 67, 93, 177
Croatia
Badinter and 38–40, 47, 50, 65
Belgrade and 64, 66
effects of recognition 40, 110–114, 144
European support for 106–108
independence 1, 15, 16, 26, 35, 103, 110
international personality 27, 103
secession 66
Serb minority in 19, 28, 30, 33–34, 50, 69, 70, 109, 113–120, 169, 184, 185

war in 15, 19, 22, 26, 108, 109, 110–113
see also EC recognition policy and Germany
Cutileiro Plan. See Bosnia and Herzegovina
Cyprus 4, 51, 104
Czechoslovakia 1, 62, 160

De Michelis, Gianni 35, 100, 101, 102, 103
De Visscher, Charles 90
Dejammet, Alain 23, 35
Demaçi, Adem 143
Denmark 15, 22, 106, 158, 165, 166, 184
Divjak, Jovan 121, 123
Donnelly, Jack 81, 84, 186
Dubrovnik 22, 109
Dumas, Roland 17, 19, 23

EC recognition policy
controversy about 3
and democratization 93–94
development of 16–25
effects of 40–41, 96–98, 144–145, 183–184, 185
implementation of 35–40, 166, 176
opportunities created by 105–6, 130, 184
strategic logic of 1–2, 16, 25–29
See also Bosnia and Herzegovina, Croatia, Kosovo, Macedonia and Slovenia
El Salvador 93, 162
Elleman-Jensen, Uffe 99
end of Cold War 1, 10, 24
aid policies 153, 156–161
democratization 153–157
German foreign policy 43–44
and minorities 41, 169–170
and new political conditionalities 157
and recognition of states 11, 24, 50–51, 86
self-determination 1, 186
Yugoslavia 1, 105, 106, 156
Eritrea 54, 85, 177
ethnic conflict 5, 6
European Convention on Human Rights 93
European Political Cooperation (EPC) 20, 162

Falk, Richard 77
France
and aid conditionality 154, 163
and Germany 47
and recognition of new states in Yugoslavia 15, 17, 19, 23–24, 35, 103

Katanga 55, 65, 85, 114
Katzenstein, Peter 8
Kellogg–Briand Pact 83, 131
Kelsen, Hans 76
Kennan, George 78
Kenya 166, 169, 173, 175
Keohane, Robert O. 80, 81, 83, 84
Kirkpatrick, Jeane 150
Kissinger, Henry 78
Kljusev, Nikola 136
Kohl, Helmut 18, 43, 44, 46, 47, 98, 107
    see also Germany
Kosin, Marko 100, 101, 103
Kosovo
    Badinter and 138
    and Carrington Plan 30, 32, 139
    and Dayton negotiations 140–141,
        142, 143
    Kosovo Liberation Army (KLA) 143
    and Macedonia 137, 143
    NATO campaign 32, 138, 143, 144, 186
    recognition of 12, 70, 97, 137–144, 186
    Serbian policy towards 128, 138, 143
    Serbs in 119, 141
    status in Yugoslavia 138
    and war in Yugoslavia 3, 140, 144
Kostić, Branko 111, 134
Kovács, László 170
Krasner, Stephen 81
Kučan, Milan 101

Lauterpacht, Hersch 59
League of Nations 62, 69, 75, 87, 145
Legal positivism 76
legitimacy
    and conditionality 157, 174–176
    and ethnic territories 115, 129, 142, 167
    and international law 75, 86–87,
        91–92, 176
    and recognition 2, 25, 63, 86–87,
        91–92, 179
Letica, Slaven 113, 115, 118
Levine, Alicia 119
Libal, Michael 107, 124
Limongi, Fernando 155
Lomé Convention 149, 159

Maastricht summit 23, 24, 41, 44, 48
Macedonia
    Badinter Commission and 37, 39, 50, 69,
        135, 177
    and dissolution of Yugoslavia 67, 134
    and ethnic minorities 40–41, 134,
        136–137, 143
    Greece and 24, 37, 133, 134, 135–136,
        167, 168

and Kosovo 143
and national identity 134, 167–168
recognition of 12, 35, 37, 39, 50, 58, 59,
    69, 97, 120, 133–137, 144, 167–168
Serbia and 133, 134, 168
Machiavelli, Niccolò 91
Marković, Ante 105, 123
McDougal, Myres 79
McGarry, John 5
Mill, John Stuart 168, 180
Milošević, Slobodan
    and Bosnia and Herzegovina 121,
        123, 128
    and Croatian Serbs 33, 34, 116, 118,
        119, 176
    and Germany 46, 47, 68–69
    and Kosovo 140, 141–142, 143–144
    and peace negotiations 19, 21, 22, 34,
        107, 110, 131, 139
    and Slovenia 110
    see also Serbia
minority rights
    and conflict management 4, 5, 28, 114
    and human rights 175
    in post-Cold War Europe 185
    in post-World War I Europe 62
    and statehood 184
    in Yugoslavia 37, 38, 40, 139, 183
    see also Carrington Plan
Mitsotakis, Constantine 134
Mitterrand, François 23, 154
Mock, Alois 98, 99, 100, 102
Montenegro 35, 62, 109, 140, 171
Montevideo Convention 52, 53, 55, 56, 60,
    71, 84
Morgenthau, Hans J. 59, 60, 61, 62, 63, 64
Müllerson, Rein 59, 60, 70, 139

Nelson, Joan 169
Netherlands, the 15, 93, 131, 162,
    165–166, 167
New Haven School 79
Nicaragua Case 92
North Atlantic Treaty Organization
    (NATO) 21, 108, 170, 171
Northern Ireland 4
nuclear non-proliferation 9, 24, 187
Nye, Joseph S. 12, 80

O'Connell, D. P. 61
O'Leary, Brendan 5
Osimo agreement (1975) 101

Pakistan 4, 51, 55
Panić, Zivota 111
Pavelić, Ante 115